ACCLAIM FOR

BARRY SANDERS'S

A is for ox

"Absorbing . . . a learned, wide-ranging, well-written, intellectual-ly engaging exploration of how cultures and individuals acquire and use speech, language, reading and writing. Sanders' descrip-tion of oral cultures, of the different kind of thinking that takes place in such cultures, is fascinating. [*A Is for Ox*] ought to be required reading." —*Boston Globe*

"In answer to the well-documented fact that children don't read and write the way they used to, Sanders refreshingly declines to give the explanation that Barney has murdered Mother Goose. . . . It's his thesis that without a literacy rooted in orality there can be neither self, as we understand it, nor self-consciousness. . . . TV still plays the villain, but it works its evil less by displacing reading than by replacing verbal interaction with parents and peers." —Jonathan Franzen, *The New Yorker*

"[*A Is for Ox*] is a reminder that the simple acts of reading and writing may not be so simple as they appear. . . . Barry Sanders argues nothing less than this: Human beings as we know them are products of literacy—and as literacy declines, as each suc-ceeding generation distances itself further and further from those literate roots, the result will be nothing short of apocalyptic." —*Albuquerque Journal*

"A brilliant, disturbing reflection on the collapsing moral order of post-modern America. If literacy is the wellspring of self-hood, as Sanders makes clear, our aggressive, image-addicted society is unwittingly committing cultural suicide."

—Mike Davis, author of *City of Quartz*

"Language is interchange between persons. Sanders shows how this feature of language makes some skill in oral discourse a pre-requisite for literacy, how familiarity with writing is needed to mature today's sense of the self and of social structures, and how electronic media can seriously disturb the sense of communication as interchange. A fascinating book for parents, teachers of writing, other teachers and scholars, and in fact for everybody."

—Walter J. Ong

"A learned, fascinating, and thought-provoking book that makes you think harder about the sources of our humanity."

—Jerome Bruner

"A meditation on the nature of orality, and on literacy and its relationship to our violent culture. Sanders describes an entire generation dispossessed of both oral and written language and envisions a 'vernacular solution' that returns to orality for the formation and realization of patterns connecting us to one another and to culture. *A Is for Ox . . .* moves with grace from idea to brilliant idea. It presents a visionary and elegant prescription for the future."   —Robert Falk, Associate Director, Boys Republic

"Sanders argues persuasively that reading and writing, the activities which for the last seven hundred years have structured our thinking, are giving way to images passively received from television and video. His range of reference is astonishingly wide. . . . *A Is for Ox*, is, in fact, an elegant brief for language."

—*El Palacio*

BARRY SANDERS

A is for ox

Barry Sanders is the author of *Sudden Glory: Laughter as Subversive History* and coauthor, with Ivan Illich, of *ABC: The Alphabetization of the Popular Mind* and, with Paul Shepard, of *The Sacred Paw: The Bear in Nature, Myth, and Literature*. He is professor of English and the History of Ideas at Pitzer College in Claremont, California.

A is for ox

A is for ox ———————

The Collapse of Literacy and
the Rise of Violence in an Electronic Age

BARRY SANDERS

VINTAGE BOOKS

A Division of Random House, Inc.

New York

FIRST VINTAGE BOOKS EDITION, OCTOBER 1995

Grateful acknowledgment is made to Tavistock/Routledge
for permission to reprint an excerpt from
"A Mother's Contribution to Society"
from *Home Is Where We Start From*
by D. W. Winnicott. Reprinted by permission
of Tavistock/Routledge, London.

The Library of Congress has cataloged
the Pantheon edition as follows:
Sanders, Barry.
A is for ox / Barry Sanders.
p. cm.
Includes bibliographical references and index.
ISBN: 0-679-41711-7
1. Oral communication—Social aspects. 2. Literacy.
3. Mass media and youth. 4. Mass media—Social aspects.
5. Children and violence. I. Title.
P95.S26 1994
302.2'242—dc20 94-9779
CIP
Vintage ISBN: 0-679-74285-9

Manufactured in the United States of America
10 9 8 7

For Ivan

CONTENTS

ACKNOWLEGMENTS

The person who usually first hears my ideas is Grace, my wife. They come back truer. I have learned much from Kali, my daughter, and Pebber, my son. They have given me inspiration and have made me question, for both of which acts I thank them deeply.

I would also like to thank Majid Rahnema, Al Schwartz, Lew Ellenhorn, Robert Falk, Paul Livadary, and Jim White. Their contributions have meant a lot.

Finally, I would like to thank Miriam Altshuler, my agent, and Peter Dimock, my editor, for both believing me and believing in me.

Certain fundamental concepts seat themselves so deeply in our daily lives that they seem to disappear from consciousness altogether. We act without thinking about them at all and become aware of them only in times of change or trouble. Perhaps the most striking example is the concept of the self that shapes our lives from behind the scenes in just this way. People may find the self too knotty or too elusive to define, but no one questions its presence—no one doubts its importance. Most people would agree that it is almost impossible to imagine life without a self.

But the self as we understand the term shows up relatively late in the history of Western thought. This book argues that the idea of a critical, self-directed human being we take for granted as the working foundation of our humanness develops only in the crucible of reading and writing. Human beings as we know them are products of literacy. In the West, alphabetic reading and writing begin to take hold some time in the fifth or sixth century B.C. What happens to the self several thousand years later, we must now ask, as today's young people find less and less appeal in bookish things. What happens, that is, to the creature to which we have grown so accustomed? That is the profoundly shocking question facing contemporary society, for the self that came into history as a result of literacy is on the verge of passing out of history. This agent called the self that came to life as a social and intellectual construct tied to the culture of the book is in the process of deconstructing and falling away entirely from the human repertoire. With its disappearance will go the human being we now know.

This book describes a world peopled with young folk who have bypassed reading and writing and who thus have been forced to fabricate a life without the benefit of that innermost,

intimate guide, the self. It does not take a powerful imagination
to describe such a world. The details can be found in the morning newspaper. It is a world marked by pain and death, a world
filled with despair and drop-outs, teen-age suicides, gang killings,
broken homes, and homicides. It is a world in which young
people seek revenge and retaliation rather than self-reflection. It
is a world in which persons kill without remorse or regret.

We must try, with every ounce of our beings, to stop the
nightmare from continuing. The solution begins in recapturing
the self. Such a task cannot be done by schools and teachers
alone. Literacy is a social enterprise, which, to be effective,
requires both a redefinition of what literacy means and a strategy
for achieving it. Every person or group of persons who move into
literacy first build a foundation for reading and writing in the
world of orality. Orality supports literacy, provides the impetus
for shaping it. The skills one learns in orality are crucial because
literacy is more than a series of words on paper. It is a set of
relationships and structures, a dynamic system that one internalizes and maps back onto experience. A person's success in orality
determines whether he or she will "take" to literacy. The way to
literacy lies in the very first act the infant engages in—the act of
breathing. The human voice, like a great alarm, sounds the way
to literacy.

But the way has been blocked. It has been blocked by electronic machinery of every conceivable kind, from TV and movies, through records and CDs, to PCs and video games. Before
teachers or parents begin to think about raising literate children,
they must first ensure their beings as creatures of orality. PEN
International, a political organization of professional writers,
takes up the cause of imprisoned writers around the world. It
protects the word against state terrorism. These days, it would do
well to turn its attention to young people, who have been barred

from reading and writing by becoming prisoners of electronic media. On January 12, 1986, PEN held its forty-eighth International Congress at the New York Public Library. Its principal speakers were Nadine Gordimer and Norman Mailer, both powerful writers who addressed the theme of the conference, "The Writer's Imagination and the Imagination of the State." As the President of the American Center, Mailer opened the ceremonies with an impassioned declaration of the power of the word:

> We are in love with the word. We are proud of it. The word precedes the formation of the state. The word comes to us from every avatar of early human existence. As writers, we are obliged more than others to keep our lives attached to the primitive power of the word. From India, out of the Vedas, we still hear: "On the spoken word, all the gods depend, all beasts and men; in the word live all creatures. . . . The word is the navel of the divine world."

Let Mailer's words serve as a threshold to this book. I use the first letter of the alphabet, *A*, for my title. In its earliest form, in the Phoenician writing system, the letter *A*, called an *aleph*, stood on its head or its side— ≮ —intended as a depiction of a cow or ox. (*Aleph* is the Phoenician word for "ox.") *A* did not represent a vowel for the Phoenicians but a breathing (vowels did not have symbols). Ask a small child to spell the word *ox*, and he or she is more than likely to reach a phonetic inscription like *ax*. After all, *A* often gets sounded as *ah*. In orality, there are no spelling mistakes. This book attempts a move back into orality, and so I choose a title as close to orality as letters can come. *A* is indeed for *ox*.

A is for ox

CHAPTER ONE

Conservative, liberal and left-wing thinkers in contemporary schools of linguistic
philosophy agree about one thing; man
became man not by the tool but by the
Word. It is not walking upright and using
a stick to dig for food or strike a blow that
makes a human being, it is speech. And
neither intelligent apes nor dolphins whis-
pering in the ocean share with us the ability to transform this direct communication
and commune between peoples and generations who will never meet.

—Nadine Gordimer, "The Unkillable Word,"
The Essential Gesture

Humans speak. Humans listen. But very few oral peoples
in the world—that vast assembly of speakers and listeners—ever
make the radically disruptive move into literacy. According to
the United Nations' latest count, of the approximately three
thousand languages spoken in the world today, only some
seventy-eight have a literature. Of those seventy-eight, a scant
five or six enjoy a truly international audience. Literates make up
a very small minority of the world's population, but they make
their force felt out of all proportion to their number. In a sense,
that is the lesson that literacy teaches: it empowers people to

speak their minds in a way that oral peoples can never know. Literacy—that mysterious, elusive force that carries human beings into a particularly powerful kind of consciousness—is the subject of this book.[1]

The great majority of people in the world today have the opportunity to walk out of orality and to cross into that other world of literacy. But vast numbers of them never even take the first step. Perhaps they sense the paradox underlying literacy: the bridge does not permit two-way traffic. Once a person makes it into that territory called literacy, he or she can never return. Literacy admits of no visitors, no tourists. It is a world with no exit, an experience which offers no possibility of ever coming back. The world of orality can barely be discerned from the other side. One can make out only the vaguest outlines, as if having dwelled there once in a dream.

No wonder that the world of orality, where people live having no contact with reading or writing—what anthropologists term "primary orality"—baffles most literate minds. It's nearly impossible to fathom how non-literates really think, or to understand how they actually perceive the world—a bit like trying to recall one's own life before reading and writing. The true feel and recollection of our earlier, pre-literate times gets eradicated by new categories of thinking and remembering. But it's important to try to enter the perceptual framework of orality, for that state that everyone has more or less passed through and forgotten provides the foundation for literacy. Literacy cannot be truly understood without exploring its relationship to orality.

----

[1]*Consciousness* is one of those words people use freely but find impossible to define. Its etymology provides some help. Derived from the Latin, *con-sciere* means "to have knowledge together with someone else," which suggests that in its earliest stages, consciousness was actually a communal affair. A communal consciousness begins in orality, developing into an individuating, self-reflective activity only in literacy.

Stories are the lifeblood of oral cultures, and the storyteller is the heart of the tribe or group. He or she keeps the stories circulating throughout the entire system. His are not just ordinary stories, casually told at random, but stories that people wait for and expect, and whose outlines they know by heart. His stories reassure the people who they are and remind them what they believe; they bind the group together. In the net of his stories, he catches everything—history, truth, heroism, religion, philosophy, morality, love. The leader who recounts these stories— usually a man, usually older—has arrived at his privileged position through years of experience. He has earned the right to speak for everyone—to act as their "mouthpiece." As Walter Benjamin has noted about storytelling in oral cultures, "Counsel woven into the fabric of real life is wisdom." Storytellers in orality occupy the position of wise men in a sense that modern, literate cultures can no longer know.

In some Native American tribes, the storyteller holds in trust the sacred instrument of storytelling, the pipe, for his breath is sacred. The leader lights the pipe and puffs, the narrative imitating the shape of the smoke, moving out and curling back on itself, dropping, and finally drifting far off and disappearing. Because he holds the secrets to their very survival—and shares them with everyone—the tribe or group treats him with respect and deference. Every bit of essential knowledge that the tribe needs drops from his mouth in units of narrative time.

In literate cultures we tend to think of storytelling as an activity assigned to various literary genres—the novel, the short story, and so on. In truth, however, storytelling—with its deep ties to the world of orality largely, if unconsciously, preserved intact—still permeates life in literate societies. Many psycholinguists even compare the process of living itself to narrating a story. The psychologist Jerome Bruner has led the way in linking narration to self-consciousness itself. He reached his conclusions after analyzing the transcripts of scores of people of various ages talking nonchalantly about themselves and their lives:

> In some important sense "lives" are texts: texts that are subject to revision, exegesis, reinterpretation, and so on. That is to say, *accounted* lives are taken by those who account them as text amenable to an alternative interpretation. When people reinterpret their life accounts, they do not deny the prior "text" . . . but deny the interpretation they have placed on it. It is a lifelong habit.
>
> I wish to equate "text" . . . in this sense with a conceptually formulated narrative account of what a life has been about. That it is an account carried in memory, or carried in memory in such a way as to be capable of generating shorter or longer versions of itself, does not exclude it from status as a text open to alternative interpretations.[2]

For Bruner, as well as for other socio- and psycholinguists, living means weaving together a series of events into an intricate narrative pattern called a life. At times, during confession, say, or in psychoanalysis, or even in relaxed conversation, people unravel their lives in sessions of highly charged and carefully shaped storytelling.

Self-help groups like Alcoholics Anonymous and Narcotics Anonymous take advantage of such group storytelling sessions to move people out of their isolated, destructive patterns and into more healthy ones. People who in all other ways remain strangers to one another stand up and confess the content of their lives in an effort to discover the universal truths that hold alcoholics

---

[2]Jerome Bruner and Susan Weisser, "The Invention of Self: Autobiography and Its Forms," in David R. Olson and Nancy Torrance, eds., *Literacy and Orality*, 129–30.

or drug users together. The process transforms isolated individuals into members of a tribe or a small community—a therapeutic transformation. Designers of twelve-step programs exploit elements of orality, relying on formulaic phrases, repetitions, oaths, declarative sentences, and myths, to inculcate group participants with their doctrines. In such meetings, one person assumes the role of storyteller.

Every tribe needs the storyteller, just as every storyteller needs the tribe, for storytelling means little without attentive storylistening. A story, no matter how interesting, must be heard to be effective: A loose tongue always craves a friendly ear. The storyteller, too, must be a person possessed of acute hearing. But he listens in a different way from the tribe, and he hears different things. The Maya in the highlands of Guatemala call their wisest storyteller the "echoman."

Moving beyond the boundaries of ordinary life, the echoman, Robert Bly points out, loses gender and becomes "a person who hears all grief, all intuition, all response to sound. He does not act but rather listens to the community and to the ancestors and tries to figure out to whom our debt for living is to be paid."[3]

Through magic—in a trance or other ecstatic states—the storyteller turns seer, and in that altered state travels to the edge of experience and beyond. A boundless traveler, the storyteller roams outside himself—goes journeying—without ever leaving his favorite spot. Indeed, *ex-stasis* means to "move out of place," to be "beside oneself." The storyteller serves as the guiding spirit of the group: From the broadest perspective possible, he can describe the entire range of human imagination, and provide direction for the ultimate trip—life's grand journey. He allays fears and raises hopes. He changes without looking changed. If consciousness can be described as standing outside oneself and

---

[3]The Maya recognize four stages for men: the boy, the warrior, the community man, and the highest of them all, the echoman. See Robert Bly, "What the Mayans Could Teach to the Joint Chiefs."

observing, then the storyteller offers a living embodiment in oral cultures of the consciousness produced within individuals by literacy.

With such wisdom to pass around, the storyteller must narrate the truth so that everyone—from the oldest man and woman to the youngest boy and girl—understands. His voice must reach the ears of the entire group; no one can be left out. Even momentary interruptions, like rambunctious dogs and crying babies, will get woven into the fabric of the tale by a skillful wordsmith. He gives back to the tribe what belongs to them. What he tells them feels as familiar and as necessary as a heartbeat. The author G. F. Michelsen captures the essence of this kind of storytelling in orality:

> "You see," he continues, "every man's life is in itself a story, where there are heroes and monsters and perils to overcome. There is lust and defeat and humiliation. A man finds his life in the story he tells of it. Like when you first go into the bush, hunting with your father, and something exciting happens, a rogue leopard comes close, you hide, and you come home and tell your friends-of-the-same-age, and you make a story of it. It's the same for a people, for a country. A people make up a large tale in which every separate man may place his own smaller tale. And soon the story and the people are one and the same. It's these stories that help us, that tell us how to live."[4]

The master's stories are born out of the fluency of the group—the tribe. *Fluency,* a watery essence, best captures the nature of storytelling in oral cultures: Elements of the story appear with the regularity of ocean waves, and disappear in just the same way. Like the ocean, regular and recurring waves come to feel familiar and provide the illusion of change within sameness—G. F. Michelsen's smaller tale within the group's large

---

[4]G. F. Michelsen, *To Sleep with Ghosts: A Novel of Africa,* 93.

tale. The storyteller takes his audience sailing on its adventures by riding the crest of an endless succession of waves.

Literary scholars call these wavelike patterns in storytelling formulaic phrases. Such phrases, repeated over and over in the same story and across stories, permit the tribe to "store" pieces of information for a time. The classicist Eric Havelock believes that what anthropologists call tradition in oral societies consists of these "ritualized utterances":

> When a society relies on a system of communication which is wholly oral it will, like ours, still have to rely on a tradition expressed in fixed statements and transmissible as such. What kind of language can supply this need and still remain oral? The answer would seem to lie in ritualized utterance, a traditional language which somehow becomes formally repeatable like a ritual in which the words remain in a fixed order.
>
> Such language has to be memorized. There is no other way of guaranteeing its survival. Ritualization becomes the means of memorization. The memories are personal, belonging to every man, woman, and child in the community, yet their content, the language preserved, is communal, something shared by the community as expressing its traditions and its historical identity.[5]

The simpler formulas have survived into the world of literacy, and are still recognizable today. When a wise king has children, he always has three. When the hero wanders off to fight, he always faces challenges in three separate episodes. At some point, the poor orphaned child will reveal his high-born background. The sea always washes ashore in wine-dark waves; the steed always gallops away with a red-roan coat.

To turn to the Alcoholics Anonymous meeting again, participants repeat set phrases periodically throughout each meeting— short, ritualized utterances so that the entire group can finally

---

[5]Eric Havelock, *The Muse Learns to Write*, 70.

repeat them automatically, without thinking: "We come to believe that a Power greater than ourselves can restore us to san-
ity." Each member tells a slightly different story, but marked by
regularized phrases, so that the group recognizes each meeting
as slightly different but almost like the last one they attended.
The process promotes an atmosphere of safety and comfort;
strangers feel reassured and welcomed.

Or to use a more immediate example from the world of
literacy, consider the experience of telling stories to children.
Anyone who has ever made up a story on the spot, and told it
out loud to a child at bedtime, has actually put a toe into the
waters of orality. I allow only a toe because, after all, parent and
child both live deeply in literacy. The parent's sentences have
been shaped by literacy. The child has been listening to those
sentences his or her entire short life. Neither of them can ever
know primary orality, but storytelling gets them fairly close.

The mother, let us say, struggles for a beginning to her tale,
falling back on a formulaic phrase: "Once upon a time," or
"There was a boy who lived on the other side of the valley," or
"The king had three children, two of them were bad and one was
very, very good." Whatever formula the mother chooses, it helps
get the story on track. And if the mother manages to keep a
regular rhythm going, a little train with a full head of steam, then
the tale seems to tell itself. What starts out as a chore gradually
turns into fun. The mother begins to feel real satisfaction as all
the pieces of the story move inexorably toward resolution—the
dragon's heart splayed wide open, or the wandering child reunited with her mother, or the king's seemingly wicked daughter
finally revealed to everyone as a saintly soul. As the mother
brings the story home, she concludes it by using another formulaic phrase: "They all lived happily ever after," or more
simply, "The end."

A formulaic phrase slides into place with all the reassuring
sound of a dead bolt—providing protection against intruders
and strangers. For those used to literacy, such phrases sound like

clichés. But that is only because in literacy authors strive, as Ezra Pound counsels, to "make it new." Formulas can be better understood if they can be seen as the equivalents of proverbs or sayings in our own lives—little nuggets of truth, many of which have been washed downstream, unchanged, from the Middle Ages to the present moment. With one major difference: they no longer occupy a central place in literate lives. They do not roll off our tongues with ease. In orality, these formulas reflect a life that is deeply patterned—a life that, in turn, comes to be perceived through patterns. Hearing those patterns out loud, people find their worldview reaffirmed and strengthened. The scholar Walter Ong assigns great practical importance to them:

> Homeric Greeks valued clichés because not only the poets but the entire oral noetic world or thought world relied upon the formulaic constitution of thought. In an oral culture, knowledge, once acquired, had to be constantly repeated or it would be lost: fixed, formulaic thought patterns were essential for wisdom and effective administration.[6]

In that unfamiliar world of orality, wisdom and the dissemination of wisdom inhere not in any institution, but within the heart and soul of a single person—the storyteller.

Orality admits of no authors—not in the contemporary sense of a person who makes up stories out of his or her own imagination and who assumes the mantle of authority. So, for instance, when a mother tells a story or a fairy tale to her daughter, as far as the daughter is concerned, the mother seems to be calling up images and ideas and actions out of the daughter's own inner life—her dreams, desires, and fears. In fact—according to the Jungian psychoanalyst Marie-Louise von Franz—that is the point. Stories and fairy tales serve to bring the child's darkest fears and doubts out into the open where they can be discussed.

---

[6]Walter Ong, *Orality and Literacy: The Technologizing of the Word*, 23–24.

The child no longer feels that only he or she holds a fear of the dark.[7]

With the idea of authors comes something brand-new—originality. Rather than speaking *with* the tribe or the child, the author speaks out of a singular experience shaped by a singular perspective. Through originality, the author tries to stand out from every other author who ever set pen to paper. And through that originality, the author speaks in counterdistinction to—in differentiation from—the community.

The word *original* sounds its own warning through etymology: its root entices one to return to "inceptions" and "beginnings." But in orality beginnings quite naturally map onto endings, a cycle that informs all storytelling in orality: the hero leaves and comes back home to the same spot. The oral mind craves the reassurance of what is familiar; it survives through tradition. Even though words fly away as soon as they are spoken, orality encourages a sense of stability unknown in literacy. A poet in orality stitches together adventures that the group already knows and describes those adventures with details that repeat themselves in a string of formulaic expressions. Whatever sounds "original," in our modern sense, or brand-new, the tribe cannot ingest, and throws off as extraneous or foreign.[8]

This book is a plea to reestablish the connection between literacy and orality—and a warning that a failure to do so will

---

[7]Marie-Louise von Franz, *An Introduction to the Interpretation of Fairy Tales.*

[8]*Gesta*, the Latin word for "deeds" and by extension "story," spun off words like *gestation, gesture,* and, interestingly, *ingestion.* Significant connections bind eating and storytelling together. The good storyteller has to ingest experience, digest it, and give it back to the group. Groups can employ dietary laws to prohibit subjects—"sacred cows"—as taboo or unclean.

The art historian Michael Camille links the "active rumination of the word with the succulent and juicy forms, both animal and vegetable, which decorated letters" on medieval manuscripts, as monks savored the alphabet "as part of the slow and deliberate repetitions in a daily digested diet" (Michael Camille, "Seeing and Reading," *Art History,* p. 29).

have catastrophic consequences. A rich experience of orality is an indispensable prelude to literacy. Orality provides a proving ground, a safe place, where a child's imagination can unfold without fear of judgment or censure. Authority and originality hold no sway there; tests and measurements have no place. Stories bring everyone together in a commonality of closely shared knowledge. In orality, knowledge is a social phenomenon, not an individual experience, so no one can be classified as dumber or smarter than anyone else. Myths and stories and poems for the tribe, fairy tales and stories for the youngster—that is how knowledge begins to weave itself among each and every person as *con*-sciousness, a knowledge arrived at *with* others.

In orality, one need not memorize a thing. Indeed, it's quite impossible to actually memorize anything. For memory in orality functions quite differently from literate memory. An oral person, or a child, learns certain truths, so to speak, by hearing them repeated, time and again, in stories and poems and fairy tales, and learns also that, because the words so quickly evaporate, he or she must listen intently.

In practice, most children listen so closely they do not want a story to end. They demand to hear it repeated again and again, for it gives them great pleasure. Repetition casts a powerful spell in orality. "But mere repetition of identical content will not get you very far," Eric Havelock theorizes, "the range of oral knowledge thus supplied will be limited. What is required is a method of repeated language (meaning acoustically identical sound patterns) which nevertheless is able to alter its content to express diverse meanings." Havelock concludes with this remarkable claim: "The solution discovered by the brain of early man was to convert thought into rhythmic talk."[9] The rhythm provides a pleasurable and reassuring repetition, like a heartbeat, so that the meaning, riding on top of it, can change slightly— and advance the action—over the course of the narrative.

---

[9]Havelock, *The Muse Learns to Write*, 71.

Thus, Havelock describes nothing less than the birth of a new
form in orality, one born out of the desires for a sense of change
within sameness, a form that literary historians call *poetry*.

Let us now turn our attention from storytelling in primary
orality, to poetic composition in a society like ancient Greece,
where oral forms persisted in the midst of a rudimentary form of
literacy, a transitional period not unlike the one in which young
people find themselves today as they enter elementary schooling.
Playing, performance, improvisation, entertainment—these
terms describe poetic composition in epic poems like Homer's
The Iliad and *The Odyssey*, just the sort of things young people
experience in orality, and just the sort of things teachers can take
advantage of in their classrooms.

The best way to understand poetic composition in the ancient
world is by listening to jazz improvisation from the late twenties
to the forties, in such groups as Count Basie's Kansas City bands,
in Duke Ellington's and Benny Goodman's small bands—in a
whole array, that is, of what have been termed "swing bands."
Every player knows from years of playing and listening exactly
what is allowed; performance means that a group of players
improvises around bits of melody from a tune using certain
chords. What have these musicians actually memorized? The
tune, perhaps, and the chord progressions; but not necessarily
note for note. Rather, they can hum the tune—make it oral—
and play it. On their favorite instruments, they can offer variations on some discernible theme, drawing in an audience as it
slowly begins to recognize the composition. The audience may
even begin to hum along as its recognition of the melody grows
stronger. Jazz musicians do not need to read music. In fact, they
may even be able to improvise better if each of them plays "by
ear."

Classical musicians must be able to read a score; and they

must be able to retain their part in the entire symphony in their heads. Memory plays its own crucial part in the success of the performance. The violinist knows he must play exactly the same notes each time he performs Beethoven's Fifth Symphony. Which means that classical musicians have to be literate. Musical notes can be preserved one way only, and that is on the page. Like words themselves, music flies away into the ether. The page freezes things forever. Only in literacy does the page become something that is visualized in the mind's eye. There, on that internalized page, we inscribe the information that needs to be remembered. When we refer to a person having a "photographic memory," we mean that that person can review a scene with all the clarity and precision of images that appear on film paper, or of words that appear on the pages of a text. Again, Walter Ong:

> A literate person, asked to think of the word "nevertheless," will normally (and I strongly suspect always) have some image, at least vague, of the spelled-out word and be quite unable ever to think of the word "nevertheless" for, let us say, 60 seconds without adverting to any lettering but *only* to sound. This is to say, a literate person cannot fully recover a sense of what the word is to purely oral people.[10]

That kind of exact recall simply cannot exist in orality. In oral cultures, memories are neither storehouses from which bits of information can be retrieved at a moment's notice, nor wax tablets into which experience has been deeply impressed, nor sheets of parchment on which key words have been inscribed. These images all characterize a memory that has been formed in literacy. A more elusive image is needed to capture the way memory functions in orality. The ancient world provides the most suggestive model of how this kind of memory probably worked.

------

[10]Ong, *Orality and Literacy*, 12.

To the imagination in orality, all of reality hangs on to its life with astonishing tenacity. Once alive, everything stays astonishingly alive. The story of Christ's death and resurrection also tells of the death and rebirth of the Logos—the Word. Orality basically erases the line separating the living from the dead: every telling of a story brings its characters back to a fully animated life. Young children have such a difficult time with death not just because the concept is so utterly abstract for them, but because it is also such an alien one for their imaginations shaped by orality. A child's imagination has the power to bring back to life even a person long-buried underground. Just hearing a mention of the dead person can sometimes be enough for the child's resurrective imagination. In ancient Greece poets had the galvanizing power to bring the dead back to an animated and vigorous life.

That poet in ancient Greece—more accurately a *rhetor*, a person who "stitches together"—would ritualistically invoke the mother of the Muses, Mnemosyne, in order to guide him in composing his poem. Mnemosyne bubbles and roils as the wellspring of life. She persists in ancient mythology as a limpid brook, babbling away for all those who chose to hear her song. In her waters float the remains of past lives—the memories that Lethe had washed free of the dead, so they could pass on, as transparent shadows, to the Other Side. At her banks, one could hear Mnemosyne sing of what is, what was, and what shall be. By drinking from her waters, the rhetor could re-collect the memories of an entire group that in the course of time had actually passed into individual forgetfulness. Every memory was a collective one, just as every ladleful of Mnemosyne's water consisted of an infinitude of droplets.[11]

---

[11]The connection between water and poetry is a truth that lies buried deep in the most ancient languages. The word *poem* can be traced all the way back to ancient Hebrew, where it translates literally as "the sound of water flowing over pebbles."

The poet could then sing these memories out loud, chanting one event after the other in what would sound to us perhaps like a "primitive call." The strum of the lyre or harp, the cadences of the poet's own singing, the rhythmic regularity of the narrative, the inhalations and exhalations of the poet's breath—all of these propelled the poet along on his narrative journey. He chanted the very rhythm of living itself. He introduced no surprises. His hero always wandered away from familiar ground; but the group could always rest assured that the hero would return home safely. The king might plummet into despair, stripped of everything but a remnant of power, but the group could rejoice over his inevitable recovery.

Each time the poet recounted the story, he would tell it slightly differently. He would have to: He himself had heard different things; he had had different experiences; he felt differently. Every telling forever changed the teller, as well, for the poet ingested the story himself—between each telling, he lived out its truths. He could only deliver a believable telling if he believed those truths himself—*and* acted on them. That is, the story had to mean as much to the poet, each time he narrated it, as it did to his audience. The poet did not tell his tales to put the community to sleep, but rather to wake it up.

Since the poem could not be written down, there could be no "authorized" version, no standard against which all other versions could be measured. Without an original version, there was no precise, no accurate way—in a literate's sense—of narrating the action. In oral cultures, reality was experienced in the poet's terms. The planets engage in a kind of improvisation, but tell roughly the same story day in and day out. The sun rises each day radiating more or less heat than the day before; the moon rises each evening slightly larger or smaller than the night before. But the sun and moon remain recognizable as the same celestial bodies. On a larger scale, the seasons complete their yearly cycle in the same way—some winters colder, some slightly warmer, but a period of time experienced always as winter. The plant life, too, blooms and dies away in this same fashion. The natural world reverberates with poetic meaning.

By imbibing from the waters of Mnemosyne, the poet allowed the dead to remain in touch with the living, as the dead carried on their quiescent lives just below the waters of Mnemosyne. Literates, on the contrary, talk about the dead in the past tense. Literates read signs of the dead in the cemetery—on gravestones and plaques and mausoleums—reminders that once upon a time they lived full and spirited lives. But no more. When literates tell stories about the dead, they rekindle a poignance, a sadness, as the finality of the departure of the dead hits them all over again. If the stories come across vividly enough, literate audiences might recognize the face of someone departed, or see their characteristic walk, once again, in their mind's eye. They might hear that distinct, departed voice in the mind's ear. Those who died in the ancient world could be experienced in a more radical way, through all the senses—they could be tasted and smelled and touched. People in pre-Socratic Greece could address the world of the dead and even provide precise directions for getting there.

A rhetor, charged with the task of resuscitating dear, departed ones, made it possible for them to walk among the living as ghosts. No sharp divisions separated the dead from the living. This characterizes all of experience in orality, which runs on without the literate's categorical breaks and discrete divisions. The dead, to focus on our example, fade into the living, the way one color in the rainbow seems to be absorbed by an adjacent color. Oral peoples know no other way of being but to situate themselves within the totality of their experiences. As I will show later in this chapter, orality simply does not possess the tools for high levels of abstraction. Walter Ong puts it this way: "Oral cultures tend to use concepts in situational, operational frames of reference that are minimally abstract in the sense that they remain close to the living human lifeworld." He points out that even in an area as sensitive and demanding as justice, which requires the application of universal principles, the pre-Socratic Greeks "thought of justice in operational rather than formally conceptualized ways. . . ."[12]

To analyze and abstract, the mind must be able to return to a subject over and over, for review and revaluation. The eye must see exactly what it saw the time before. Writing—in particular, as we shall see, alphabetic writing—enabled this major change to take place. The reader could go over the same sentence time and time again, puzzling out its meaning, analyzing its structure, teasing from it every nuance of meaning. A sentence could be scoured and sifted, finally, for the very last drop of its truth. Reading and writing provided the key exercise for the literate mind, allowing a critical eye to be turned to everyday experience.

The Clarence Thomas confirmation hearings can serve as a recent example. For days, what dominated casual conversation in America was one, maybe two questions: Did Clarence Thomas sexually harass Anita Hill? Was Anita Hill lying? These questions could of course be reframed another way: What was the truth? Most people, led by the stance of certainty from members of Congress, believed it was possible to discover the answer to this very knotty question. Citizens who did not know the rules or the procedures for uncovering the truth, and who were for the most part unfamiliar with the art of cross-examination, somehow believed the truth could be uncovered. How could they spot it? Some listened carefully to the details as Thomas retailed his story, others watched his every facial expression, still others studied his body movements, or those of his wife sitting by his side. People took sides, and argued over the eventual confirmation. Everyone sounded like an expert.

In orality, words disappear as soon as they are spoken; ideas

---

[12]Ong, *Orality and Literacy*, 49.

evaporate into the ether. One simply cannot recall them exactly. Nothing in orality really stands still or stays exact. Orality renders "analysis" impossible. No one could remember Thomas's words exactly; they had to be read in transcript. When storytelling provides the model for people's lives, "truth," in a literate's sense, is not possible. No one can narrate an event exactly the same way twice. The narrator fabricates a different version every time he opens his mouth. He takes his hero down one route one day, and down a different one the next time. But it's always the same hero, and he comes home to exactly the same welcoming arms every time. No one, however, would ever accuse the weaver of stories of perpetrating lies. No one would suspect him of telling something so abstract and absolute as the truth.

One can only accept each description, each story, each account of an event, at face value. No conclusion can ever be reached, for no standard of truth exists against which to measure a sentence or a story. Certainly all thought, in both primary oral and literate cultures, is to some degree analytic, in the sense that it breaks its materials into various components. But an abstractly sequential, classificatory, explanatory examination of experience or of sentences uttered out loud cannot be effected without the aid of reading and writing. People in oral cultures learn a great deal and possess and practice great wisdom, but they do not acquire their wisdom through what we know as "study." They learn by discipleship—a form of intimate apprenticeship—by listening, by repeating what they hear, by ingesting proverbs and learning ways of combining and recombining them, by assimilating other formulary bits of wisdom, by participation in a kind of collective recollection.

Writing and reading privilege the eye, by forcing attention on the visual. To reach meaning, the eye must continually scan. The eye constantly hungers for experience, and captures everything within its view. To decipher reality, the eye must dominate whatever comes into view by immediately breaking everything it sees into discrete parts. It analyzes spatial relationships, and sends this information back to the brain for processing. The slightest variations in light and shadow raise the most basic questions. Is that shape concave or convex? Does that edge lie closer or farther away from me? In this way the eye "handles" reality. A person who utters the phrase "I see what you mean" indicates that he or she understands in an architectonic way, that he or she understands the world of ideas in terms of a complicated maze of spatial relationships: Some ideas rank higher or lower than others; some stand in the foreground and some in the background. Perception shapes understanding, which in turn shapes perception.

But the eye, like every organ, has limitations. In order to determine what lurks inside a vessel, or even how much it contains, for instance, the eye needs to peer inside. What the eye cannot actually see, the person can only guess about. But a thump on the side of that same sealed container sends critical information reverberating back to the ear. A container half filled with water sounds different from a full one, and a solid sounds different from a liquid. Humans possess their own special kind of X-ray vision, but one which has to be processed through the ear. The ancients understood the ear's capacity for seeing. *Deaf* in an etymological dictionary leads to a Greek homonym for "blindness." (Likewise, the mouth does its own kind of listening. As we shall see later, an ability to hear well bears directly on the ability to speak clearly.)

Medieval doctors took advantage of the subtle connection between ear and eye, as a way of getting inside a patient's body. They determined the "soundness" of a patient by listening to his or her body as it was being thumped. Each of the four humors that coursed throughout the body echoed with its own unique sound. Too much yellow bile sounded quite different, for instance, from an excess of black bile. Phlegm reverberated differently from blood. To render an accurate diagnosis, the doctor had to "attune" himself to the patient. He had to listen to what the patient was saying through his or her own body—a highly articulate version of body language.

Ancient writers like Aristotle and Porphyry anthropomorphized the eye as a military strategist—a commanding general that sends out powerful rays imprisoning every object its gaze fixes upon; seeing constituted something physical and aggressive. Acting with noticeable force and persuasion, the eye moves out among the flotsam of experience and captures this bit and that. (This imagery characterized the earliest days of the camera—the eye turned mechanical—as George Eastman and others typically "captured" this or that image for all eternity.) But if the eye functions as an organ of aggression, the ear performs practically as its opposite—an organ of passive receptivity. It welcomes stimuli. In fact, unlike the eye, which can stop seeing at will—resting by closing its lid—the ear must be plugged up in order to stop hearing. The ear has no independent way of taking a break. It continually hears—during sleep, unconsciousness, and, according to some neuropsychologists, even during periods of prolonged coma.

As we have seen, sometimes the ear acts like an additional pair of eyes. The ear, too, can perform double duty; it seems to have an indirect line to the mouth. People who do not hear, or do not hear very well, cannot speak with clarity. The relationship is such an intimate one that we might more accurately think of listening and speaking as a hyphenated activity, like hunting-gathering, rather than two distinct operations. Diane Ackerman, in her book *A Natural History of the Senses,* corroborates this twin relationship by uncovering an interesting bit of etymology:

> In Arabic, *absurdity* is not being able to hear. A *surd* is a mathematical impossibility, the core of the word "absurdity," which we get from the Latin *surdus,* "deaf or mute" . . . which

in turn is a translation from the Greek *alogos,* "speechless or irrational."[13]

The ear resembles a dish for good reason. It functions best in the midst of noise, collecting the sound that washes over its surface. The ear harmonizes as it receives. It integrates and brings together. Think about being in an *audience.* The word itself points to a certain wholeness: *audience* is a mass noun, and refers to an indeterminate number of individuals. Fill an auditorium with one hundred people, or one hundred thousand, it still remains an *audience.* To reach the equivalent in literacy requires a borrowing; publishers often refer to a "reading audience," but the term is ghostly and hollow—a theoretical construct—pointing ultimately nowhere: to a theoretical conglomeration of common readers poring over books in individualized living rooms. Since orality by definition exists apart from literacy, it has very few critical terms by which it can describe and evaluate itself. Even so basic a term as *volume* must be borrowed from literacy, a word which initially meant a "scroll," from the Latin *volumen,* "anything rolled," and came to mean "intensity of sound" only through analogy—a large volume presumably speaking much more loudly than a slim one.

Sitting in an audience—in a theater, a music hall, or a lecture hall—constitutes a community experience. Everyone in the room hears the same sound at virtually the same time. Reactions tend to be group-motivated, fairly immediate, and noisy: the room fills with hissing, booing, cheering, applauding. Reading is a much more individualizing, personal experience—a single person facing an imaginary world reacts to a text in silence. The reader can enjoy the luxury of daydreaming and drifting off, returning to the text whenever he or she chooses, without missing a bit of the story. (Saving one's place in a theater audience,

---

[13]Diane Ackerman, *A Natural History of the Senses,* 175.

and saving one's place in a book, refer of course to two different kinds of space and thus require two very different acts.) The reader can even keep his activity a secret, by reading undetected in a remote, hidden spot, or behind closed doors.

Orality is practically synonymous with communal, group activity, in part because speaking and listening—an utter dependence on words—demands human interaction. (Talking to oneself in a literate culture stands out for most observers as a sure sign of craziness. A person must have a book propped up in front of him if he is going to talk out loud, and even then he is suspect.) In oral cultures, survival itself—where to find game animals, water, other friendly tribes—may hang on a word or gesture. In a subsistence community, one has to listen, and listen well. Social distance plays a critical role in coping with the environment. Stand close enough to the master and you can hear every word; stand too far back and you may not even be able to pick out facial expressions. Since orality knows no lying, messages tend to be, as they say, out in the open—loud enough for everyone to hear. Arguing can be heard for great distances. Laughter and crying also carry over great distances. The community in orality can harbor few secrets: What would you want or need to keep secret? To get away with telling a secret, one has to move out of eye-sight and ear-shot. There is no way to avoid it: True conversation feeds on the intimacy of face-to-face contact. Gesture and gesticulation underscore word and sentence. The whole body gets called into action during social intercourse. The Latin infinitive *sentire*, "to feel," produces both *sentence* and *sentience*.

Marcel Jousse, the Jesuit priest and scholar, who grew up in an essentially oral, peasant village, coined the term *verbomoteur* (verbomotor) to capture the essence of social intercourse in oral cultures. Jousse hoped to convey the way that words in oral cultures become somatized—incorporated, in the way perhaps that the Christians refer to the Word becoming enfleshed. In an oral culture, words incubate like so many bacteria deep inside a person. Gesturing, dancing, clapping—rhythmic movement of all kinds—help to get the word out. The ancient Greeks called education *mousiké*, Modern English "music," because they danced and clapped and sang out loud their mathematics and poetry and rhetorical exercises. Aristotle makes no distinction between rhythm and education, between *motion* and *emotion*. In both cases, one is "moved."

We can find contemporary examples of *verbomoteur* behavior. Watch a congregation in a synagogue chanting prayers aloud and you will witness an entire room of Jewish penitents rocking back and forth. *Davaning* is the Hebrew word for this kind of animated, rhythmic prayer activity—as if instead of praying, each person were enticing words to rise up from the innermost recesses of his or her body. Or try to buy something in a small village in Mexico and you will immediately find yourself witness to a living example of Jousse's *verbomoteur*. Villagers carry out business transactions through bantering and bargaining, a give-and-take that animates both buyer and seller, pitching their voices high above the crowd, tossing their hands here and there—a sideshow. When it's done well, an audience will slowly gather. They know that they will soon be watching something much more exciting than business. For what's really being traded here is not so much goods and money but rhetoric and skill. Everyone in the village expects the marketplace to erupt in bouts of bargaining, but natives place special value on those who have the skill to pull it off with style. A supermarket with its tidy aisles, fixed prices, and relative silence—individual selves each behind a cart—may represent the *mercado* in its most literate form. The supermarket says take it or leave it. If you find this product too expensive, choose another brand—much like changing channels on a TV set. You can grouse, but you cannot bargain. You can express yourself only through your cash—or with your feet. The buyer and the seller remain as silent as the fixtures: "Money talks."

Negotiations in the marketplace take on the appearance of storytelling—buyer and seller each improvising his own part of the narrative, both enjoying a carefully staged antagonism as they move toward a satisfactory conclusion—the eventual sale. The seller says he must have this amount of money, the buyer responds by saying he has, unfortunately, only this amount to spend. "But my product is special, mister." "Ah, but not that special, sir. I can get the same thing down the road for half the price." And on and on they go, spinning out their stylized dialogue of duplicity, each avoiding being trapped in the other's web. Neither party walks away insulted, neither party really offended, but both have played their indignant parts to the hilt. All this goes on, until the object of desire has been exchanged, and the event finally culminates in the *purchase:* a word that reveals the chase, the hunt, that underlies those colorful, vernacular transactions.

A Soviet psychologist, Alexander Luria, conducted a series of simple experiments with peasants who lived in remote areas of Uzbekistan and Kirghizia in the Soviet Union, in the early 1930s. His remarkable findings did not appear in English until some fifty-five years later, in a volume titled *Cognitive Development: Its Cultural and Social Foundations.* Luria provided a firsthand look at how the mind in orality conceptualizes reality, and offered a glimpse at the intellectual framework behind the term *verbomoteur.* He gathered his data from a group of peasants—mostly nonliterates, a few with a smattering of reading and writing—in relaxed, social settings over tea in neighborhood cafés.

Luria began with a simple test. He presented his interviewees with pictures of basic geometric figures. The peasants who were free of any contact with reading and writing never assigned the figures their abstract, categorical names, like circle, square, triangle, and so forth. Rather, they saw a circle as a plate, or the moon; a square could be nothing but a door, or a house, or an apricot drying board. The figures all had to be *like* something from their experience. Their reasoning did not go the other way around: a round thing from their immediate environment was never abstracted into the concept *roundness*. Since a circle cannot be tasted or touched or smelled, it cannot be assumed to exist. A circle appears only in various concrete instantiations—tire, moon, and so forth—and not as a Platonic form.

In another experiment, Luria showed his interviewees four objects, three belonging to one category, and one that did not belong. Again, his non-literate subjects responded in the most specific, situational way. Shown a drawing of a hammer, a saw, a log, and a hatchet, and asked which one did not belong, the peasants talked past the question, as if Luria were speaking nonsense. They focused on the log, the thing that needed to be cut and hewn into shape to make of it something useful. One man said, "They're all alike. The saw will cut the log and the hatchet will chop it into small pieces. If one of these has to go, I would throw out the hatchet. It doesn't do as good a job as a saw." When Luria tells him that the hammer, saw, and hatchet are all tools, the peasant persists in thinking in concrete, operational terms: "Yes, but even if we have tools, we still need wood—otherwise we cannot build anything." Which raises a serious existential question: Is a tool still a tool when it's not being used? Or does it only become a tool when it's being defined that way, and the definition gets put to a practical end? In a literate world, it seems, the hammer always carries its label, *tool*. In orality, the hammer must be used for very specific tasks.

All language is to some degree abstract. *Log* is already an abstraction—a category—into which various real logs can be stuffed. Circle and square engage language at a higher level of abstraction. But Luria's subjects grapple with experience at the most concrete level. What they cannot handle—quite literally touch and finger—they cannot get a handle on, and so cannot even entertain as something useful or reasonable, or even real.

When Luria's subjects could read or write even just a bit, they responded very differently. They immediately showed signs of categorical, abstract thinking. Asked to complete the series ax, hatchet, sickle, from saw, ear of grain, log, for instance, one semiliterate chose saw, defending his answer by pointing out that they were all farming tools. A few seconds later, however, he added, as if not to appear totally impractical, "You could cut the grain with the sickle."

Luria began to deduce certain features of "critical" thinking from his non-literate peasants. He concluded that his subjects did not use formal deductive logic. Which does not mean they did not think, or did not think in a logically ordered way. It means rather that they could not handle purely logical forms. Syllogistic problems, disembedded from actual experience, simply made no sense. Here is one of the examples Luria presented to the group: "In the far North, where there is snow, all bears are white. Novaya Zembla is in the far North and there is always snow there. What color are the bears?" One man's response typifies the entire group reaction: "I don't know. I've seen a black bear. I've never seen any others . . . each locality has its own animals."

Notice that this man breaks through the confines of the syllogism and roams outside it to find his own answer; he moves into the world itself. That's the only place to look for answers, for that's the *only* world. The peasant cannot construct an imaginary one in his mind. As Walter Ong so nicely observes, "the syllogism is thus like a text, fixed, boxed-off, isolated."[14] The riddle, on the other hand, an almost universally popular genre in oral cultures, requires the canniness of a hunter, searching beyond the confines of the riddle itself, to spot the answer. Figuring out the answer to a riddle requires falling back on past experience. For a person in orality, the syllogism is comparable to a game out of virtual reality—a hologram that lacks the substance and solidity of actual experience. Put your mind to it, and it disappears.

Any problem, in fact, that demanded Luria's peasants to stay within the confines built out of words only, met with disaster.

---

[14]Ong, *Orality and Literacy*, 53.

"Define a tree," Luria asks one of them. His subject gets indignant, even slightly angry, to be asked something so stupid: "Why should I? Everyone knows what a tree is, they don't need me telling them." Luria tries another way into the idea of definition: "If you went where there were no cars," Luria asks, "what would you tell people a car is?" The peasant responds in exactly the same operational, direct way: "If you get in a car and go for a drive, you'll find out." In oral cultures, there is simply no substitute for actual, real-world experience. Abstract talk will not take a person anywhere.

Finally, and really the most important of Luria's discoveries emerged from his series of questions to try to see if those Soviet peasants conducted their lives with any concept of self. To be aware of a concept of something called the self may require, in a most isolating way, the highest degree of abstraction and disembedding. All surrounding context must give way while attention gets focused inwardly on . . . what else can we call it? . . . that certainty called self. But if we remember how oral thinking tends to be so operational, it should not be surprising to learn they could not grasp the idea of self-analysis.

Self is another one of those terms, like consciousness, that defies definition. In fact, self and consciousness move through history together, and perhaps even as symbiotically connected as Siamese twins. Both self and consciousness force a division in a person and both arise only in literacy. Consciousness seems to require the idea of a self. But as I have tried to show, a certain kind of group consciousness begins to develop in orality where the self does not exist. An individualized consciousness, however, forms only in literacy. And that particular kind of consciousness does require a self. A history of consciousness can be traced, very roughly, through the word *self*.

The word *self* in English did not initially imply a reflexiveness—a pointing back to the "I"—but indicated an emphatic underscoring of a person or a thing. The first reference to that *self* comes from an early-tenth-century poet named Cynewulf:

"Nu is rodera Weard, God sylfa mid us" ("Now is the guardian of heaven, that self-same God, with us").[15]

The Oxford English Dictionary claims that *self* gained its reflexivity through an accident of spelling; it provides the following history: "The substantive use appears to have developed chiefly from collocations in which the Old English masculine and neuter genitive *selfes* admitted of being taken as the genitive of a neuter substantive. Thus, in *his selfes, Godes selfes,* it was easy to interpret *selfes* as a substantive governing the preceding genitive [because of similarity of spelling], instead of as a pronominal adjective in concord with it." The phrases should have read, "self-same God" or "God's own," rather than "his self" or "God's self."

It seems unlikely that a word so essential for talking about human life should come about through a casual mistake. In England, it was a growing literacy that prompted the need to give independent life to *self*. By 1300, when *self* fully emerged as a noun, in phrases like "my own self," "your dear self," "our two selves," literacy had already worked its way through society down to the level of the laity. The word carried such potency that, in only one century, it came to designate the interior object that could divert people from their religious devotion. In 1400, the Rule of Saint Benedict, verse 577, offered this cautionary advice to all monks: "Oure own self we sal deny, And folow oure lord god al-myghty."[16] To achieve monastic purity, the self had to be turned aside.

As the nature of reading changed from sounding words aloud to reading them in silence, it enabled a person to read letters and reflect on their meaning at the same time. The activity forced the reflective self into existence. In orality, words fly away too fast to be remembered or analyzed. The birth of the self requires what Horace observed as the characterizing feature of literacy: "Litera

---

[15]From "Cynewulf II," 1.134, in *The Poems of Cynewulf,* trans. C. W. Kennedy.

[16]This fifteenth-century translation is cited in *The Oxford English Dictionary*. For the original, see *Acta Sanctorum Ordinis S. Benedictii,* vol. 4, 191.

scripta manet"—"The written word remains." Only when words stand still can they be viewed and reviewed. The self is always a reflective self, and as it reflects acquires an individualizing consciousness.

Luria thus faced an impossible task in trying to draw out of his oral subjects anything more than the most rudimentary discussion of the literate self. But he persisted, and thought he could even ease them into talking by sipping tea with them and chatting leisurely about differences and similarities among village folk. When he got them to talk about other villagers, they characterized their neighbors and friends by their work habits, or daily routines. When asked about themselves, Luria found his subjects quickly turning to a discussion of their immediate surroundings or to their own behavior:

Q: "Are you satisfied with yourself, or would you like to be different?"

A: "I would like more land so I could plant more wheat."

Q: "People are different—calm, hot-tempered, sometimes their memory is poor. What do you think of yourself?"

A: "We behave well. If we were bad, no one would respect us."

Although Luria carried on his work over fifty years ago in conditions that could hardly be called controlled, his research can still help in understanding the world of orality. People who have not been trained in reading and writing—essentially a schoolroom education—do not think in highly abstract categories, all of which derive, as Ong and others have pointed out, not simply from tutored thought, but from "text-formed thought." Reading and writing radically alter perception. There seems to be no such thing as a little literacy. Even the smallest amount of literacy begins to alter perception. Almost immediately, it has the effect of lifting a person out of group thinking and setting him or her back down in a more self-centered and abstract world. Plato, the first real man of letters in the West, quickly moves to cast out from his Republic all poets—those old-fashioned rhetors—who retail stories of the here and now, in favor of abstract thinkers and philosophers. Modern philosophers use the technical phrase Platonic Forms to refer to abstract categories like the idea of the triangle, or of a circle. Plato's poets represent an antiquated way of thinking, old-fashioned in the immediate way they try to render reality. Plato wants thinkers, theorists—he demands philosophers for his new Republic. The idea of the future, of all that's forward-looking, lies buried in Plato's vision. The intellectual, like Plato, now participates *in* the body politic without being *of* it.

Through his interviews, Luria could describe the broad out-lines of thinking under the conditions of orality, but in the end he could learn little if anything of the native intelligence of his peasants. Any paper-test—indeed, most questions posed by a literate interviewer—strains the oral person to do something he or she seems unable to do, which we can call by any number of different names—decontextualization, abstraction, disembed-ding, defining, describing, categorizing—things the average grammar school child does every night in homework assign-ments. For Luria's peasants, however, these concepts seemed foreign. They lived fully in their sensory world. They saw no reason for removing themselves from it, and they had no tools for accomplishing that task. In the end, they refused to be pulled out of their immediate situation. Categorical terms held no practical use for them. "Tree" does not exist. But *that* tree stands over there; it provides shade and drops fruit. The pre-literate or non-literate remains deeply situated, and confronts experience by walking right up to it and grabbing hold of it.

Every young child who enters a classroom for the very first time, who crosses the threshold into his or her educational life, walks into that room as a miniature version of Luria's peasants, trailing all the magical excitement of the world of orality. That child enters school not only with unfathomable qualities, but with a way of perceiving the world that is alien to the teacher and to the school. So alien, in fact, that the child cannot be measured or tested by any of the great phalanx of teachers or administrators that he or she will face in the next eighteen years or more of school life. The child's solid connection in orality defends it, like Luria's peasants, against such untimely psychometric invasions. No one can calculate the child's native intelligence, for all the measuring instruments have been designed for literates. A youngster in that condition can only be observed, his or her behavior can only serve as matter for discussion. Does he play with the group; does she share? Is he a loner? The questions all try to get at the quality of the child's relation to the larger group, for the child still feels himself or herself as a member of the tribe. Young children reason just like Luria's peasants, accepting questions and statements at face value. They recognize shapes and figures as objects from their immediate environment. Circles *are* moons, and squares *are* blocks.

In kindergarten or the first grade, the child lives to hear stories—anticipates and expects them. Delights in their details. The child invests the teacher with all the power of the wise tribal master, the keeper of all the secrets, of group magic, and a deep repository of talking animal stories, every last one of them ending happily ever after. The good teacher, like the good storyteller, brings the entire world startlingly alive. Once children feel friendly enough with one another—that is, when they begin to "fit in"— the kindergarten classroom begins to resemble more and more the tribe or group at its rudimentary and basic, oral stage.

I do not mean to equate oral peoples with children. Far from it. Rather, I am suggesting that very young children participate in the only world they know, and that is a fairly lively kind of orality. After all, making sounds and noises is what they do— almost the only thing they do—from birth. Without uttering a single word, the child in its earliest years makes its needs and desires known; it signals hunger and discomfort and desire for love, all with a whimper or a gesture. Children express an orality so potent that they easily turn their mothers into skillful partners, training them to listen with what sometimes seems the acuteness of a clairvoyant, or a Guatemalan "echoman."

But why all the fuss? Why so much attention to what seems so ordinary—to talking and listening? What's the big deal about the human voice? The answer is a simple and direct one: Without a full experience in orality a person cannot truly embrace an animating and invigorating literacy. Orality is the armature, the framework, on which literacy takes its particular shape and fills out its contours. Orality makes social and emotional development possible. As many psycholinguists have argued, one's basic perception is molded by speech.[17] By swapping stories, a person learns that he does not have to accept things as they are. He can conjure his own world and manipulate it to his own liking. Young people thus talk themselves into a whole and consummate life: they hear out loud how they feel. Without practice in speaking and telling stories, without the joy of playing with language—which includes telling a few lies—youngsters quite literally *self*-destruct. It is not just that they have a weakened sense of self, but that without the formative power of language, the inner life never fills out and takes shape. That leaves nothing, no substance, for literacy to embrace.

A child who has not grown up in the bosom of orality can still reach literacy. No doubt about it. But in the majority of those cases, the youngster approaches reading and writing with caution or suspicion—as brand-new and alien processes—rather than coming to them with enthusiasm. For orality and literacy are not truly discrete categories. They both partake of sounds

---

[17]John L. Austin, *How to Do Things with Words*, sparked interest in speech and perception. See Jerome S. Bruner, *Child's Talk: Learning to Use Language;* Eve W. Clark and Herbert H. Clark, *Psychology and Language: An Introduction to Psycholinguistics;* P. M. Greenfield and J. Smith, *The Structure of Communication in Early Language Development;* M. A. K. Halliday, *Learning How to Mean;* and George A. Miller, "Dictionaries in the Mind," *Language and Cognitive Processes.*

and meanings. They both try to get a point across. Literacy, a much later development in the history of civilization than speech, feeds off orality.

To say it more graphically, literacy fits over orality like a protective glove, following every contour and outline that orality hands it. Orality provides the rhythms, the intonations and pitches, the very feelings, that find final expression in writing. Orality thus serves as a preparation—a necessary and powerful foundation—for the construction we call literacy. Children need to hear language in order to learn language. This may sound like a tautology, but a child must hear language spoken by a live human being. Conversely, a living human being must listen to the child, and suffer through all the millions of questions and complaints. An electronically simulated voice will not work. Breyne Arlene Moskowitz, a linguist who studies language acquisition in children, relates the following story. A small boy who had normal hearing but deaf parents, remained indoors most of the time because of a severe case of asthma. His parents, who communicated with him in American Sign Language, placed him in front of the TV set every day so he could learn English. By age three, he could sign with ease, but could neither understand nor speak English. After studying this child for years, Moskowitz reached the only conclusion possible. Just as bottles of poison come banded with skulls and crossbones, her conclusion should be plastered across every TV set. She writes: "A television set does not suffice as the sole medium for language learning because, even though it can ask questions, it cannot respond to a child's answers. A child, then, can develop language only if there is language in her environment and if she can employ that language to communicate with other people in her immediate environment."[18] By this standard, most American children today grow up in an environment from which language has in effect been stripped.

---

[18]Breyne Arlene Moskowitz, "The Acquisition of Language," in *The Emergence of Language: Development and Evolution,* ed. William S-Y. Wang, 135.

Historical example tells us that cultures first pass through a phase of orality before they move, if they ever do move, into literacy. Every young child recapitulates that same history. Every youngster did, that is, until quite recently. Fewer and fewer young children in this country ever fully enter the world of orality, with disastrous implications for their lives. High school dropout rates across the country hover around 40 percent, climbing even higher in the inner-city schools. Reading scores in California have declined every year for high school seniors for the past decade. If America hopes to continue producing generations of young people whose lives have been shaped by reading and writing, then I am describing a major crisis. The vast majority of young children now experiences the human voice primarily through TV and movies, records and the radio—electronic wizardry that has mesmerized two or three generations into accepting electrical impulses for the real thing.

"In present-day America we encounter difficulty in teaching our children to read. Is this possibly because we do not take pains concurrently to teach them the art of oral recitation?"—this is the classicist Eric Havelock's question.[19] While Havelock might ask the right question, he skims over a basic, underlying issue. No one can teach oral recitation effectively in a classroom when students do not experience true orality in their own lives. Havelock senses that underlying problem: "Unless the developing child is first grounded in the oral culture of his ancestors for which his developing brain has been formed to cope, how can he be expected successfully to take the artificial step of converting his oral recognition of language into a visual act?" A child does not have to learn to speak and to listen; he or she learns orality by imitation and participation. Reading and writing are a differ-

---

[19] Eric Havelock, *The Literate Revolution in Greece and Its Cultural Consequences*, 45.

ent matter: they must be learned. They demand memorizing the alphabet, and understanding certain rules. That's what Havelock means by an "artificial step." But practice with language, preparation for understanding words and sentences and meanings, begins in orality.

Conventional wisdom these days argues that CDs and TV offer young people the opportunity to immerse themselves in the world of orality. Children watch on the average of five hours of TV every day—seven days a week. Don't they get a large dose of the human voice? Don't they hear a lot of conversation—on talk shows, news shows, sitcoms, and so on? In truth, young people watch and listen to a staggering amount of electronically generated media. The average child from the ages of six to eighteen will have watched about sixteen thousand hours of television and spent an additional four thousand hours listening to radio and recordings or watching movies. They will have passed more hours with these media than in the classroom or with their parents. In less than two decades, daily television viewing by youngsters from six to eighteen has increased 70 percent. Noting this increase over the past twenty years, savvy electronic firms have introduced young boys and girls to personal computers and video games. In a 1983 study, Godfrey Ellis found that in the sixth grade students he studied in Oklahoma schools, 73 percent of them reported owning a video game and 17 percent a PC. They spent on the average two hours a day playing video games. More than half the boys (52 percent) in addition played games at arcades at least once a week, and 35 percent of the girls played at least once a week.[20]

But all of this does not add up to orality. Anyone who speaks through electronic media has had his or her patter carefully shaped by a script; the delivery—tone, intonation, emphasis—has been rehearsed. Every program is a playlet. Few if any

---

[20]Godfrey J. Ellis, "Youth in the Electronic Environment: An Introduction," *Youth and Society*.

programs can dare risk spontaneity or improvisation, let alone freewheeling conversation. Corporate sponsors are not paying to be surprised. Even the most relaxed and human-sounding programs consist of a wall of sound—no pauses or apologies, no false starts, no dead space. Silence means a loss of revenue.

No one listening to electronic media participates in orality. An electronic medium violates the cardinal rule of conversation: The listener must be able to interrupt. And interruption, along with argument, questions, and repetitions—people roaming out of control and then back in—lie at the heart of orality. In conversation, the participants have the option of breaking the rules. Rudeness threatens to burst on the scene at every moment. Radio delivers a packaged, highly orchestrated message. If two people cannot see each other's faces, conversation can hardly be said to take place.

Television stands several steps removed from orality, for the box projects the illusion of actual human beings speaking with a free and easy give-and-take. Even a situation that purports to carry tremendous importance for the nation, such as a presidential press conference, and which comes off as immediate and real and personal, has been meticulously rehearsed and shaped. The president has prepared responses handed to him, answering at times with prescribed hand and body gestures. Press conferences are video events every bit as routine as a prime-time sitcom. From the standpoint of true orality, TV broadcasts an auditory and visual lie.

TV kills the human voice. People cannot argue with anything on the screen. TV images pass by too fast for young minds to consider or analyze them. Young people mistake the stuff of commercials for real satisfaction. Of course, if they don't like what's on the screen, they're free to turn the channel, or wait for the next show or commercial break. Better yet, they can tune it out. Which requires little effort these days—the push of a button on a handheld remote.

What has to be understood is that children transfer that kind of behavior to real-life situations. They come to believe that tuning a human being out requires no more effort, and carries no more significance, than turning a screen off, or changing a channel. One of the most intense cries of contemporary life has come to be "Let's turn off the TV and talk about this!"

Even more important, TV makes of young people passive recipients of hundreds of thousands of images of violence, of sex, or of sexual violence, each and every day and each and every evening. Even if a child takes issue with those images while sitting in front of the screen—a monologue with a light and sound show—the images still work unrelentingly, leaving their indelible impression on the imagination. Between the ages of three and five—the height of the brain's critical period of cognitive and linguistic development—the average child watches at least 28 hours of TV per week. The average viewing time for elementary students is 25 hours a week, and for high school students, 28 hours a week. By the time that child reaches five years of age, he or she will have already watched a staggering 6,000 hours of TV programming. Given what we know about the effects of TV, that statistic can be restated this way: By age five, the average child has received 6,000 hours of programming.

Training like this thoroughly debilitates young people. It short-circuits the natural, emotional development they need to become healthy human beings; it strangles the development of their own voices, and denies them their own imaginative powers. Some neuro-anatomists argue that excessive TV viewing—more than four or five hours per day, seven days a week—ultimately takes a serious cognitive toll. They believe that the limbic system of the brain—the mysterious, subcortical part of the brain that researchers designate as the image-making center—develops more slowly when a young person spends half of his or her waking life in front of the TV set.

The limbic system, sometimes called the emotional brain, among its other functions regulates the body's immune system and thus controls the body's ability to heal itself. This helps explain the current interest in conjuring images of good health as a way of achieving health. But the limbic system serves a much more specific function in the child's developing, interiorized emotional life, providing the "seat of all the emotional bonds, from that of mother-infant, child-family, child-society, the foundational pair-bond of male-female, and so on. It is involved in dreaming, visions of our inner world, subtle-intuitive experiences, and even the daydreams and fantasies spinning out of its upper neighbor, the neocortex."[21]

The limbic system seems to feed on self-generated images. According to some researchers, when young people conjure their own scenes in the mind's eye—while reading, for instance, or during sessions of storytelling, or while sitting and daydreaming—the heart produces a hormone that feeds the limbic system, strengthening it to generate more images of a more and more vivid nature. A strong limbic system provides a natural defense against the constant bombardment of images of sadism and violence that permeate contemporary consumer culture.[22]

The real issue is not whether a child who sees images of violence on TV runs outside and commits his or her own acts of violence in imitation. It is to understand the biological, neurological effects of watching media; it is to understand the way TV washes the child clean of his or her own images. If these neuroanatomists are right, a young child fed on TV or movies or video games faces a difficult task of trying to imagine a world in which depersonalized violence is *not* the prevailing signature of validation and stimulation.

Joseph Chilton Pearce has written about child development

---

[21]Joseph Chilton Pearce, *Evolution's End: Claiming the Potential of Our Intelligence*, 44–45.

[22]See Keith A. Buzzell, *The Neurophysiology of Television Viewing: A Preliminary Report;* Robert Cloninger, "Three brain chemical systems"; Paul D. MacLean, "The Triune Brain in Conflict," P.O. Sifneos, ed., in *Psychotherapy and Psychosomatics.*

throughout his life. In recent years, he has focused on the adverse relationship between TV and the old mammalian, or limbic, neural structure of the brain. His findings have great importance for literacy:

[T]elevision floods the infant-child brain with images at the very time his or her brain is supposed to learn to make images from within. Story telling feeds into the infant-child a stimulus that brings about a response of image making that involves every aspect of our triune system. Television feeds both stimulus *and* response into that infant-child brain, as a single paired-effect, and therein lies the danger. Television floods the brain with a counterfeit of the response the brain is supposed to learn to make to the stimuli of words or music. As a result, much structural coupling between mind and environment is eliminated; few metaphoric images develop; few higher cortical areas of the brain are called into play; few, if any, symbolic structures develop. $E = MC^2$ will be just marks on paper, for there will be no metaphoric ability to transfer those symbols to the neocortex for conceptualization, and subsequently, no development of its main purpose: symbolic conceptual systems.

An equally insidious effect is habituation—the natural condition of our two animal brains with their hard-wired response to "concrete information." Unable to adapt to novelty, these primitive systems avoid it. They seek out compatible stimuli and feel "comfortable" with familiar input unless moved by the novelty seeking of the neocortex . . . each new story requires a whole new set of patterns to accommodate the new stimuli, requiring entrainment of all three brains over and over. The brain is challenged anew and continually enlarges the number of neural fields involved in new image-pattern flows.[23]

---

[23]Pearce, *Evolution's End: Claiming the Potential of Our Intelligence*, 165–66. The "triune brain" is made up of the reptilian, the old mammalian (limbic), and the new mammalian.

By the time a child leaves elementary school, if that child watches on the average only two to four hours of TV a day, he or she will have been witness to over eight thousand murders. But the word *witness* has to be carefully considered here, for the child has been silent about, complicitous to, has learned to accept as normal, habituated behavior, the most graphic dramatizations possible of the most heinous crime against humanity—premeditated murder. TV makes of the child a witness who has been denied the opportunity to act—a creature of impotence who has the power to speak but who has had his or her vocal cords cut. Youngsters can reveal what they harbor in their hearts only to themselves, and only in the darkest, most private moments—in secret, or in dreams. In an eerie scenario, the child views the most horrible of those images inside his or her mind twice, once when he watches them on the TV or movie screen, and once again when they return to haunt his dream life.

Watching TV creates the most vicious of cycles: It makes a person more susceptible to manufactured images by diminishing that person's ability to generate his own, a condition akin to the suppression of the immune system. Watching TV also weakens the will. With TV near at hand, the child has no need to fall back on natural resources and confront a state such as boredom. It prevents the child from entering into what one critic of the medium calls "down time"—those moments when a child's schedule has fallen apart and he falls helplessly into the flow of time. Facing afternoons with "nothing to do," children once made up games, or figured out something interesting to occupy themselves. Nowadays, children do not have to engage their imagination. They have no need to make up new stories, or invent new games, or concoct different versions of reality. TV studios do the work for them. TV says, No one should ever experience loneliness or boredom; no one should ever spend a single moment without being entertained.

TV broadcasts with such power that it has even affected the definition of boredom. Television programs—and films, as well—create the expectation that to be satisfying an experience must reach the highest pitches of intensity. That translates into scenes of shooting and fighting and killing and making love. Anything short of such intensity, for TV fans, does not constitute meaningful experience. Boredom, a subject little discussed by most child psychologists, passes without comment as a non-activity. But boredom can serve as a meditative opportunity, a quiet space where youngsters can discover what things they find interesting. As the social critic Walter Benjamin points out, "Boredom is the dream bird that hatches the egg of experience."[24] Underlying boredom, where nothing at all seems to be happening—opposite of the TV's image—lies the possibility for a child to discover something of extreme importance: himself or herself. That moment of expanded quiet—and a child knows very few such moments—offers the young person an opportunity to learn what he or she believes, and thinks, ultimately providing moments of great strength. If the youngster can persist in that down time, boredom can turn into an episode of self-reflective insight.

But not when the TV interferes. The TV distracts the young person from his or her boredom, and defuses the frustration and anxiety of a child's lassitude. On the TV, something happens all the time, a powerful model of what life should look like. Once the child turns on the TV for something "to do," the set begins to dictate what the child needs and desires, not just through commercials, but through action programs as well. The youngster uses the set as an electronic mother, one who will attend to every need without having ever met the child. But the set can only function as a universal mother who can deliver only depersonalized, standardized solutions.

TV thus delivers one of the most debilitating psychological blows in denying the youngster the chance to turn inside himself or herself and to have a silent conversation with that budding

---

[24]Walter Benjamin, *Illuminations: Essays and Reflections,* 91.

social construct, the self. The TV short-circuits the developmental process, replacing emotional and psychological needs and desires with consumer values: Instead of listening to his or her own inner voice, the young person pays attention to the loudest commercial or the noisiest cop show. Adam Phillips, a child psychotherapist, has recently written about the developmental possibilities of boredom:

> [B]oredom is actually a precarious process in which the child is, as it were, both waiting for something and looking for something, in which hope is being secretly negotiated; and in this sense boredom is akin to free-floating attention. . . . But to begin with, of course, the child needs the adult to hold, and hold to, the experience—that is, to recognize it as such, rather than to sabotage it by distraction. The child's boredom starts as a regular crisis in the child's developing capacity to be alone in the presence of the mother. In other words, the capacity to be bored can be a developmental achievement for the child.[25]

How does one come to feel confident and strong? The process is obviously a long and complicated one, and different for each person. But the first steps come out of thin air—the human voice. Speaking sentences to another human being, listening for a response, marshalling thoughts in order to respond again, and on and on, encourages a person to care about other people—to pay attention to their "story"—and to weave their story into one's own. It generates trust. In the exchange of stories, the hope arises, as the poet Robert Browning writes, that the other will "rap and knock and enter in our soul."[26] When the door opens, we pray that someone interesting is at home. But the self—that

---

[25]Adam Phillips, *On Kissing, Tickling, and Being Bored: Psychoanalytic Essays on the Unexamined Life*, 69.

[26]Robert Browning, "Bishop Blougram's Apology," line 37, in Ian Jack, ed., *Browning: Poetical Works, 1833–64*, 650.

instrument of reflective subjectivity and humane coherence that modern society assumes as its ultimate experiential and moral reference point—cannot and should not be taken for granted. Without a literacy based on a fully experienced social orality, that self remains a psychological and social impossibility.

A child's literacy begins with the mouth and ear. Courtney B. Cazden, professor of psychology at Harvard University, found that children benefit less from adult correction of their speech errors than from straight conversation. They learn by talking. And they learn faster without being constantly corrected. Conversation constitutes the child's introduction to a sophisticated rhythm, to the "shape" of an argument, to suspense and climax, to self-correction and modification, and most important, perhaps, to resolution. Talking offers an introduction, in effect, to life—to the stories that one begins to tell and that make up an accountability to one's experience. As a child continues to engage in discussion with other people, he must constantly draw on his inner life, his capacity to feel and his ability to reason, in "coming up" with a response, as the discussion rolls around, like a large wheel, turning and returning, to this point and that. The bulk of a relationship consists of stories that people tell to each other—about everyday things, or more personally about their hopes and desires, or even more intimately, about love and fear. Obviously, people touch each other—relationships thrive on physicality—but how much more passionate that embrace when we feel tightly held, like a parenthesis, by that other person's story. At those moments, we feel doubly touched—both physically and emotionally.

By narrating his version of things, a child shapes the world to his liking. By changing his story, that same child goes one step further, and re-creates the world. What a lesson to learn "by heart"—to know that he or she does not have to accept things as they are, but that he can transform them with his breath. What power in a sentence! What *playful* power. In the mouth of a skillful person, words become plastic. Imagining is most imme-

diately a semantic operation. Through language we remain playful creatures—each one of us fulfilling ourselves as *homo ludens*.

How someone comes to be a person is an infinitely complex
process, perhaps the most mysterious of life's journeys. But telling stories, in both senses—narration and lying—is one way of
getting there. It is misleading to think of stories as words that
merely emerge from the mouth, affecting only the tongue and
lips and vocal cords. Stories spring from emotional roots that
grow as large underground as the stories we hear above: Every
time a child rattles one off, he taps deep into those emotional
roots, for the stories get told from the "inner senses" out. A
person, after all, is a "sounding through," a *per-sonare*, or a
"telling through."

Very few parents today tell stories to send their children off to
sleep. Most children watch TV and then drift off, carried into
bed still dreaming, perhaps, of the images they have just witnessed on some evening program. TV does not tell complicated
stories. In fact, it tends to tell the same story over and over.
That's the meaning of *program* and *format*. The overwhelming
majority of TV programs intentionally avoids the complicated
nuances of real social conflict. They resolve things neatly and
tidily, and in a prescribed time limit of a half hour, or an hour.
Unlike novels and short stories, which require readers to confront ambiguity and encourage them to ponder meaning, TV
programs sum up and synthesize. Whatever questions the program raises, it will also quickly answer. Each show offers a
catharsis; each show provides information.

A child without the ability to make up stories—a child whose
imagination is shaped by plot summaries and comedies of situations from the season's latest, popular series—cannot conjure
stories and tell them silently to himself or herself. The child can
only recount clichés. Packaged stories have the same effect as
junk food, standardizing taste and eliminating surprise. Clichés
put the clamps on one's life; they dampen excitement by emphasizing regularity and predictability. They close off the possibility

of penetrating through the surface of experience to reach meaning at a deeper level. When everyone watches the same shows—
the goal of national networks—everyone receives the same
education. In an electronic perversion of the communal experience in orality, every member of the community not only hears
the same message but also sees the same images. Something out
of the ordinary, like a new idea, or a new slant on an old idea,
can only startle and shock. Innovation gets easily missed or
dismissed—except when it comes as a special effect.

In contemporary TV programming, it's the commercials,
quite often, rather than the programs that hold a child's interest,
so that children receive as a side benefit an education in consumerism. In a 1993 study, Michael Morgan, a sociologist at the
University of Michigan, discovered that more schools from low-
income areas have subscribed to Channel One—the channel
that is beamed into classrooms, complete with commercials—
than those in middle- or high-income areas.[27] This means that
poor children not only get an education each morning in acquisi-
tive consumerism, but since they cannot afford most of the
objects dangled in front of them, they receive an education in a
kind of frustrated consumerism. The screen says, Buy this stuff.
But the parents say, We can't afford it. Some of those youngsters
will go to extremes, of course, to find a way to get those goods.
Which means that some of those youngsters will wind up telling
their stories to a judge.

In its programming and in its commercials, TV creates an
atmosphere that actually prevents live storytelling. It fosters the
absolutely wrong attitude for developing the foundations for
powerful literacy in its full sense. Young children need to feel
lost, confused, and bewildered enough to concoct their own
stories in order to climb out of tight situations. They need to
string together narrative threads from here and there to reach
meaning in their lives. TV trivializes problems by offering swift

---

[27]Michael Morgan, National Public Radio interview, June 1993.

and pat solutions. It reduces the complexity of living to a simple set of equations. It projects conflict and the most serious of social problems as entertainment—material shaped into a spectacle that is privately consumed.

We need to understand the full implications of this situation if we hope to address the deeper issues lying beneath contemporary society's much discussed, but, in fact, little heeded, "literacy crisis."

I sense that we shall not come home to the
facts of our unhousedness, of our eviction
from a central humanity in the face of the
tidal provocations of political barbarism
and technocratic servitude, if we do not
redefine, if we do not re-experience, the
life of meaning in the text, in music, in art.
We must come to recognize, and the stress
is on *re*-cognition, a meaningfulness which
is that of a freedom of giving and of recep-
tion beyond the constraints of immanence.

—George Steiner, *Real Presences*

You can read the sentence you are reading now as many
times as you like. You can pass it on to a literate friend, and he
or she can read it, too—without ever having seen that combination of letters before. If you close your eyes, the image of that
sentence will most likely linger dimly in your mind's eye. With
only twenty-six letters, I have the unbounded freedom to write
anything about anything else. Or I can pull off other tricks just
as remarkable. I can fabricate lies—create a convincing fiction.
And, according to many linguists and philosophers, two even
more spectacular feats find expression in writing: I can compete
with prevailing, accepted notions of the truth by constructing
what philosophers call counter-factuals; and, I can talk about

events that might arrive some time in the future.[1] This congeries of miracles has been made possible through just one simple act: the transformation of speech into a visual act.

This transformation—the one you are experiencing this very instant—brought the Greeks into a consciousness they could never have imagined in their world of orality. What a breathtaking invention—so elegant, the Greek alphabet had to be invented only once. Unlike hieroglyphics where meanings of figures must be agreed upon by the group in advance, alphabetic letters could be arranged in any order and deciphered by any member of the group who had committed its sounds to memory. A person did not have to recognize pictures, or recall ideas or syllables, but instead had only to recognize a series of characters and to remember what sounds they represented. The combinations could never be exhausted. Vocabulary could be expanded indefinitely. Hieroglyphics had to mirror reality; experience placed a cap on expression. If you had not seen the picture *before,* you lost the meaning. But with the alphabet only the writer's imagination limited expression. Vocabulary could certainly throw up a serious barrier to meaning. But pictures no longer had to match up with one's experience. The text no longer held a one-to-one correspondence with reality. The alphabet could expand the possibilities of experience by re-creating the world in the reader's imagination.

W riting had been around for thousands of years when the alphabet appeared on the scene. The alphabet made its special mark mainly because with it retrieval—the transformation of marks back into sound—became so easy. Where did this amazing invention come from? If it was invented only once, then it

---

[1]See Herman Wekker, *The Expression of Future Time in Contemporary British English;* and Frederick J. Newmeyer, *Grammatical Theory: Its Limits and Its Possibilities.*

must have appeared full blown one day. What does the earliest extant alphabetic inscription say? It was incised into a vase—commonly referred to as the Dipylon Vase—roughly between 750 and 690 B.C. The line, in hexameter, written in Phoenician order from right to left reads: "Who now of all dancers sports most playfully?"

That the earliest surviving alphabetic line—a piece of graffito, oral in its syntactic structure—should refer to dance and play, to the lightness of the individual heart and the lightheartedness of the entire group, reflects one of literacy's strongest and most poignant claims: the ability to take the ephemeral quality of reality, the dancing fragility of experience, and freeze it forever like Keats's lovers on *his* famous Grecian Urn: "For ever panting, and for ever young."

One theory of the invention of the alphabet supposes that it was an improvement on the writing system used by Phoenician sailing merchants, who carried on trade with the Greeks. To convert the Phoenician system into one that would capture all the Greek sounds, and thus make communication possible, the Greeks adapted the softer Phoenician consonants as vowel sounds. This theory would suggest that the impulse behind the invention of alphabetic writing was a commercial one, that the alphabet simply made record-keeping possible for the first time. Archaeologists have substantiated this mercantile theory with evidence that connects writing with accounting, a connection that persists in words like *conte* and *raconteur* for "story" and "storyteller" in French, or phrases in English like "recounting a story" or giving "accounts of an event" or even "summing up" a story.

Because the Phoenicians did not represent every sound in their writing system, their readers must have stumbled over those sentences that seemed unclear, having to reach an interpretation through context or informed guessing. The Greeks, on the other hand, left nothing to chance. Their alphabet allowed for economy of expression, and at the same time, for accuracy of expression. That was the great advance over the Phoenicians' alphabet—full disclosure. The Greeks succeeded in devising a writing system that carried all the exactness and accuracy of a number system. Indeed, letters and numbers share a similar history. In every culture, when literacy rises, numeracy also increases. They both require people to abstract ideas and concepts from a concrete reality.

Writing, a system of making permanent marks that could be held in storage and deciphered at a later time—bringing its contents back to life, as it were—did not, then, initially perform any task so sophisticated as recording the fullness of speech or the intricacies of thought. The earliest writing appears to have been used to keep track of domesticated animals, such as cattle.[2] Archaeologists date this kind of writing to roughly eleven thousand years before the birth of Christ, using as evidence small clay markers in the shape of circles, ovoids, diamonds, and double diamonds, unearthed in ancient Mesopotamia, now part of Iraq. These markers, which appear in the early Neolithic period, just as hunting-and-gathering gives way to plant and animal domestication, perhaps enabled proto-farmers to carry out their new way of life in agriculture. No longer at the mercy of the migrations of game, or the vagaries of weather, farmers could guarantee a continual supply of food, but only by storing excess during times of bounty and redistributing it, later, during leaner times. Writing thus not only moved the world toward thinking abstractly—one thing, one token, standing in place of something else, a cow—but also prepared people to accept some vague notion of time, distinct from the natural rhythms of seasons and stars, in which events that had not yet occurred could still be anticipated. People thus began to live with a new, extraordinary idea: the expectation that something was about to happen. This

---

[2]"Keeping track" literally means finding an economical way of recording an animal's tracks, so the beast could be re-collected later. Making marks on a piece of clay or parchment may simply imitate the prints left by animals.

remarkable fiction was an embryonic form of what we call the future.

Some three thousand years later, and in roughly the same area, a significant change takes place in the way the tokens themselves are presented, moving this crude counting system much closer to writing. Like the cows, the tokens themselves have now been stored, inside the egg-shaped ceramic cases called *bullae,* their shells marked with the precise number of tokens stored inside. This method of representing reality—tokens inside bullae—turned the *actuality* of inventory into a *model* of inventory. (While this development suggests a certain degree of abstraction, it is undercut by the concreteness of the clay objects themselves. Tokens can still be turned over, felt and smelled, in the hand.)

This crude form of writing, dating from as early as eight thousand years ago, unwittingly captures the very nature of writing: Scratches announced that a living message lies stored inside this system of script, but you, the outsider, have to figure out how to crack it open, how to break the code, without shattering the shell itself. In an eerie, uncanny way, these bullae make clear the metaphysical interior that writing posits, an interiority that the reader himself or herself internalizes in the act of reading. Those tokens of reality—markers or scratches—hold out their promise of some mysterious, inner meaning. Once again: the code only needs to be cracked and the contents spilled. But that must be done by a sleight of eye, in a deft turn of magic, for the breaking must occur while the shell remains intact.

Five thousand years later—around 3,500 B.C.—this same crude marking system takes yet another step toward writing. In roughly the same general area in the Middle East, archaeologists have unearthed what have been called the first tablets, on which were inscribed figures that stand for livestock and grain. These tablets resemble not at all the crude stone slabs that Moses holds aloft in countless paintings. Rather, they look like the top half of the bullae, a carapace sliced off some giant insect: convex clay shells.

The tokens have disappeared. The scratches on the surface of the shell now serve as a record of what once could be found inside the complete bulla. Here, for the first time, writing has truly emerged from its "shell." The "reader" must take on faith the prior existence of real cattle or actual sheaves of grain, the actuality of which has faded into abstraction. Writing now by-passes the tokens altogether and refers, in a much more abstract way, to a reality that it tries to take into account. That the scratches refer to some phantom tokens can only exist as a memory. That they refer to some invisible cattle or grain can only exist as an idea. The reader has to have faith in the certainty of the record.

Writing, which served the purpose of keeping track of goods in inventory was itself a storehouse of sorts. Messages were held inside letters and could be called up on demand.[3] This double idea of inventory can be expanded. Anyone who plays with a writing system for very long internalizes various levels of inventory keeping: sound retrieved from letters, meanings retrieved from sentences, ideas retrieved from the memory, and so on. And of course reading and writing, literacy itself, is one great inventory of technical inventions: punctuation marks, spaces, chapters, capitals, and other advances that made reading, and, in particular, silent reading possible.

The entire process seems like smoke and mirrors. No wonder that Merlin, that wily professor of magic, assumes the title of the patron saint of writing by the early Middle Ages. For writing can effect the most amazing feats of magic. Writing successfully

---

[3]The word *inventory* derives from the Latin root *veneri*, "to come to," or "come upon," hence "to discover," a root crucial to the act of reading. Letters constantly beckon the reader; and the reader indeed "comes to" a reading or interpretation of the text. The reader also "comes to" letters with anticipation and expectation, for he senses that knowledge and information reside in every sentence, in every letter. (*Invention* comes from the same root.)

transported the idea of certainty—reliable, precisely reportable information—across the barriers of time and space. With a small amount of effort, for instance, you can not only read this sentence as many times as you desire; you can also read it practically anywhere you please. Today, everyone takes all of this for granted, but it represents a change of the highest order over orality, where sentences disappear into the ether as soon as one utters them. Writing defies time, in a sense, by reaching for a kind of immortality. I can read a manuscript today that was completed in the Middle Ages, or even centuries earlier.

With alphabetic writing, the mantic act—the magic act—continues in a semantic of undisguised hope.[4] The highly literate writer knows how to deconstruct real space and time and reconstruct an imaginary universe through casting counter-factuals: "If Marilyn Monroe were president of the United States." Counter-factuals speak of a supreme, human arrogance, a profane *IF* set against the intolerable *IS* of God's creation. But an *IF* has sufficient power to negate even the fact of Kennedy's presidency with the delightfully frivolous notion of Marilyn's. For a moment, Kennedy is placed in doubt, or vanishes altogether. History turns tail and hides; the writer has something

---

[4]*Semantics* originally referred to divination through changes of weather. What stories do the clouds contain? The imagination can find all kinds of shapes in the fluffy stuff: out of nothing comes significance. Recall the playful exchange between the distracted Hamlet and the accommodating Polonius, who changes as rapidly as the weather.

H: Do you see yonder cloud that's almost in the shape of a camel.
P: By th' mass and 'tis, like a camel indeed.
H: Methinks it is like a weasel.
P: It is backed like a weasel.
H: Or like a whale.
P: Very like a whale.

Hamlet insinuates his madness on Polonius through semantics: for Hamlet, like the Queen of Hearts, things mean what he says they mean—at least for the moment.

better up his sleeve. In our mind's eye we see Marilyn occupying the Oval Office. At this level, language carries all the dynamic charge of good fiction.

As if that didn't grant humans enough raw power, we have George Steiner's observation: "Of all evolutionary tools toward survival, it is the ability to use future tenses of the verb—when, how did the psyche acquire this monstrous and liberating power?—which I take to be foremost. Without it, men and women would be no better than 'falling stones' (Spinoza)."[5] The future, counter-factuals—these two very crucial grammatical constructions serve as vessels into which we pour dreams and desires of change, of progress, of hope.

The Greek alphabet filled out Semitic writing systems by making language more "stream-lined"—"fluent"—and meandering as a river. In Hebrew, the reader confronts a series of consonants grouped into what can best be called "roots." To consider Hebrew in the context of language's beginnings in accounting, Hebrew can never give a full record, for it leaves out, does not keep track of, vowels. It leaves that task up to the reader, who sounds the consonants out loud by supplying the missing vowels—that is, by supplying the human voice. Without vowels, consonants (*consonare*, "with sound") lay dead on the page. Every consonant—an *f, g, k*—can only be heard as an *ef,* or *gee,* or *kay*—that is, they only come to life with the assistance of vowels. So Hebrew presents this special burden of responsibility for the reader: As one scans each root on the page, he must at the same time interpret it for all possible meanings, making certain that the word created will make sense in the context of the entire narration. Without this mental exercise (a "dry run" really), the reader remains uncertain what vowel sound to add in order to transform a root into a word. Slight variations in vowel sounds can produce very disparate meanings from the same root. *Tsahok,* for example, means "laughter"; *tsahak* means "sexual inter-

---

[5]George Steiner, *Real Presences*, 56.

course"—two quite different, though perhaps emotionally related, meanings. The reader has the freedom of sounding both
of these words from the same root. Only context will dictate the
appropriate level.

The rabbis of the third and fourth centuries condemned reading silently as a dead activity. When the Torah is read silently,
one rabbi warns, words can only fall from the mouth like stones.
The rabbis mean what they say, for in the Hebrew tradition,
reading situates one as a participant in the act of creation. Which
gives to reading a special ontological status: only a certain class
of males—the Kohanes—enjoy the supreme privilege of being
able to read from the Torah. Reading is a God-like activity. Just
as God breathes into dust and brings Adam to life, readers bring
characters on the page to life by breathing them aloud. Voice
must be taken as something quite real here, something palpable
and physical: the words must be *uttered*. (The word for *word* in
Hebrew, *dabar*, also means "thing.") Because Hebrew must be
read aloud, it appears to be a language of community: everyone
overhears the same thing at the same time. But the appearance
is slightly deceiving. Without the text in front of them, an audience has no way of deciding whether the reader has made the
correct vowel selection. The audience must take the reader's
interpretation on faith. A reader delivers the truth to a group the
way Moses receives and then delivers the Ten Commandments.

In fact, the Hebrew reader has decided what words will mean
for the entire group in collaboration with a group of rabbis, who
have argued over the choices of certain vowels until they arrive
at a collective interpretation. Interpretation by committee implies, of course, that another committee can revise it later. Meaning always remains in flux. The alphabetic reader decides for
himself in a self-fulfilling dialogue, creating out of the reader
both editor and authority. He takes his finalized interpretation to
the group in the form of solid opinions and decisions, and not as
proposals or tentative offerings. No one edits or revises with him,
for his reading is a private affair. His interpretation is a "read-

ing." "The Torah is indeterminately synchronic with all individual and communal life," George Steiner points out, "the Gospels, Epistles and Acts are not."[6] Vowels hold the key to the secret of the Hebrew writing system, and they hold the key to the Greek alphabet. To understand literacy—to understand the rise of modern consciousness—we must turn to the most ethereal of things, the human voice, and that means to turn to vowels.

Even though it sounds like a simple thing, this was the great Greek invention—a notational system that could account for that seemingly endless variety of sounds that vibrates through the vocal cords and gets shaped by the mouth. This invention, which occurred roughly 700 B.C., carried enormous social significance. It radically shifted the status accorded to the individual under every other system of writing. The Semitic reader shouldered a linguistic responsibility for the entire community as the Great Interpreter. He "makes up his mind," as we have seen, with each eye movement across the parchment. Hebrew permits so much freedom that a reading must be negotiated by a team of readers—a counsel of rabbis. The alphabet lifts that responsibility from the Western reader. Meaning—surface meaning at least— has been totally encoded in the letters. Every Semitic reader brings, let's say, Hebrew characters to life with characteristic individuality: the reader uses his intelligence to interpret just so he can accomplish the complicated task of reading. In Hebrew, reading *is* interpretation. Nonsense gets read *out* of sentences as a mistake in interpretation.

The alphabetic reader knows no such individual responsibility: everyone—priest or peasant—sounds the letters exactly the same. Interpretation comes *after* the reading has been accomplished, not during it. Both sense and nonsense get an equal

---

[6]Steiner, *Real Presences*, 44.

hearing. In the early stages of literacy, in the Middle Ages, a person who knew the alphabet would read a text—an edict from the king, or a capitulary from the Church—out loud for a group of non-literates in what has been called by one medieval historian "textual communities."[7]

In these small communities, the reader in a sense opened the document so that it could be discussed by everyone as a collective enterprise. (This is the literate counterpart of the storyteller imparting wisdom to the tribe.) These textual communities combined orality and literacy in a complementary fashion to arrive at meaning and instruction. But with the spread of literacy, these groups quietly disappeared. It was not until the ninth century that technical innovations made silent, alphabetic reading possible. Saint Augustine in his *Confessions* gives us the first description of someone reading silently. He sees his teacher, Ambrose, Bishop of Milan, reading to himself one day and it puzzles him. He cannot understand why his great and generous teacher would want to conceal information from him by reading so quietly. Augustine reaches the only conclusion that makes sense for him: Ambrose must have a sore throat and cannot sound the words out loud.

Rabbis could argue over the correct vowels during the act of reading; meaning could be debated at the level of sound. But the alphabet locked in sound as tightly as the printing press would later lock in paragraphs and pages. The addition of written characters to mark the vowels predetermined both sound and sense. For the first time, even nonsense could be written down and read.

This alphabetic wholeness had the effect of spreading authority throughout a collection of individuals—anyone who knew how to read could read for meaning. Such a democratizing shift could of course transform an entire society. Indeed, the Greeks believed so strongly in the democratic vigor of their alphabet that

---

[7]See Brian Stock, *The Implications of Literacy.*

they even characterized it as *a-tomos* (atomic): whole and complete—indivisible. This atomic notion, buried deep in the heart of the alphabet, got translated into the Greek idea of the *polis*— the elevated Semitic reader giving way to a collection of literate readers that make up the body politic. It has been suggested that the perfect tense in Greek—the urge toward completion—resulted in such things as a desire to found the ideal republic. But the Greeks also believed in the ideal, whole republic so emphatically, in part because their language—their system of passing information back and forth—infused everything they saw or read or wrote about with that very same ideal of wholeness. The alphabet quite literally authorized the ideal of the republic. Plato, the first Western man of letters, articulated an idea that cannot be disembedded from the accomplishment of literacy itself.

Reading and writing are the most powerful tools imaginable. They are able to reshape the way a person views the world. But how? Even though every person who can read and write sentences has had his world rearranged in this same way, none of us can remember exactly that dramatic change, quite simply because literacy furnishes us with a new way of remembering. Literacy gives us the memory we do have. Prior to literacy, as children, we are not only *in* experience, we *are* experience. Somehow, Walt Whitman managed to retain the uncanny ability to recall that special time:

> There was a child went forth every day,
> And the first object he look'd upon and received with
> wonder or pity or love or dread, that object he became,
> And that object became part of him for the day or a certain
> part of the day. . . .
> Or for many years or stretching
> cycles of years.[8]

---

[8]Walt Whitman, *Leaves of Grass,* 1855 edition.

Literacy forces a separation. Once the child begins to play with letters, he must say good-bye forever to those objects that he encounters around him. He can enjoy them only at a distance. Literacy pulls the child away from "becoming objects," urging him into "becoming himself." Once inside the world of language, whenever the child sees an object, he analyzes and describes it, turns it over in his mind and categorizes it. He stands back, metaphorically, from all the objects that surround him. The more objects he sees, the more he becomes separated from everything around him. The child moves toward consciousness by "reading" the things of this world as if reality were a text—interpreting and analyzing at the same time. That child moves toward full consciousness once he begins to read himself as another one of those objects in the world. The process may be the most mysterious and misunderstood phase of our maturing. As the child develops a sense of self, that self drifts out of the body and watches and observes the child in action. Like holding a finger closer and closer to the eyes until it goes out of focus and finally divides, in a certain way literacy forces a child to split in two. Standing outside one's self and observing one's self doing the normal things of ordinary life— the "I" split into both subject and object, with subject sometimes talking silently to object—may be the most organic way of understanding literate consciousness.[9]

---

[9]Jerome Bruner suggests that something called "cultural psychology" is needed to explain the "classically central concept in psychology—the 'self.' " As a way into the subject, he suggests Hazel Markus and Paula Nurius, "Possible Selves." See also Anthony R. Pratkanis, Steven J. Breckler, and Anthony G. Greenwald, eds., *Attitude Structure and Function;* Robbie Case, *Intellectual Development: Birth to Adulthood;* and Tory E. Higgins, "Self-Discrepancy: A Theory Relating Self and Affect."

For the idea of a running dialogue with the self, see Mikhail Bakhtin's notion of "heteroglossia" in his *Dialogic Imagination: Four Essays;* and Lev Vygotsky's "inner speech" in his *Thought and Language.*

On self and literacy, see Ivan Illich and Barry Sanders, *ABC: The Alphabetization of the Popular Mind.*

Commonplace but complicated ideas like consciousness can sometimes be understood best by looking at aberrations. To understand consciousness as a grammatical construction—a concept that develops inside literacy—we can look at an obscure, nineteenth-century interruption of its development. A wild boy "tottered" (according to one eyewitness) into the city of Nuremberg on May 26, 1828.[10] While he appeared to be around seventeen years old at the time, he spoke not one syllable and uttered only grunts and groans. He had no Mother Tongue. His vernacular consisted of guttural sounds. When in captivity, he was immediately taught Latin and Greek—both written languages.

A criminologist, Anselm von Feuerbach, who met the wild boy on July 11, "made it his business to find out, from witnesses and police reports, how the lad had behaved on arrival in Nuremberg."[11] Von Feuerbach composed the most detailed account of the boy's life. When someone offered the boy pen and paper, he scribbled the name Kaspar Hauser; and that is the name he has been known by ever since. A short time after he met Hauser, and having taught him some rudimentary German, von Feuerbach made the following observation: "I directed Kaspar to look out the window, pointing to the wide and extensive prospect of a beautiful landscape, that presented itself to us in all

---

[10]From Michael Hulse's introduction, *Caspar Hauser* by Wassermann, vii.

[11]Of "wolf children" alone, some fifty accounts have been written since the fourteenth century. Literature on the wild child includes the following: Jean-Claude Armen, *Gazelle-Boy;* Susan Curtiss, *Genie: A Psycholinguistic Study of a Modern-Day "Wild Child";* Theodore Kroeber, *Ishi;* Harlan Lane, *The Wild Boy of Aveyron;* Lucien Malson, *Wolf Children and the Problem of Human Nature;* Russ Rymer, *Genie: An Abused Child's Flight from Silence;* Roger Shattuck, *The Forbidden Experiment: The Story of the Wild Boy of Aveyron;* J. A. L. Singh and Robert M. Zingg, *Wolf Children and Feral Men.* For an interesting summary, see Douglas Keith Candland, *Feral Children and Clever Animals.*

the glory of summer. . . . He instantly drew back, with visible horror, exclaiming, 'Ugly! ugly!' " Later, when he had learned sufficient German, Kaspar explained his reaction: "When I looked at the window it always appeared to me as if a window-shutter had been placed close before my eyes, upon which a wall-painter had splattered the contents of his different brushes, filled with white, blue, green, yellow, and red paint, all mingled together. Single things, as I now see things, I could not at that time recognize and distinguish from each other."[12] At this point in his life, Kaspar Hauser knew very few names of things, and very few definitions, and thus he held very few categories. Without these guides, as odd as it sounds, he could not delineate one thing from another. This became apparent to him only after he had acquired language.

Later, as Kaspar Hauser learned to read and write, one subject absolutely captivated his interest and imagination—himself. But it did so in an unusual way. Hauser rarely if ever used the first person singular "I." The effect was to erase him as a personality, and to leave behind merely an object. Since he did not grow up in and actually develop and mature in literacy, he had a hard time settling into anything that might be called an inner life. He could only be excruciatingly aware of himself as this new creation, Kaspar Hauser. And so in his autobiography he refers to this strange entity, this fleshy stranger, in the only way he knows how, in the third person:

> As long as he can recollect, he had always lived in a hole (a small low apartment which he sometimes calls a cage), where he had always sat upon the ground, with bare feet, and clothed only with a shirt and a pair of breeches. In his apartment he never heard a sound. . . . He never saw the heavens. . . . He never perceived any difference between day and night. Whenever he awoke from sleep, he found a loaf of bread and a pitcher of water

[12]Anselm von Feuerbach, *Kaspar Hauser,* 284.

by him. He never saw the face of the man who brought him his
meat or drink.[13]

In an odd way, Hauser is all consciousness, passing his days
forever hovering outside himself. The door stays forever shut,
however, to a deep understanding of his inner life, to his self, for
he has not developed anything like a reflective self. Kaspar
Hauser can only move through his environment like a
camera—a dybbuk—a product of a late-blooming literacy, followed by an even later-blooming ability to speak. One way of
understanding literate consciousness is to see it as an integration
of the first person with the third person: I can be myself—I—and
I can also observe myself—he. Hauser cannot pull off that integration; he cannot descend into himself. Even in the short
paragraph about his apartment, Hauser reveals no real emotions—no longings, no desires, no fears—only surface descriptions. Kaspar Hauser has importance for this book, because his
life reverses so startlingly the ordering of orality and literacy.

Normally, of course, orality comes first; but literacy does not
supplant orality. Rather, literacy comes to dominate one's life,
while orality remains omnipresent in the background. Literacy
has to dominate since normative consciousness develops out of
the foundation of reading and writing that a child learns as a
skill—the primary skill in a child's life. Nevertheless, even though
it takes place gradually and passes virtually unnoticed, a rift
develops between a child's predominately oral world and his or
her entry into literacy. In Kaspar Hauser, this rift is dramatically
obvious, since Hauser has almost no experience—and certainly
no early experience—with orality. He hardly ever uses the pre-

---

[13]Ibid., 304–5.

sent tense, since events continually pass him by, leaving him nothing to do but contemplate and comment.

This separation generated by literacy is no less dramatically wrenching, no less important, than the break an adolescent makes when he or she leaves home. This literate fissuring may quietly prepare the way, emotionally, for the child's eventual flight from the nest. In fact, the movement from orality into literacy gives the youngster the first experience with abstracting, with distancing—requisites for all breaks in later life.

The archetypal rigor, and absolute exhilaration, of this kind of separation is best expressed through analogy. Separation characterizes virtually every creation myth in every culture, even the act of creation in the Old Testament. In order to bring the world out of the formlessness of chaos, God must separate the waters that reside above from the waters that reside below. He faces that most arduous, painful task on the second day of creation. The second day describes a battle of the most violent, cosmic proportions. The waters cry and protest, refusing to be separated from each other. God eventually accomplishes the task, but ends the second day differently from all the rest. On each of the other days He ends His labors by saying, "And it was good." But not on the second day. God persists, though, and He persists because without this separation there could be no division or form or category, no day or night, no naming of the animals and plants   in short, no ultimate creation that could be conceptualized as *earth*.[14]

This biblical separation creates the wholeness of the universe. Linguistic separation creates consciousness. By converting speech into a written artifact, the alphabet separated it forever

---

[14]Priests re-enact this duality of fracturing and completeness in the liturgy: the consecration of the bread and wine, in which the bread is broken and the bread and wine are given in communion to the congregation.

from the speaker and in the process created something technical called *language*, which could then be inspected, analyzed, and discussed. Once language became an object of study, rules could then be formulated and applied to govern its usage. The experience of language gave birth to standards of correctness—and excellence—which in turn were applied to all aspects of life. Those people with the most developed capacities for reading and writing came to be seen, themselves, as models of correctness, who then commanded great authority. Such wide-sweeping effects led Eric Havelock to make the following basic and profound claim for the alphabet: "The Greek alphabet . . . is a piece of explosive technology, revolutionary in its effects on human culture, in a way not precisely shared by any other invention."[15]

That explosive revolution took many forms. For one thing, the artifact called language made the many things of the world preservable without the intervention of memory. Whatever needed to be remembered could now be stored inside sentences. Twenty-six letters could hold the entire world! For another, ideas could be considered in a leisurely way by returning time and again to the very same sentences to uncover their messages. Unlike a listener, a reader can set his own pace, or skip whole sections of an argument or a story. Sentences that remain stationary on the page can also be rearranged, reordered, and made generally more complicated than those that come out of one's mouth. And since language is the medium through which we perceive reality, the more complex the sentences the more complex our experience. Sentences formed in orality typically take the form of subject/verb/object, and those kinds of sentences keep reality neatly and predictably in line. Breaking the hold that simple grammatical construction has on language permits us to gain a fresh insight on old things—everyday experience, commonplace ideas—in a radically new way.

---

[15]Eric Havelock, *The Literate Revolution in Greece and Its Cultural Consequences*, 6. See especially pages 51–53 for a discussion of literacy in China.

But the most revolutionary effect of all carries implications of staggering proportions. It appears at first glance as a terrible drawback: literacy forces a separation between the knower and the known. For the literate person, reality exists out there, somewhere, at arm's distance. One can only recapture it again, ironically, by describing and analyzing, categorizing and defining, through the very thing that created the separation in the first place—language. In that dead space between subject and object, between reader and text, critical analysis and self-consciousness are miraculously born. The fact that sentences can be read many times—re-searched for content silently by a person and in seclusion—slowly feeds and fills out that activity we call self-reflective, critical thinking.[16]

That is something not possible in orality. In orality, speaking and thinking run at the same time—in the uttered sentences. In orality, one cannot say, Let me think about that out loud. In orality, one cannot hold one thought, one idea, in mind and say something entirely different. That kind of intentional misleading—a lie—also comes out of literacy. That internalized text called "thought" has not yet come into existence in oral cultures. Reading a sentence is to consider time and space in an abstract and conceptual way. Every reader internalizes that newly formed conceptualization: literate people take on an inner space and with it fill out their personalities. "Volume," as the pitch of a voice, has somehow been extended to refer to the metaphysical depth of a self's "interior."

Serious consequences follow. The rise of Western civilization can be traced to that contemplative open space between knower and known. The separation is vast enough, as I have indicated, to accommodate the creation of individualized consciousness.

---

[16]For a view of the neuroanatomical literature on language and critical thinking, see D. L. Mills, S. A. Coffey, and H. J. Neville, "Language abilities and cerebral specializations in 10-20-month-olds," in C. Nelson, ed., *Neuro correlates of early cognition and linguistic development symposium.*

But it also provides a place where people can stand at ease in order to gain some control—we commonly say "to gain some distance," or "to gain some perspective"—over their lives. Just as a person must step back from a written sentence in order to get its meaning, he can just as easily step back from an experience, critically evaluate it, without necessarily being overwhelmed by it. Being able to rearrange and reorder experience means something crucial to everyday life: it suggests that a person has choices.

Anyone with enough literacy to read these sentences will find it hard to imagine dealing with experience in any other way. Every literate person has the capacity to analyze and critically evaluate a situation. But literacy can also blind us to the pre- or non- or even anti-literate world. Literacy dominates perception so thoroughly that, as adults, we find our own childhood recognizable only barely. We know it only in fleeting images that pass through our minds, or as we reconstruct it at the prompting of old family photographs. Most of us have moved decisively and irrevocably from orality into literacy.

For many young people today, this is not happening. Many of them have wound up on the streets after only a few years in elementary school. As literates, we have as much difficulty imagining their lives—and the life of the gangs they enter into—as we do in remembering our own childhoods.

In that other world—a tough, angry, and violently distorted version of childhood—a gang kid gets tossed and tumbled around as the daily flow of events washes over him. He lacks the skills that would enable him, like some other youngsters, to sit on the sidelines, contemplatively, and watch those events pass by. Many of them live like Kaspar Hauser, still caught in their holes, unable to observe their own actions. Gang children basically surrender and drift along with the current. They enjoy no distance from events going on around them. The events appear, in fact, to be happening *with* them or *through* them, certainly in spite *of* them. They feel victimized, at the mercy of experience, unable to see meaningful choices that would allow them to exercise true agency. They are reduced to choosing what caliber gun to buy. No wonder youngsters feel overwhelmed and give up on finding any way out of their crazy life, "la vida loca." Literacy certainly does not promise a way out of gang life, but it may offer one of the most effective ways of never falling into it in the first place. It is literate consciousness that controls the world. A dropout can struggle against the odds, but the climb out of the hole is a steep one indeed.

It is crucial for every parent, every teacher, every citizen to recognize that simple but powerful fact. A good many young people cannot perform the mechanical operations of reading and writing. But that is the least of our problems. It is only, in fact, the thin surface of a much deeper problem. It is the emptiness in the hearts and souls of the illiterates who drop out—the destruction of their emotional and psychic lives—that really constitutes the deepest and severest loss. That loss can be partially brought into view by briefly summarizing the consciousness that is formed in literacy.

Words do not come into existence until the entire range of spoken sounds can be written down. Only then can we actually see that one group of sounds begins and ends, and another string takes up. A speaker in orality merely utters a continuous stream of definable sounds called phonemes. But he or she utters no words. The speaker's sounds get defined in performance—make the sound for *tree*, for instance, and point to a tree. Oral peoples have no need of dictionaries, just as they have no need for grammars, for orality holds to no standards of correct usage— neither in syntax nor in spelling. Language not only makes sounds visible as words, it freezes those words so that a reader can ponder each sentence in an attempt to figure out meaning. Writing thus freezes memory. I can return time and again to the text, rather than try to recall what someone said. The reader can also recall those words or sentences in his mind's eye. He can even carry on conversations with that other alphabetically constructed creature—the most important construct of literacy by far—the self. This is to describe, in rudimentary terms, the way literacy sponsors and authorizes the process of reflective thinking—how it produces what we often term *insight:* a looking inward.

A literate person ingests reality—takes it in, sorts out what he needs and does not need. A metaphor for eating is appropriate, for in reading one learns to be an omnivore, devouring every kind and substance and shape of idea. Reading and writing generate an interior, where an active and sometimes contemplative life goes on, carried out through those essential elements that constitute the modern human being: a memory, a conscience, and a self. Once alphabetized, people take on a particular metaphoric shape. They get characterized as deep or shallow, hollow or full of life. They can hide deep within themselves; or they can appear self-conscious or self-absorbed. Cut someone open and this space vanishes. It cannot be found amidst the muscles and organs and vessels of a splayed cadaver. It can only be suggested through metaphor. Ivan Illich tries to take a peek into that elusive space:

> As soon as I say that I have "come to know something," I have already "looked at it," "searched for it," "figured out" the "right angle" to "approach it," "reached out" for it, and finally "grasped it." All these verbs that allow me to describe the "process" and "progress" of my thinking are, of course, spatial metaphors, and they all refer to space that is within me. When I use any one of these expressions, I am aware that the space which I experience between myself and the world that I have come to know is not "in" the same kind of space "in" which I perceive the things around me. I am told "in my mind" is a systematically

misleading expression and that I should dispense with it as thoroughly as I can.

I cannot follow such well-meaning advice.[17]

Notions of foreground and background, closeness and distance—the grid of perspective itself—exist first as a volumetric idea in the mind and then get projected back into the world. Youngsters deprived of language generally find those spatial relationships baffling. That is, they do not participate in the reciprocal relationship between what is out in front of them and what is inside them. They lack the *me* from which distance is judged. Again, Kaspar Hauser can illuminate this problem. Here is Anselm von Feuerbach describing a short walk with his charge: "He had not yet learned by experience, that objects of sight appear smaller in the distance than they really are. He wondered that the trees of an alley in which we were walking became smaller and lower, and the walk narrower at a distance; so that it appeared as if at length it would be impossible to pass [through] them."[18] Von Feuerbach thinks it a matter of experience "that objects of sight appear smaller in the distance than they really are," but experience has relatively little to do with it.

The case of "Genie" makes the point clearer. A thirteen-year-old girl came into a welfare office with her mother in Temple City, California, in November 1970; she had been imprisoned in her bedroom since birth, hearing hardly any language. Caseworkers assigned her the name Genie. Clinical psychologists who worked with Genie report that she had great difficulty negotiating space and walked with her hands in front of her to avoid banging into things. When given objects to hold, she would first

[17]Ivan Illich, *H₂O and the Waters of Forgetfulness*, 72.

[18]Von Feuerbach, *Kaspar Hauser*, 354.

touch them to her face to determine how hard they were, how sharp, and even how large they were.[19]

A person must first hold the abstract notions of space and volume in mind before perspective can be described and analyzed, and certainly before it can be translated onto paper as vanishing-point perspective. That level of abstraction flourishes in literacy. Vanishing-point perspective requires more than mere seeing; it requires abstracting and shaping reality through conception and perception. Tuscan painters began rearranging reality through this new spatial grid in the thirteenth century. Before that time, artists depicted the world vanishing into a Euclidian space where parallel lines never converge. In the thirteenth century, a new conceptualized reality—a new relationship, that is, between viewer and experience—begins to appear on canvases. Painters found themselves in a more volumetric space, and they depict a world that has been conceptualized differently. Literacy develops a new space inside each individual—a mental space that gets projected out in the world. The new space gets "produced" through a reciprocal relationship negotiated between a literate mind and experience. This is what Tuscan painters record, the discovery of seeing the world in a new, self-centered way: "The vanishing line, the vanishing-point and the meeting of parallel lines 'at infinity' were the determinants of a representation, at once intellectual and visual, which promoted the primacy of the gaze in a kind of 'logic of visualization.' This representation, which has been in the making for centuries, now became enshrined in architectural and urbanistic practice as the *code* of linear perspective."[20]

Internalized space houses feelings of all kinds. Certain feelings, however, remain unique to literacy, specifically those that

---

[19]Russ Rymer, *Genie: An Abused Child's Flight from Silence.*

[20]Henri Lefebvre, *The Production of Space,* 41. Susanne K. Langer, *Philosophy in a New Key,* makes the point that painters depict what they and their epoch see. Erwin Panofsky, *Idea,* makes much the same point.

get inscribed on an internalized text or page, and get carried through time by the person. Guilt and conscience, for example, inform a person's inner life with as much permanence, in effect, as a historical document. Periodically, a person can consult that text and make public its contents—in confessions, apologies, or as simple declarations. "Conscience" and "guilt," as these psychological categories are elaborated and experienced in Western culture, are fundamentally constructions of literacy. Literate people behave as if every act, every event, takes place in the outside world and, at the same time, impresses itself indelibly on an invisible text inside their fleshy selves. While the actual act fades, its outlines remain permanently imprinted inside the literate's conscience or memory.

Oral peoples—those who have no contact with reading and writing—do not structure their lives around such an internalized textual system. Not that they do not feel. On the contrary. But oral peoples learn not by internalizing a set of rules or regulations, not by following the dictates of conscience, but through example. They fill out their emotional lives by listening to myths and stories of right behavior repeated over and over again, much the way Bruno Bettelheim or Marie-Louise von Franz argues that fairy tales provide young children with a moralized landscape. Guilt and remorse do not structure lives or institutions in orality. An act in an oral culture does not leave an after-image as it does in literate societies. The completed act disappears totally, like words themselves.

As soon as literacy had sifted down to the laity, the Catholic Church seized control over this newly formed interiority. The inner life had indeed become a much more complicated issue. As a way of exerting control, the Fourth Lateran Council in 1244 demanded that every novitiate participate in yearly, auricular confession. The edict directed every parishioner to narrate through the screen of the confessional the sinful acts he or she had committed during the year. In passing this edict, the Church clearly recognized that Christian lives had taken on the quality of an internalized and sometimes knotty text that could be consulted at will and recited out loud. What got narrated, spun out like a spidery filament for the priest's scrutiny, was the internalized self. The book itself became the controlling metaphor for managing life, a metaphor that would dominate civilized, Western life for the next seven hundred years. Today, the computer is making a strong bid to unseat it.

This emphasis on the text is reflected in a corresponding shift in Church iconography around the middle of the twelfth century. During this period, the sculptures that decorate the tympanum of cathedrals—the space above the archway entrance—take on new imagery. Before then Christ appears holding a pair of scales in his right hand, weighing each soul to determine who will ascend to heaven, and who will descend to hell. Saintly souls exhibit a characteristic lightness of being *(levitas)*, the less pure a decided gravity *(gravitas)*. After 1150 or so, sculptors depict Christ with a quill in his right hand, recording deeds in a book—the Book of Life. Christ will open that book on the Day of Judgment and read out loud the accounting of each person's life, for on that Day of Reckoning, each person's life will indeed turn into an "open book." (*Reckoning* is about computation. Christ participates in writing and inventory-keeping.) In anticipation of that momentous day, each year medievals were directed to ceremonially open their own book themselves, and to read aloud to a priest all that had been inscribed there. A medieval walked the earth with an inventory—of all the events that had affected him or her during a lifetime. Over the centuries, a name develops for this interaction between the inner textual life, and what gets presented to the outside world. The nineteenth century calls this dynamic a personality.

Consider the self as the mediator, the voice, for this articulation between the inner life and outer swirl of events. The self provides the armature, the framework, around which or on which the complexities of personality accrete, like so many annoying grains of sand inside an oyster. Vestiges of the self as grammar still appear in the reflexive endings of verbs in a language like Spanish—*venderse, llevarse:* "It sells itself," "It washes itself."

It is that invisible thing, the self, that makes the world rich and complex for people. The self is the regulating agent, the negotiator, the avant-garde that first meets with reality and brings the news back home. Is it safe out there, or not? Is it time to act, or not? (That is Hamlet on center stage, in his first soliloquy: all *self*.) By promoting consciousness, the self seems to separate an individual from his or her physical and biological environment. Separation, as I pointed out earlier, liberates an individual. What once felt like enmeshment begins to look like control. Psychotherapists call this process individuation, sociologists call it human nature, psychologists call it personality, parents see it as just growing up. Whatever the name, the self is synonymous with personhood.

We do not have to wonder how human beings would behave if they lost the sense of self. We now face a significant portion of a generation of young people who have given up struggling with letters, or working their way through a sentence or a paragraph, let alone a book. They have abandoned the book, even express open disdain for it. They have gone beyond believing in the power and strength—the efficacy—of reading and writing. At the same time, they enjoy none of the advantages of pre-literates: they derive no inner strength from an early immersion in orality. They fit neither of the standard categories. They might better be referred to by some new term like *post-illiterates*. I am describing something practically unthinkable only a decade ago: a generation dispossessed of language—both verbal and written. In the classroom and on the streets, this new kind of illiteracy is culminating in the worst tragedy imaginable: the spiritual degradation of America's youth.

These children have altered what it means to be a human being at the most fundamental level. Not only have they been unable to construct a sense of self out of reading and writing, they cannot draw on the reserve of orality. Experience overwhelms them. Finally, disconnected from literacy, soured on school, they spend their time hanging out in malls, or joining gangs for thrills and excitement.

These children are America's Kaspar Hausers. It is not far-fetched to think of them stumbling into our cities last year, or the year before, or the year before that. Like Kaspar Hauser, they have been kept for hours on end in darkened rooms without being comforted by human touch or touched by the human voice. They speak only a trace, a shred, of the Mother Tongue. Schools ignore this and teach them instead to read and write. Against all odds, teachers try to make them literate. Attention must be paid to these youngsters—as much attention, or even more, than is paid to those who remain safely and solidly in school, for these new illiterates can help everyone understand how things have gone wrong. They display extraordinary skills; they just happen to point them in the wrong direction—toward violence, drug addiction, despair, and cynicism. They can be blamed for their misdeeds, but that misses the point. Having bypassed literacy, they have bypassed the social contrivances—and resources of self—that come with literacy.

Statistics tell the story: Reading abilities among young people have steadily declined over the past decade, high school dropout rates have increased.[21] Newspapers and magazines meanwhile

---

[21]Jan La Bonty, professor of education, Southern Illinois University, notes that only "10 percent of the population reads 70 percent of the books. Of the 159 members of the United Nations, the United States ranks 49th in literacy" ("College Students as Readers," Presentation at the Fortieth Annual Meeting of the National Readers' Conference, Miami, Florida, November 1990, p. 3). But statistics can also hide the deeper truth of reading. The Scholastic Aptitude Test scores, for example, may be a better gauge of reading levels, in the sense that the test tries to measure reading comprehension. According to the College

wonder about the possible decline in the number of books published, and the decline in the intellectual rigor of those books. But
those issues only hit the most tangible, the most obvious signs of
a decline in a shrinking pool of readers and writers. The more
insidious changes take place inside each person who abandons
the book. With the disappearance of the book goes that most

Board's annual SAT score report, August 28, 1990, SAT scores have declined
nationwide from 1988 through 1990. They reached an all-time low in 1991
(James Lichtenberg, "Reading: Does the Future Even Require It?", *Liberal
Education,* vol. 79, no. 1, Winter 1991, p. 4). They reached another record low
in 1992. Daniel J. Singal points out, in "The Other Crisis in Education " (*The
Atlantic Monthly,* November 1991), the average SAT verbal scores at selective
colleges have dropped 50 to 60 points in the last twenty-five years. Singal is
quick to say that these schools have not slipped in relative standings. Students
are simply much poorer readers than they used to be: "So much escapes them;
even those of above-average ability absorb no more than a dusting of detail
from a printed text. And without such detailed information it's impossible for
them to gain a real understanding of what the author is saying."
    Dropout rates are harder to come by, and vary greatly by geographical
region and economic class. Even the term *dropout* requires definition and interpretation. When do schools conclude that a student has actually dropped out?
According to the *Los Angeles Times,* May 11, 1990, roughly one out of every four
youths drops out of school before entering the workforce ("Reading the Signs
of a Crisis," Section A-1). These figures reach 40 percent or more in some
inner-city schools. According to Michelle Fine, in "Dropping Out of High
School, An Inside Look," *Social Policy* (Fall 1985), 43–50, students in urban
areas graduate at rates approximating only 50 percent.
    The National Center for Education Statistics, Washington, D.C., deter-
mined that, in 1983, 73.9 percent of ninth graders in the United States would
complete high school. But that means grossly high dropout figures in some
inner cities. Sara Rimer of the *New York Times,* March 12, 1991, set the dropout
rate in New York City in 1990 at 46 percent (Based on the "Annual Dropout
Report," April 1990, New York City Board of Education). The *Chicago Tribune*
has at various times placed the high school dropout rate for Chicago at 55
percent. Jonathan Kozol, *Savage Inequalities* (New York: Crown Publishers,
1991), p. 112, has even more shocking news: "According to a recent study
issued by the State Commission of Education, 'as many as three out of four
blacks' in New York City 'and four out of five Latinos fail to complete high
school within the traditional four-year period.' "

precious instrument for holding modern society together, the
internalized text on which is inscribed conscience and remorse
and, most significant of all, the self.

Illiteracy leaves behind shells of people—ghosts who take to
the streets in a terribly dangerous state. They are unable to feel
remorse or sorrow or guilt about their actions, even those of the
most violent and gruesome kind. Society needs to fear ghosts
who feel no more real than the shimmering of an image on a
computer screen. For them, others are no more real than they
are. Under those conditions anything can and does happen.
Behavior becomes literally antisocial.

It will do no good to lock up these young people. The efficacy
of the penal system rests on the basic civilizing matrix of a
conscience and a sense of remorse—feelings of guilt and thus a
desire to change. But these new post-illiterates—at home neither
in orality nor in literacy—prowl the neighborhoods as truly
aberrant beings. They abide by different rules. They have joined
their own tribal units, but their behavior is anything but communal. The impoverished stories they pass around speak not of
heroes who face moral dilemmas, but of gangsters who vent their
rage and despair. They need to feel important and powerful, just
like the literate folks around them. They crave recognition and
a sense of identity. Drugs give them a rush—of hope, of power,
of invulnerability.

Whatever the problem, the new post-illiterates crave a quick
fix. They get high. When they come down, society locks them up.
But surely that's a last resort. Prisons stand as a testimony to a
colossal social failure.

The solution has to lie elsewhere. It will lie—in all its insub-
stantiality, evanescence, and invisibility—in the human voice. In
voiced breath. What those young people want is to feel and to be
empowered through their own voices.

CHAPTER THREE

Every solid in the universe is ready to
become fluid on the approach of the mind,
and the power to flux it is the measure of
the mind. If the wall remain adamant, it
accuses the want of thought. To a subtle
force it will stream into new forms, expres-
sive of the character of the mind.

—Ralph Waldo Emerson, "Essays"

Historians tunnel back through time in search of origins—the ultimate sources—of virtually everything under the
sun. The first scratchings that can be called writing, as we have
already seen, were discovered in Mesopotamia, and date back
some eleven thousand years before the birth of Christ. The
origins of fiction—consider those pre-historic scratches pushed
to the limits of sophistication—turn out to have much more
recent beginnings. I focus on the roots of fiction because they
carry crucial importance for understanding literacy today, and
even more importance for teaching reading and writing.

Given the way that most schools currently teach reading and
writing—the primary, traditional tools for knowing and reasoning—an observer might readily conclude that fiction has developed out of a spirit of determined seriousness, and that teachers
have quite naturally committed themselves to continuing that
somber tradition. But history actually reveals quite the contrary:

the roots of storytelling lie buried deep in play and joking, a fact that the majority of teachers appears to have forgotten. But anyone who hopes to achieve literacy at its deepest level would do well to remember those playful beginnings.

Schools draw on an opposite scenario. Young children give up the freedom and formlessness of play, and struggle to "get it right" in reading and writing. Teachers make a sharp distinction for their students between the schoolyard and the classroom. The outdoors is reserved for play, the indoors for serious work. But a young person who hopes to make a living connection with letters cannot do so without a playful attitude. The teacher has to allow that outdoor spirit to seep into the classroom. Ezra Pound, one of the most influential and decidedly serious poets of the twentieth century, coined a term for this attitude, *logopoeia:* "The dance of the intellect among words." That is Pound, the literate giant, talking back to that earliest Greek inscription, "Who now of all dancers sports most playfully?"

The spirit of play characterizes storytelling both in orality and in literacy. It has to. Every telling dances and sports with reality in order to coax and tease a brand-new world out into the open. At the same time, every story can be nothing more than that—a story: a collection of sounds and images and emphases. A story—even the best-told story—offers only the illusion of reality. Things of this world persist with a stubborn self-sufficiency. They simply will not surrender their essence easily to language.

Every story not only sports and teases but hits with the punch of a gently delivered joke. Pre-literate cultures know the devilish nature of language only too well, and they unashamedly display it on every formal occasion. By fabricating a subversive critter called a trickster, they guarantee that audiences will not take their stories seriously. This cultural imp devotes his entire exis-tence to plotting his own elaborate practical jokes aimed at upsetting the established order—wherever he finds it. Through his joking nature, he makes it evident that the story, too, is only a joke. The audience applauds the efforts of the storyteller, and laughs at the pranks of the trickster. The two sounds—clapping and laughing—complement each other.

Tricksters appear in different forms in different cultures—as a spider in African tales, a coyote in Native American stories, as Reynard the Fox derived from Aesop's fables, as Tar-Baby in the Uncle Remus tales—but they always pop up whenever stories are told, to prevent them from being taken as the gospel truth.[1] While the storyteller spins his yarn, the trickster carefully and deliberately unravels it; while the storyteller gives, the trickster takes back. The audience is supposed to be bewildered, standing there, helplessly, in the no-man's-land between storyteller and trickster. The audience must find meaning in the exchange between those two combatants, storyteller and story-taker, in the interplay between what the anthropologist Claude Lévi-Strauss calls "the binary opposition" of the two actors, an opposition characteristic of all oral cultures. Seen from the perspective of our own technological times, this binary opposition stands as a parody of the binary system of the computer. The computer aims at achieving clarity, but the trickster delights in producing ambiguity.[2]

For Native Americans, this binary opposition constitutes the heart of storytelling. In Zuni storytelling sessions, clowns, called Koyemshi or more popularly Mudheads, stand at one end of the pueblo parodying with grotesque and exaggerated gestures every word of the storyteller, who occupies the opposite side, or moiety, of the pueblo. Dressed in parti-colored costumes, or more

---

[1]The Greek god Hermes, in his various guises and most notably as a thief, belongs to the extended family of tricksters.

[2]For a good introduction to the trickster, see Paul Radin, *The Trickster*. For cross-cultural studies after that date, see Mehadev L. Apted, *Humor and Laughter: An Anthropological Approach*, especially "The Trickster in Folklore," 212–36.

often as women, the Koyemshi make very clear to everyone that information, even the most important information, can always be read in an entirely different way—even in an opposite way. The trickster quite literally puts a different "spin" on the story by turning it completely around. While words can render a new reality, the clowns remind everyone that words can nullify that reality, and on and on the dance of assertion and negation goes, like an infinity of mirrored reflections.

Even cultures without a formalized trickster tradition work out ways to graft the comic onto the serious. For example, in medieval England, France, and Germany, a series of festivals shadowed even the most sacred religious rituals by mimicking them with a light-hearted travesty. The French, for instance, performed a special mass to commemorate Mary's flight into Egypt. To undercut the seriousness of the ceremony, a mock priest led a procession of asses into the cathedral, and at the conclusion to each part of the mass—Kyrie, Gloria, and so on—instructed the congregation to bray their approval like a pack of asses. Everyone—Mary, the priest, the congregation—all acted like asses. Mary's flight represents a serious religious moment in the Church liturgy, but in the end, at bottom, when we try to capture it in words, assign it meaning in language, we can seem as assinine as Shakespeare's Bottom. A world built out of letters is indeed a "Midsummer Night's Dream," where anything is possible—in word or deed. But therein lies the rub: While it's language that can make us play the fool, language also offers the only way out. The lesson: Do not take things so seriously; don't lose sight of the comedy of all this. We are all trapped inside our own sentences, caught in our own grammatical constructions.

Through the role of the trickster, non-literate people make it graphically clear that language always casts a distorted shadow of itself. Through the Mudheads, or in the Mass of the Asses, or with any of the great many Festivals of Fools—that same, reassuring laugh goes up to warn the entire community: Do not take this stuff so seriously! Sure, the story's real, but it's also not real. Every Persian fairy tale acknowledges that truth by opening with this contradictory formula, *Yeki bud, yeki nabud:* "There *was* one, there was *not* one; this *happened,* this did *not* happen." The Zuni clowns should be seen as doing something more rigorous, more radical, perhaps, than cutting a story or an audience down to size. They are broadcasting a message similar to the one in Persian fairy tales: When the wise man picks up his pipe and begins to tell his story, his words may ultimately point to nothing more than the story itself. The Mudheads in effect erase everything that the wise man says by laughing him off. In this linguistic give-and-take between clown and storyteller, the audience can do little more than enjoy the performance: Pound's "dance of the intellect." That is what they are left with. But that should suffice. Language comes most alive when it most closely resembles performance.

In literate cultures, the tricksters disappear. They have climbed inside the sentences themselves. While reading silently to ourselves, we need to remain continually aware that some invisible Mudheads are quietly at work, erasing each sentence as quickly as we read it. They pull the rug out from under our magic carpet ride. They make us wake up and realize we have fallen into a fictional dream. The writer creates a reality, raises the book to ontological status. But sooner or later the bubble pops, the dream ends.

That practical joke, a cultural vanishing act into thin air, dominates so thoroughly the very heart of language that it became the object of study for a group of modern linguists known as the Natural Language Philosophers.[3] They became interested in the way sentences travesty—the word must be understood in

---

[3]As an introduction, see John L. Austin, *How to Do Things with Words;* Hilary Putnam, "Is Semantics Possible?" and "The Meaning of Meaning," in Hilary Putnam, *Mind, Language and Reality;* and Donald Davidson, *Truth and Interpretation.*

its meaning as *transvestite,* "to put on clothes of the opposite sex," what the Renaissance called "to counterfeit"—themselves. In effect, they took up the study of that binary opposition between storyteller and clown as a literate phenomenon, which they found written into each and every sentence. Every author plays the serious storyteller and the joker at the same time.

Language continually plays its practical joke, no matter what, and it fools both the speaker and the reader in the same ways. People rely on language as if every utterance corresponded absolutely with reality. That is, people invest their sentences—spoken or written—with so much importance that they dupe themselves into mistaking sentences for reality itself. We describe a tree, either in the most poetic, metaphoric language, or with the most precise, scientific detail, and believe that in doing so we "know" nature.

While language entices us into believing we have found the truth, in fact all that we wind up knowing for certain is something about language itself—the grammar and syntax and intonations of the sentences we fabricate. Confirmed literates, those who have fallen hopelessly in love with language, trick themselves even more thoroughly than those in orality. How is it, after all, that grown men and women burst into tears after reading *King Lear?* The eighteenth century even chose to rewrite the ending of the play, complaining that it was too painful and bleak—too hopelessly unredeeming. No one can deny it, Shakespeare wrote himself into heaven with that play. The language sings. But Lear is not a real king, Cordelia only a character. We can get as worked up as we like over *Lear,* but the play remains mere scratches on the page. Still, readers cry, or feel sorrow, or express horrible outrage or regret, after finishing the final scene, a testament to the awesome power of language. And a testament, as well, to its ability to pull off the most improbable and all-consuming practical joke: To dazzle readers into falling headfirst into that dreamworld on the page.

Beginning with Ferdinand de Saussure and Ludwig Wittgen-

stein, a group of linguistic philosophers have explored language's
most teasing, practical joke—how it gives all the appearance of
building a solid and straightforward bridge between word and
world. After a lifetime investigating the nature of language, Wittgenstein came to see that the superstructure of language was
shaky, that it could never support the tremendous weight and
stress of reality—and so he found himself laughing at our hapless
condition. Language, he was forced to conclude, records better
than any other function it performs the break between what we
take pains to describe and what essentially exists out there.
Human beings will never be able to cross the chasm between
experience and their desire to understand their experience.

At the end of the *Tractatus,* Wittgenstein could only advocate
silence—a begrudging mysticism—as the linguistic state that
best catches the essence of human experience. The sensible part
of our selves, he declared, "keeps its peace." He ends the *Tractatus* by emulating language's true nature, its jocular spirit, and
so leaves his readers with a joking, final line: "Whereof one
cannot speak, thereof one must remain silent." For Wittgenstein,
one could not really speak of anything, if by *speak* one truly meant
embracing the spirit of that thing. Even knowledge of ourselves,
consciousness, since it is a phenomenon of language, may also be
a futile effort. Eavesdropping on our selves, what we hear may
be nothing more than background noise.[4]

For George Steiner, that break in our linguistic confidence—
the umbilicus that keeps us connected to experience and sustains
us in that experience—marks the beginning of the modern period, a moment that Steiner places at the end of the nineteenth
century: "Mallarmé breaks (*rupture* becomes a cardinal term) the
covenant, the intimacies between word and world. This move in
turn generates the potential discontinuities between the word
and previous or subsequent usage of the word as they are ex-

---

[4]Ludwig Wittgenstein, *Tractatus Logico-Philosophicus.* See also D. F. Pears, *The
Development of Wittgenstein's Philosophy* and his *Wittgenstein.*

plored in *The Philosophical Investigations*. We are at sea, uncompassed."[5]

While Mallarmé wrote his major works during the 1890s, his "uncompassing"—that is, the linguistic break that Mallarmé effected—erupted in artistic revolutions of laughter, in movements in the twentieth century like surrealism and Dada: canvases and constructions and works of literature marked by poetic absurdities and visual punch lines. As more and more artists gradually got the joke at the very heart of language—the recalcitrance situated deep in its DNA—laughter took over other art forms, even critical, theoretical pursuits like deconstruction, in which one of its principal figures, Jacques Derrida, uses puns and jokes to make his point about the playful nature of language. That spirit even permeated something that seems so seriously monolithic—architecture. But even architecture, so heavily dependent on physical laws and engineering principles, responded to the surprises of language. One has only to look at contemporary architects such as Frank Gehry and Michael Graves to see how a sense of humor—playing with various elements from several styles—has been turned into concrete jokes in their postmodern designs. This group of architects breaks the discrete boundaries separating one historical style from another in a kind of insider's joke. Such postmodernist jokes undercut the seriousness of a profession that erects lofty, monumental structures through a playful dislocation of styles. Postmodern buildings are buildings, as well as parodies of historical buildings. Their archi-

---

[5]George Steiner, *Real Presences*, 104. Notice that *rupture* comes in several forms. One linguistic variant is *corruption*. John Gardner's novel *October Light*, which plays with, among other things, levels of language and life, opens this way: " 'Corruption? *I'll* tell you about corruption, sonny!' The old man glared into the flames in the fireplace and trembled all over, biting so hard on the stem of his pipe that it crackled once, sharply, like the fireplace logs." Morals, fire, relationships, and pipe all crack with the same intensity, that same intensity with which Gardner finds language cracking its jokes. It's the jokes in the novel that keep a usually heavy month like October exceedingly light.

tecture destroys the importance and permanence of historical building styles by wrenching them out of history and placing various elements together in one building. A single, contemporary building, for instance, might feature a Renaissance column alongside a late eighteenth-century cornice. The subject of these architectural designs is the rupture of history itself—the collapse of categories—into an assemblage of historical forms. Postmodern buildings aim at being concrete jokes—*double-entendres* of design.

Every time we use language we create a similar kind of break, not consciously or deliberately, perhaps, but a break nonetheless. Whatever we try to capture in words—a table or a chair or a bowling ball—we reshape into an object that is capable of being rendered in words. In the process, that table or chair gets stripped of some of its individuality, so that it can be categorized by shape and size and color and texture. That's the little practical joke that language continually plays on us: the real object that we want to understand or appreciate gets lost in the tangle of language.

Literate consciousness, the great Bringer of Light, delivers a similar joke. With the gift of consciousness comes the awful awareness of our own mortality. By coming to know ourselves—the Delphic oracle's mandate—we also stare at our own certain deaths.[6] When Plato tells the story of Thoth delivering the alphabet to mortals, he calls literacy a *pharmakon*, a medicine. Like all medicines, it can heal or it can kill. The doubling effect of languages sticks to it like a burr.

Which leads to another reason why language just naturally encourages jesting: language is inherently plastic and malleable. Metaphor is what it does best, because language itself, since it is not reality, can only offer a metaphoric representation of every-

---

[6]The real Bringer of Light, of course, is Lucifer, who falls into darkness. Lucifer shines in the sky as the morning star, Venus, and as the evening star, Hesperus—the consummate trickster of binary, cosmological oppositions.

thing we experience. So it addresses reality most efficiently in an indirect way, grabbing hold of experience metaphorically. It hits things at the edges, through analogy, with a glancing blow at best. Irony and ambiguity underlie every utterance, every word, sentence, and paragraph. How can language be anything but ripe for joking? Only when one relaxes in the face of the alphabet—when one catches and enters into the playful spirit of language—only then can one breathe a sigh of relief and learn to really enjoy reading and writing. At that moment, one comes to see the truth about literacy: Reading and writing are truly poetic undertakings.

The majority of teachers, however, ignores the risible, absolutely playful nature of language. Exactness and precision dominate their approach. Almost everyone demands the same exactness from language as he or she has come to expect from computer programs. The car breaks down, the landing gear collapses, the PC fails—these are mechanical accidents of a minor or major order that require immediate attention and repair. In some cases, the repair signals an entire redesign. Young people immediately get frustrated in their writing when they don't "get it right," as if some repair or redesign were needed to overhaul their own circuitry. How different it would be if youngsters could think of the natural state of language as an accident. There is no getting it "right" in language. Of course standards of correctness apply to language, but only to grammar, syntax, tense, and to agreement in case and number—basics that most students can learn very fast. But the rest, the meat and meaning of sentences, can best be achieved by ignoring the rules and adopting an attitude of play. That way, one enters directly into the spirit of language.

Reading and writing are unnatural acts, more unnatural, say, than speaking and listening. No one can master them in a short time. Most people feel more comfortable around a PC than with a pen and a piece of paper, in part because PC programs admit no ambiguity and incongruity. Inside the machine, we know the computer fires circuits with superhuman precision. Those standards do not stay put inside the machine; every operator adopts them and applies them to himself or herself. The PC even gives the impression of imparting such accuracy and precision to language itself. How can anyone not expect to "get it right" with such a wonder machine at his or her service? But that standard of linguistic precision is only an illusion. Ambiguity best characterizes the nature of language. As well as one other, closely related activity: joking.

Virtually every form of joking rests on one fundamental ingredient, an ingredient that the earliest philosophers of laughter have recognized—incongruity. The eighteenth-century poet James Beattie, writing about the nature of laughter, believed that laughter arose "from the view of two or more inconsistent, unsuitable, or incongruous parts or circumstances, considered as united in one complex object or assemblage." This knotty definition is rephrased by the anthropologist Elliot Oring in his book *Jokes and Their Relations* this way: "The perception of humor depends upon the perception of an *appropriate incongruity*—that is, the perception of an appropriate interrelationship of elements from domains that are generally regarded as incongruous."[7] By appropriate, Oring means resolvable. The incongruity must make sense in some familiar context. Oring offers as an example the following riddling question: "When is a door not a door?"

Young children love riddles. So do non-literate peoples. Riddles show up the playful nature of language in an easily manageable form. They are the earliest examples of literature in Anglo-Saxon England. Here is riddle number 65 from the Anglo-Saxon Exeter Book manuscript:

Quick; quite mum; I die notwithstanding.
I lived once, I live again. Everybody
lifts me, grips me, and chops off my head,

---

[7]Elliot Oring, *Jokes and Their Relations*, 2.

bites my bare body, violates me.
I never bite a man unless he bites me;
there are many men who bite me.[8]

The answer requires listeners to sift through their experience, matching up this riddle with some specific object from their experience—in this case, an onion. As A. R. Luria tried to show, oral peoples do not function within the confines of a linguistic construct. They never leave the world of experience.

Which is not to say that they cannot be playful. To show just how playful the Anglo-Saxons could get in their riddles, here is riddle 25, also about an onion, but one that adds another thin layer, this time a layer of bawdiness, to the image of the onion:

I'm a strange creature, for I satisfy women,
a service to the neighbors! No one suffers
at my hands except for my slayer.
I grow very tall, erect in a bed,
I'm hairy underneath. From time to time
a beautiful girl, the brave daughter
of some churl dares to hold me,
grips my russet skin, robs me of my head
and puts me in the pantry. At once that girl
with plaited hair who has confined me
remembers our meeting. Her eye moistens.[9]

"When is a door not a door?"—this riddle, which every school kid knows, asks, with absolute straight face, What in the world can be both a door and not-a-door at the same time? Unlike riddles from orality, the resolution here must be found in the

---

[8]Kevin Crossley-Holland, ed., *The Exeter Book Riddles*, 85.

[9]Ibid.

context of language itself. That is, the answer lies in the question itself. On its face, the question appears unresolvable. One thing cannot be two things at once. The riddle tries to tease out of the listener some solution to the conundrum that will satisfy these two conditions—door and not-a-door. The riddle's success relies not on a fact of experience, but on linguistic ambiguity. The question, at its most basic level, can be rephrased to ask, When is language ambiguous? The answer: always. In this instance, a homophone can serve double duty and be two things at once. The answer must be, of course, that a door is not-a-door when it is *ajar*.

While this riddle belongs to the world of literacy, notice that the answer can only be spoken aloud, since *ajar* rests on the punning ambiguity of the two words *a jar*. The trick rests on a confusion created by a linguistic principle in orality called juncture. On the page, the eye sees only one word, *ajar*. The mistaken juncture—the perceptible break between sounds—that produces *a jar* vanishes when we hear it aloud. Recall, orality has no words, only phonemes—sounds.

Language gives birth, then, to fraternal twins, narration and joking, both of which are nurtured on a special formula, concocted out of one-third Truth, one-third Lying, and one-third something that literary critics call Untruth.[10] Like metaphor, narration and joking each suggests that the real feel of life can be found between the lines, with language ajar. Recall the Persian formula "There was one, there was not one." It captures the creation and dissolution, the reality and irreality of language—

---

[10]See Ivan Illich and Barry Sanders, *ABC: The Alphabetization of the Popular Mind*, especially "Untruth and Narration," 84–105; and Barry Sanders, "Lie It As It Plays," in David R. Olson and Nancy Torrance, eds., *Literacy and Orality*.

that kind of opening in the linguistic door in which an entrance also serves as an exit that is essential for an understanding of the psychosocial dimensions of both language and literacy.

The vocabulary of narration reveals this delicate balance: Fiction, fable, tale, story—each at times claims to be true, at other times, false. A child begs to be told a story; an irate parent scolds a child for telling a story. Mark Twain can capture the Yankee truth in King Arthur's court through fiction; Charles Manson gets convicted for telling his fictions in a superior court. Jokes, too, vacillate between the twin poles of lying and the sharpest truth-telling. While they start out as lies, interesting and enticing, even exciting, jokes usually cross the line and hit with the stinging accuracy of truth. Even Saint Augustine, not noted for hilarity, held mixed feelings about jokes. The narrative style intrigued him, and their shady character bothered him: "Jokes should never be accounted lies, seeing they bear with them in the tone of voice, and in the very mood of the joker, a most evident indication that he means no deceit, although the thing he utters be not true. . . . A person should not be thought to lie, who lieth not."[11] Augustine does not have in mind the aggressive, nasty form of joking that Freud so brilliantly analyzed. For Augustine, jokes still remain very much enmeshed in benign storytelling. The Latin word in Augustine's time for "deeds" and "exploits" and thus by extension "story," *gesta*, produces the later Modern English word *jest*, "a funny story." Performing, narrating, and joking branch from the same etymological root.

In writing fiction, every author weaves an intricately beautiful lie—a metaphoric reality—so that his or her story will be taken seriously. The author plots in order to perpetrate his story on the audience, to hoodwink it into accepting his fabrication as real. To be successful, the author must master the art of "appropriate incongruity" by taking seriously his storytelling and, at the same

---

[11]From *De Mendacio*, Book One, Chap. 2, p. 488.

time, by taking delight in playing his practical joke on the audience. Since both author and joker must enjoy being playful, it makes sense that Thoth, the god of writing in the ancient world, is also the inventor of play, the one who puts play into play.

This ancient connection between narration and joking dominated the attitudes toward storytelling in eighth- and ninth-century England. King Alfred, for instance, uses the same Anglo-Saxon word *racu* in some places to translate the Latin *commoedia* ("comedy") and in other places to translate *historia* ("history" or "story"). Look up the definition for *racu* in an Anglo-Saxon dictionary, and you will find both "laughter" and "narration." Anglo-Saxons called their poets "laughtersmiths" and "minstrels" (singers of stories), *mimi* and *scurrae*, but most often they referred to them as purveyors of laughter, *gleemen:* laughter-guys.

Medieval England, France, and Germany developed such a rich and elaborate tradition of jesting and narration—and, of course, laughter—that they produced an extraordinary array of traveling performers, jugglers, storytellers, and acrobats. The medievals have many names for these figures, a testament to the fine gradations they could make in risibility, and to their great appreciation for them: mimi, scurrae, scenici, goliards, poetae, parasites, tragoedi, commoiedi, comici, joculatores, jocistae, corauli, cantatores, historiones, cytharistae, thymalici.[12]

By the thirteenth century, these various entertainers, all derived from the ancient Greek actors ("players") called mimes, were being described by one inclusive French word, *jongleur,* Modern English *juggler,* derived in turn from the same Latin root as *joke, iocus.* Traveling from village to village, these juggling

---

[12]An interesting survey of itinerant medieval performers is in J. D. A. Ogilvy, *"Mimi, scurrae, historiones:* Entertainers in the Early Middle Ages." The standard work on mimes remains Hermann Reich, *Der Mimus;* on the bridge between the ancient world and the medieval, see Allardyce Nicoll, *Masks, Mimes and Miracles: Studies in the Popular Theatre.*

raconteurs left a trail of laughter across the countryside. One contemporary historian in the fourteenth century referred to England as a *terra ridentum*, "a land possessed by laughter."[13]

From the account books of colleges and monasteries, from councils, synods, and capitularies (Frankish ordinances), it is clear that men and women of the cloth were forbidden the company of *joculatores*. Capitularies in particular make it obvious that the *gestae*—the stories—being circulated were nothing more than thinly disguised *jocistae* (jokes). In addition, many are preserved under the name that Cicero gave them, *facetiae*—short, mostly funny, and bawdy vignettes. They resemble the modern joke in subject but not yet in form.

Given the playful nature of language, the joke makes sense as the most natural expression of writers. The joke turns language into a powerful weapon of retaliation. It will take the informing power of literacy—reading and writing and most importantly an author—to sharpen those *facetiae* into their distinctive shape as the modern joke. First, however, these *facetiae* were passed around in orality for hundreds of years, kept alive and flexible, by word-of-mouth. But here is the shocking, rarely articulated bit of the story. The jesting word did not punctuate everyone's speech, but mostly the language of women. In recognizing this fact, we come to one of the most important but hidden aspects of the history of literacy—namely, that women kept the spirit of linguistic play and jesting alive. This extraordinary detail has dropped out of the history of literacy.

I spend some time here examining this part of the history of language because it represents a crucial turning point. The great child psychologist D. W. Winnicott made the point that the world will always know war so long as men do not resolve their problems with their mothers. For literacy, the problem may be

---

[13]The standard work on the *jongleur* is Edmond Faral, *Les Jongleurs en France du Moyen Âge*.

stated this way: Without a solid connection with a mother, per-haps no one can ever achieve a playful, that is a fully enfleshed, sense of literacy.

A baby's first taste of playing with language is initiated by its mother. Mothers make the first human contact with their babies. Likewise, over the course of a child's younger years, mothers generally spend more time with their infants than do fathers. The point is almost too obvious to state: Without a mother around, a child is deprived of its full exposure with orality and makes an awkward entry into literacy. These days, with children being plopped in front of TV sets, mothers—as well as fathers—have less and less contact with their children. Many children come from homes without fathers, and so mothers have to work in order to support the family. Clearly, mothers should be an equal part of the workplace, if they have the choice and that is what they choose. But their absence—particularly their forced absence—leaves a hole in the child's education. More and more toddlers spend their days in preschools, or nursery schools, or day-care centers. Teachers or day-care specialists simply cannot make the same playful contact with young children that their mothers can. Schools have to recognize the mother's nurturing, playful role and supplement it through a different approach to teaching.

The model that schools use today, however, is one that quite deliberately removes the mother's role. That attitude has very clear historical roots. For over one thousand years, from the sixth to the seventeenth centuries, men and women underwent a separate and very distinct training in literacy. Aristocratic men in England and western Europe received their education in grammar schools, where clergymen taught them a very precise linguistic artifact known as Learned Latin. Women were ex-cluded from this institutionalized program. Their education came through the vernacular, with talking and gesturing—con-tact and conversation. Educated men had an absolutely different exposure to learning, one disembedded from everyday experience.[14]

No one outside of school ever spoke a single word in Learned Latin. It was never heard on street corners, or in drawing rooms, never found utterance in baby talk, the language of love, or in the marketplace. All of that was reserved for the vernacular language: the Mother Tongue.[15] Learned Latin might be heard in schools and educational councils, but only in sentences carefully shaped by formal rules of rhetoric. Men in the universities committed its rules of grammar and correct usage to memory. They learned it by practicing the art of rhetoric, and practiced it by learning strategies of debate. Royal, legal, and religious charters assumed official status only when drafted in Learned Latin.

In a certain sense, these early educational institutions treated every young man as a kind of Kaspar Hauser. The university ignored the Mother Tongue, and substituted for it intensive training in a language those young men had never heard uttered or even seen before. This was serious work, precisely attuned to high standards of accuracy.

Play was deemed quite frivolous, an activity reserved for women's linguistic domain. Schools today teach literacy in a way that approximates that medieval model—using a system that has been designed almost exclusively for elite men, one that has been drained of play and fun and sport of all kinds. Schools insist on seeing every child as a Kaspar Hauser. If children enter schools without a Mother Tongue—and the phrase is an advisedly gen-

---

[14]In addition to Walter J. Ong, *Orality and Literacy*, 112–16, see Brother Bonaventure, "The Teaching of Latin in Later Medieval England"; Henri Irenée Marrou, *A History of Education in Antiquity;* E. Pulgram, "Spoken and Written Latin"; Roger Wright, "Speaking, Reading, and Writing Late Latin and Early Romance."

[15]On the concept of the "Mother Tongue," see Karl Heisig, "Muttersprache: Ein romanistischer Beitrag zur Genesis eines deutschen Wortes und zur Enstehung der deutsch-franzoesischen Sprachgrenze."

dered one—then teachers have to provide it. The current, severe
male model needs to be overturned, if the teaching of literacy is
ever to be invigorated.

Learned Latin—or today's equivalent, Received Standard
English, written English guided by the rules of standard grammar books—has its advantages, but they are slight.[16] While writing in general provides more objectivity than speaking by
separating the knower from the known, Learned Latin creates an
even greater objectivity, as Walter Ong argues, "by establishing
knowledge in a medium insulated from the emotion-charged
depths of one's mother tongue, thus reducing interference from
the human lifeworld and making possible the exquisitely abstract
world of medieval scholasticism and of the new mathematical
modern science which followed on the scholastic experience.
Without Learned Latin, it appears that modern science would
have got under way with greater difficulty, if it had got under
way at all."[17] In this atmosphere, Learned Latin immaculately
conceived its insulated, carefully modulated world. But it left the
commerce of the world—the hustle and bustle, the messiness of
emotions—far behind.

Only a few cloistered women managed to write anything in this
elevated, uncontaminated language. The overwhelming majority of women lived surrounded by the clutter of the vernacular—
amidst the racket of baby talk, and immersed in the hurly-burly
of conversation. More than men, women faced off in gritty
negotiations in the give-and-take of the local marketplace. For
women, life was marked by the spontaneity of oral discourse, in
sentences unaffected by the syntax of the Taught Mother

---

[16]Ong, *Orality and Literacy*, 114.

[17]Ibid.

Tongue—Learned Latin—and thus structurally less formal. Which means that women remained more attuned to rhythm, measure, and periodicity, and felt more at home with the fits and starts, the interruptions and improbabilities of discourse. They remained more in touch with the plasticity of language, as well, for rules of correct punctuation and accurate spelling and standards of correctness do not obtain in orality. But more important, all of this linguistic flexibility must have given to women a more flexible attitude toward the world in general, and thus allowed them to remain more open to playfulness and the possibilities of change, to stay more adaptable than men, who were being inculcated in the strict rhetorical training of the grammar school.

Barred from acquiring formal rhetorical skills, denied access to writing, and prevented from occupying positions of social, commercial, or religious power, women found their voice in their own intimate and private female conversations. That voice was at times understandably angry at those in power—namely men. Women circulated their own aggressive, amusing little stories in tightly knit social circles. Some of these stories were true, others embellished, or trumped up and blown out of proportion—filled with hot air. But always the bulk of them was about men. No wonder that by the late Middle Ages men found women's talk dangerous enough that they had to dismiss it as idle chatter. Women's speech was disparaged as banal by redefining it as gossip. But while the attribution of gossip may have served to lower women's voices, women refused to be silenced.

Patricia Meyer Spacks, the author of the only book-length study of gossip, tries to reinstate gossip's place in history both as a pleasurable and politically potent activity: "From outside . . . gossip often looks dangerous. It ferrets out secrets, harms other people, reveals human nature's worst propensities. Within the group of participants, gossip can feel otherwise. Freed from ordinary social inhibitions, seeking no material benefits, proceeding by established rules, forging bonds within their group, talkers pursue a game which, like all absorbing games, expresses impulses and satisfies needs."[18] As interesting as her analysis sounds, the description misses the point. Like most men, Spacks, too, concedes that gossip can be a secret, spiteful, and harmful activity. She refuses to see it as a political response—a playful but potent act of political resistance to the clearly articulated voice of power: men.

That is why critics can put down gossips for refusing "to stand up and fight like men."[19] But how could they? If women hoped to slug it out on equal footing with men, they would need to enter the ring armed with the skills of formal rhetoric. Instead, women developed their own domain of discursive power by telling pointed stories, filled with punch and bite—in that clandestine pastime called gossip. Anthropologists such as Roger Abrahams, who have studied gossip cross-culturally, find significant analogies between gossiping and aggressive joke telling within the same culture. Even in widely diverse cultures, gossiping remains a closed, more intimate and personal form of joke telling. Hélène Cixous, the French feminist critic, has written an essay about the nature of women's talk entitled "The Laugh of the Medusa," an image that corroborates Abrahams's findings. Cixous claims that, from a distance, women in intimate, secret discourse appear to be playful, joking creatures. But if people come closer, they may find themselves victims of a venomous bite from a barbed tongue.[20]

---

[18]Patricia Meyer Spacks, *Gossip,* 29.

[19]Stanley L. Olinick, "The Gossiping Psychoanalyst"; Samuel C. Heilman, *Synagogue Life: A Study in Symbolic Interaction.*

[20]For an introduction to the anthropological work on gossip, *see* Roger D. Abrahams, "A Performance-Centered Approach to Gossip"; and Clifford Geertz, *The Interpretation of Culture.* Hélène Cixous, "The Laugh of the Medusa": "You need only to look at the Medusa straight on to see her. And she's not deadly. She's beautiful and she's laughing."

This gendered distinction in joke telling has worked its way into the language. The two words *grammar* and *glamour* share a common Latin root meaning "magic," but they have branched off and developed along separate lines. *Grammar* has to do with working magic by casting correctly structured sentences, *glamour* with working magic by casting a playful eye. One is literate, the other oral; one is considered profound, the other provocative. One is perfectly acceptable, even encouraged as a sign of intelligence, the other encouraged only when it is convenient and then is generally considered a substitute—a poor substitute—for intelligence.[21] Cixous has reunited the two words in her Medusa, who gives a "come hither" glance, followed quickly by a don't-you-dare rebuff. As if that were not enough, her Medusa adds insult to injury by laughing the whole thing off.

While women were not permitted to attend grammar schools before the end of the sixteenth century, they surrounded themselves with a home-bred, but little noticed kind of linguistic instruction. The blabbing of babies, like the babbling of Mnemosyne, the mother of the Muses, provides subtle instruction in the great pleasures of social intercourse—in the luxuries of talking. The baby acts as the Muse of the mother. Raising an infant is never one-sided—in the Middle Ages or in the modern period—for the baby, in its limited but utterly sophisticated way, socializes the parents in what it means to grow up. Through cries and smiles, the infant shapes the behavior of its parents to suit its needs for comfort and food. One psychologist, Harriet Rheingold, casts this reciprocal relationship in the strongest terms: "That particular facet of socialization called parental behavior—caring for the infant in a responsible fashion—is taught to them by the infant. The specific proposition is that he teaches them what he needs to have them do for him. He makes them behave in a nurturing fashion. . . . Of men and women he makes fathers

---

[21]A similar pairing exists in French, in the etymological connection between *le chanteur* and *l'enchanteur,* "singer" and "magician."

and mothers."[22] The infant recalls for its parents the process of growing, but in particular it schools that parent most intimately connected with its welfare, the mother. And it does this at a very early age—three or four months—through its own quirky brand of communication.

Infant blather, that tiny rivulet of consciousness, noisy with unfamiliar sounds, flows without carrying along with it one pebble of a recognizable word. Each utterance, however, comes rolling along with meaning—through intonation, rhythm, and relation: a primitive grammar that would make even Noam Chomsky smile. Every mother understands that private language, knowing in an instant what her baby needs from listening to its *goo*s and *gah*s. She can distinguish questions from statements, needs from wants, and respond in turn with just the right sentence—and caring response. This language is diametrically opposed to Learned Latin: It is never written, has no formal grammar or rules of spelling, could never serve rhetorical precision. No one teaches it; it is acquired without tuition. Even for orality, infant blather seems strange in its evanescence, lasting but two or three years before it evolves and congeals into something approximating conversation. This is small talk, in its most elemental stage and form: the deepest, most emotional, life-and-death transactions get negotiated in this innocent jabber.

The infant "informs" the mother by "telling" her what it wants, keeping her in tune with the rhythm of sentences, with breathing, and with loose and unpredictable constructions kept lively and animated through giggles and laughter. The baby, that is, keeps the mother "fluid," teaching her to "go with the flow." The mother must remain flexible, willing to respond spontaneously, try different solutions to make her baby comfortable, offer

---

[22]Harriet Rheingold, "The Social and Socializing Infant," in H. W. Stevenson, ed., *Concept of Development. Monograph of the Society for Research and Child Development*, 782–83.

her breast at a moment's notice—the most fundamental *solu-tion*—until the infant gets on "schedule." It is the mother who comes to understand best of anyone the true meaning of the phrase "kidding around." By allowing the roles to reverse, she can feel like a kid again—through playfulness. And, if she wants to understand her offspring, she has to throw herself into that world with her whole being.

The associations between mothers and fluidity hold the biblical story of Moses together. Moses' sister, Miriam, weaves a small basket—weaving, recall, is one of the key metaphors for storytelling—and places her brother in it, setting him afloat down the Nile. I call on the novelist Anthony Burgess for the fictive possibilities of Moses's watery journey: "Miriam . . . probably improvised the first lullaby. It was essential that the potential saviour of his people not cry aloud and thus betray himself to the Egyptian police, who had orders to kill all the Israelite men-children. We cannot doubt that her song had *lulla* or *lolla* or *lalla* in it: the consonant called a liquid, the most soothing sound in the whole inventory, is essential to cradlesongs. Miriam, a virgin destined to be a prophetess, is the first of the great mothers."[23] Interestingly, Miriam remains in orality, singing the praises of the Israelites in crossing the Red Sea, while her brother Moses clearly ends up in ultimate literacy, handing on the Ten Commandments—on stone tablets.

The history of jesting, narration, and laughter culminated in the late fourteenth century in the literary genius of Geoffrey Chaucer, who gave those witty, oral stories a definite, written shape. The first identifiable man of letters in English, Chaucer distinguishes himself as the first person to use the word *author* in a

[23]Anthony Burgess, *On Going to Bed*, 7.

secular sense, and to apply it to himself.[24] He is an interesting figure, precisely because he straddles so elegantly and so intelligently the two worlds of orality and literacy. He can tell us a tremendous amount about the transition between the two.

I am inclined to call Chaucer the mother of English literature, for he is also our first wonderfully silly writer. He manages to bring the mother's affectionate spirit into literature by making puns and funny noises, pulling off clever rhymes, and he seems to know that the audacity and courage needed for storytelling comes from women. He gives us complicated storytellers, like the Wife in "The Wife of Bath's Tale," and crafty practical jokers, like Alisoun, in "The Miller's Tale." He also loves language so intently that he leaves the aristocratic language around him and drops down into the vernacular to give his stories their heartfelt punch. Thirty-odd pilgrims make the pilgrimage to Canterbury but Chaucer includes not one aristocrat. Chaucer knows that their rule-bound language prevented them from telling interesting stories. Their absence constitutes its own significant tale.

Since this discussion turns on the definition of vernacular language, the term deserves discussion. *Vernacular* derives from an Indo-Germanic root that indicates "rootedness" or "abode." It is a Latin word used in classical times to refer to whatever was home-bred, home-grown, home-made—be it slave, child's food, dress, animal, opinion, or most important, a joke. Joking could be accomplished only in the vernacular. The Roman poet Publius Terrentius Varro (c. 82–37 B.C.) used the word *vernacular* to designate language that is grown on a speaker's own soil as

---

[24]The Latin stem *gero* produces a wide range of meanings, from the specific "to give birth to a child," to the more general "to bear, to carry, to perform or accomplish," "to reveal feelings" or "to wear an expression." From these general meanings of *gero* arises in the later Latin of the empire "author" *(auctor)*, "story" *(gesta)*, "gesture" *(gestu)*, and "telling" *(agare)*. By analogy with growing or making, the agent-noun *augere* becomes *auctor* in Old French, passing into Middle English as *auctor*, "author."

opposed to that which was planted there by others—a transplant like Learned Latin. Varro was a learned man, with considerable influence on the Middle Ages, and so *vernacular* came into English with the restricted sense and overtones that Varro had established for it. It is nevertheless crucial to recognize *vernacular* as the speech of the living world itself.

An example might help to make the distinctions between the various levels of language clear. Take the word *suck* for our example. In street argot—slang—it means "terrible" or "totally unacceptable," as in the line "I hate that movie; it sucks!" In the vernacular, it connotes "drawing in something, like a liquid, or air." In the taught language of science, *suck* refers very narrowly to the physical laws governing vacuums and partial vacuums.

Vernacular languages are not just less-developed models of officially authorized systems of communication like Learned Latin or Received Standard English. Taught languages are imposed and colonize a person's way of being, controlling his or her perception. The vernacular, on the other hand, represents a community's shared power and authority. According to Ivan Illich:

> Language that is exempt from rational tutorship is a different kind of social phenomenon than language that is taught. Where untutored language is the predominant marker of a shared world, a sense of the shared power within the group exists that cannot be duplicated by language that is delivered. One of the first ways the difference shows is in a sense of power over language itself—over its acquisition.[25]

The vernacular develops deep inside a person, at infancy, and through it one articulates the desires and dreams of the unconscious, in a way that taught languages never can. The vernacular becomes permeated and thus shaped by the idiosyncratic

---

[25]Ivan Illich, "Vernacular Values and Education," in Bruce Bain, ed., *The Sociogenesis of Language and Human Conduct*, 482–83.

rhythms of one's own inner life. It gets passed around casually from person to person within a community. As a vernacular speaker, I may tailor what I say as I speak, face-to-face, with another. In taught languages, some outside agency sets the standards for correctness; and so under those conditions I cannot enunciate my own style, but only what others have contrived. I speak rules, not rhythms; I utter correctness, not consciousness. Taught language can be declaimed, recited, announced, but it can never be truly spoken. It would be hard to lose one's temper in taught language, since a script of some sort always underlies it, always keeps it bound. Whatever else taught language can accomplish, it cannot hold a conversation together, and so can never promote the human contact needed for community.

As a user of Standard English, I find myself immediately judged: Do I measure up?, do I violate rules?, do I know what I'm talking about? Intelligence gets equated with one's ability to observe the rules of grammar and syntax. Compared with Standard English, Black English and Chicano English turn out to be Dumb English, and their speakers appear equally dumb. Received Standard English, like Learned Latin, forces a shift away from content to an emphasis on form. What an argument sounds like, or what it looks like on a page, precedes anything that a speaker or a writer might have to articulate.[26]

---

[26]The most deliberate and obvious example of the vernacular can be heard in the "internalized grammar" of young children talking. The psycholinguist Breyne Arlene Moskowitz notes the following: "It is important to understand that when children make such errors, they are not producing flawed or incomplete replicas of adult sentences; they are producing sentences that are correct and grammatical with respect to their own current internalized grammar. Indeed, children's errors are essential data for students of child language because it is the consistent departures from the adult model that indicate the nature of a child's current hypotheses about the grammar of language" ("The Acquisition of Language," in William S-Y. Wang, *The Emergence of Language: Development and Evolution*, 135–37).

See also Noam Chomsky, *Rules and Representations;* and Anwar S. Dil, ed., *Language, Structure and Language Use: Essays by Charles H. Ferguson.*

Comic stories can be told best in the vernacular. (Slang does not get separated out from the vernacular to occupy its own category until fairly recently—late in the eighteenth century.) Chaucer understands what the vernacular is capable of doing. Because he presides over the earliest experiments with narration—*The Oxford English Dictionary* cites 1398 as the first instance of the word *fiction*—he knows how well joking dances and frolics in the vernacular. Just one of his remarkable feats was to shape the *facetiae* into the first modern joke, not of the type Augustine referred to—benign stretches of the truth—but aggressive hostile jokes with a punch line delivered to bring a rival down.

In a stroke of brilliance, Chaucer noticed that the physicality of the practical joke could be converted into a verbal punch line. When added to the *facetiae,* the punch line turned the listener into a target, a butt, no longer subject to a physical blow, but instead made vulnerable—emotionally and psychically—to an image or a word. In "The Miller's Tale," Chaucer had drawn the curtain aside and offered his fourteenth-century audience a glimpse into the literate future: The practical joke has become domesticated. While the Miller tells a story that revolves around several practical jokes—a fake flood, a misdirected kiss, a perfectly aimed fart, a singed ass—his tale itself constitutes a colossal, nasty joke, about gullibility and cuckoldry, delivered at another character, the Reeve (a carpenter).

Derisive joking in the ancient world was characterized as *aculei,* "barbed," "arrowlike." The word *butt* appropriately enough translates as "target," in archery, for instance. These key words reveal something crucial: The punch line cannot hit its mark unless victims themselves present themselves as fully rounded characters, their vulnerability made fleshly palpable. The Miller must be close enough to the Reeve to know, as the saying goes, where he "lives." A joke misfires unless it finds as its object a personality rife with consciousness and sensibility. Idiots, dolts—as the Middle Ages say, *stupidus*—will simply miss the point. Or the point will miss them—fly by without so much as a glancing blow—or pass over their heads. Which presents us with another of language's double-takes, another of its surprises: Corralling the joke into a literate context forced Chaucer into becoming a serious writer, into dropping traditional, flat stereotypes in favor of fully rounded characters. At this early stage of storytelling, characters spring to life, so they can be brought down—laid low—by other characters through hostile jokes. This paradox radically affects the storyteller as well. By writing jokes Chaucer moved to another level of seriousness. It forced him to become—in medieval terms—an "author."

Let me sketch the action of the "The Miller's Tale" to show how the form of the well-made, conventional short story follows the form of Chaucer's early joke—the confluence, as I have said, of the two streams of narration and joking. The action starts out fast. The Miller announces he will tell a tale about cuckoldry. No sooner are the words out of his mouth, than his pilgrim rival, the Reeve, protests: Tell something more wholesome, less offensive. The Reeve protests too much, of course, revealing *himself* to be a cuckold, while laying his insecurities wide open for everyone to see.

Every joker begins by asking the question "Have you heard the one about . . . ? or "Stop me if you've heard this one." The joke simply will not work without surprise. The Reeve has not heard this one—and he does not want to—but he clearly knows what's coming, and that's his problem: he cannot stop the boorish Miller.

Chaucer underscores the two men's rivalry with physical descriptions. The Miller, bully that he is, outweighs the skinny, choleric Reeve by several hundred pounds. When he punches, it hurts. The face-off between Miller and Reeve continues in modern teams of fat and lean comic pairs, like Abbott and Costello, Laurel and Hardy, Mutt and Jeff, and Ralph Cramden and Ed Norton. The straight man functions as the literate version of the Mudhead or the trickster. But the straight man undercuts, not through exaggeration and parody, but by pretending not to understand what's going on. The straight man lets the air out of the fat man by acting like the gullible innocent until he exposes his partner as a fool.

As the Miller unfolds his story, it is clear that he intends to throw his weight around, and the Reeve will undoubtedly get hurt. The Miller goes straight for his target: An old, wealthy man, who just happens to be a carpenter like the Reeve, marries a young, beautiful girl, Alisoun, and, because he feels deeply jealous, keeps her confined. He's also cheap. To make some extra money, the old carpenter, John, rents a room in the attic of his house to a young, handsome university student, Nicholas.

The young couple, Alisoun and Nicholas, immediately conspire, of course, to keep John at a safe distance so they can, as Chaucer puts it, "rage and pleye." Alisoun hatches a plan; Nicholas carries it out. In a tiny story within a story, Nicholas warns John about a fast-approaching flood, so horrendous it will make Noah's flood seem like a summer shower. To escape certain death by drowning, Nicholas counsels, John must hammer together three little tubs and secure them to the roof of the house, high above the waterline. John complies, and with the gullible old man safely tied to the roof and curled up inside his tub and fast asleep, Alisoun and Nicholas descend to the ground floor to spend the evening together in John and Alisoun's bed. The tale has settled into an uneasy balance.

But not for long. Just as Alisoun and Nicholas have settled themselves into bed, Chaucer ruins their fun by throwing in a new complication—an additional thread that Chaucer will use to knit up the climax of the story, and another angle to turn the lover's triangle into a square. Absolon, the parish priest, who has had his eye on Alisoun, comes to her bedroom window, in true courtly lover fashion, to serenade his paramour and charm a juicy kiss from her. After a few minutes of off-key singing, Absolon pops the question of a kiss. Alisoun consents, but now she is enamored of practical jokes and hatches another one. Pucker up, she coyly coos, as she eases her naked ass out the window.

Blinded by the excitement of getting a kiss at long last, Absolon unwittingly kisses her keester, as Chaucer describes, "ful savourly," producing in Alisoun one of the most resounding iambic lines in literature, as well as the first laugh recorded in English: " 'Tehee!' quod she, and clapte the wyndow to."[27]

Just as stories inspire competition, practical jokes prompt an immediate escalation. That's what we have already learned from Alisoun. "Can you top this?" is implied in every joke and story. But Alisoun should beware, for escalation sometimes backfires. As Absolon slowly understands what he has done, he resolves to get even. Which means, in trickster's terms, that he must raise the ante. He returns to Alisoun's bedroom window and begs for another kiss, just as wonderful as the one he got before; and Alisoun once more agrees. Nicholas now decides he wants to get *his* fair share. This parish fool should kiss *his* behind, too. So Nicholas slides his naked arse out the window "over the buttock, to the haunche-bone" and, because the night has fallen fast, Absolon asks his little turtle dove to let him know where she is: "Spek, swete bryd," he croons, "I noot not where thou art"— triggering a rhyme Chaucer simply cannot resist: "This Nicholas anon leet fle a fart." But Absolon stands ready this time. Taking careful aim, he brands Nicholas smack on the ass with a red-hot poker.

Nicholas has fired off no ordinary fart. No, Chaucer declares it was "as greet as it had been a thounder-dent." The noise fills the night air. The tale lacks only one element to make it com-

---

[27]Chaucer deliberately exploits play and joking in appreciation of the vernacular. Medievalists constantly argue away this kind of playfulness. Glending Olson insists that Chaucer's play serves a practical end by providing a refreshing respite, necessary to carry out serious work (*Literature as Recreation in the Later Middle Ages*).Richard Lanham argues that Chaucer must have seen the world as a game and people as players ("Games and High Seriousness: Chaucer," in Richard Lanham, *The Motives of Eloquence: Literary Rhetoric in the Renaissance*). Stephen Manning holds a similar view, in "Rhetoric, Game, Morality, and Geoffrey Chaucer," *Studies in the Age of Chaucer*.

plete—rain. Without knowing it, Nicholas has become the
weather man. Writhing in pain, clutching his smoking behind,
he manages a pathetic cry: "Help! Water! Water!" That's all
John needs to hear. In his dopey sleep, he concludes that Noah's
flood has actually arrived and dutifully cuts the rope holding him
fast. As Chaucer puts it: "Downe gooth alle." John falls three
stories headlong into the street, bringing all the neighbors running out of their houses alarmed by the great commotion. Nicholas and Alisoun also dash outside, adding to the confusion. All
three characters wind up on the street, leveled, finally, by the
action of the story.

When the Miller finishes, the pilgrims all howl with laughter—all but the Reeve, who curses and swears at the Miller. He's
angry, disgusted, and what's worse, humiliated. Thanks to the
Miller, thirty-three pilgrims now know the awful truth of his life,
and in embarrassingly graphic detail. The Miller has stepped
outside the boundaries of fiction, violating the rules of storytelling by revealing secrets of the Reeve's personal life. He has
backed the Reeve into one of society's most feared corners,
forcing him to play the butt of a joke.

Ultimately, Chaucer has thrown *every* character out of the
little house of fiction he has so carefully constructed. On examination, "The Miller's Tale" appears to follow a deliberate architectural scheme. In the beginning of the tale, the characters
stand separated by three stories—from attic to ground floor.[28] As
the action rises, all three characters climb outside of the confines
of the house and up to the roof, moving from the inside volume
of the house, to occupy its skin. (Storytelling, fiction, and architecture all deal with *volume*, each in its own peculiar way.) When
the action begins to run down, so do the principal characters—
Alisoun and Nicholas climb down from the roof of the house and

---

[28]Notice that *story* is both a fictional as well as an architectural term. The
conflation of these two terms may be due to narrative friezes carved into the
parapet above each floor of Greek buildings in the classical period.

reenter it at the first story, to the scene of the original sin, the bedroom. The punch line—the climax of the story—comes in the form of a single word, "water," that in good storytelling fashion does double duty. First, it secures the knot holding sub-plot to main plot, the inside of the house to the outside, and fiction to practical joke. Second, the story's resolution, in French called the *dénouement,* which means "untying," undoes the narra-tive threads that hold all the elements of the story together, a cutting done by the Reeve himself as he comes to groggy con-sciousness.

M other Tongue: It seems like such an innocent, benign term. *The Oxford English Dictionary* defines it as "one's native language" and cites 1380 as its first written use in English: "Secular lords should, to counter the prelates, learn and preach the law of God in their mother tongue." The citation is from John Wyclife, the English reformer. He is saying that parishioners need to hear the Gospel in English, not in Latin, so they can understand its message and take it to heart.[29]

The term obviously refers to language—but also to a time before language—and turns out to be not as benign as it looks at first glance. Its history embodies the themes I have been discussing, and therefore I want to trace its outlines, beginning with the Mother Tongue as we know it from primitive times and from mythology. Intriguing evidence for both turns up in France.

The French use a phrase, *ours mal léché,* "a badly licked bear,"

---

[29]The connection between "mother" and "tongue" is first made in Lorraine in the tenth century, at the time of a retreat of the Frankish and the advance of neo-Latin-speaking populations. See L. Weissberger, "Ist Muttersprache eine germanische oder eine romantische Wortpraegung," who traces the rise of the idea of the Mother Tongue in European cultures.

to refer to a child who acts in an uncivil manner.[30] The phrase compares that recalcitrant child to a bear cub who has not received proper licking from the sow. An ancient belief held that bear mothers must lick their cubs, who are born formless blobs of fat, into a discernible shape. Biologists in fact report that if the mother bear does not lick the cub's stomach, peristalsis will not begin, and the newborn will not mature. Indeed, it will wither and die. Hence an uncivilized French child, who continually behaves outside the bounds of civility, needs a "licking" (perhaps with a cane) or a "tongue-lashing" (perhaps with strong words) in order to "shape-up." (One meaning of the Latin *lingua* is a little leather strap.)

Bear sows provide a model from the animal world of the human mother's powerful linguistic connection to her infant. Her nonverbal exchanges help shape the infant and give it form as much as her suckling does. The difference between breast-feeding and bottle-feeding may serve as an analogy for under-standing the difference between vernacular language and taught language. Aristocrats in the Middle Ages typically gave over their babies to wet nurses for breast-feeding, a practice which may even more accurately capture the distance between the vernacular and the taught language. In both of these cases, the infant receives nourishment, but the experiences are radically different.

When we talk about the nourishing, milk-giving mother, we move to the very foundation of a child's entry into growth, education, breath, language, rhythm, and emotional develop-ment—to the nexus that connects the infant with his or her eventual being. Whoever controls and shapes this second umbili-cus exerts tremendous power over a citizenry. The early medie-

---

[30]Notice that the English meaning of the French *léché* (past tense of the infinitive *lécher*) refers to the tongue, to licking; and in Spanish that word denotes milk. (The word *tongue* comes from the Latin *lingua,* which means both "language" and "tongue.")

val Catholic Church recognized this fact, and made maternal care—the breast/tongue/language—into a commodity, repackaged the concept, and delivered it to their parishioners as the *alma mater* (nourishing mother). The medieval Church as *Mater Ecclesia* assigned formal, instrumental value to the vernacular tongue—and breast—and thus made it into something bureaucratic that required administrative oversight. Our modern attitude toward the teaching of literacy remains tied to that medieval legacy.

How did that model persist? What we moderns experience, social critics like Ivan Illich and Michel Foucault have pointed out, are basic needs that match up to commodities rather than to vernacular values.[31] Illich in particular has pointed out the ways in which technological innovations are quickly pressed into service to increase commodity production rather than to improve vernacular competence. Language has fallen in line as another one of those commodities. No matter how vividly a young person speaks, no matter how lively his slang, or her individual rhythms, schools are designed to replace the vernacular with Standard English. And Standard English is quickly recognizable because it adheres to rigid grammatical rules and follows frozen syntactic models. In elementary and secondary classrooms, teachers present that brand of literacy as a required tool of economic advancement—one that can enable a person to fill out this form, or to complete that contract. But the real stakes remain hidden. Illich reveals them:

> We have become accustomed, through Karl Marx's writings, to speak of the alienation of the worker from his work in class society. We must now recognize the estrangement of man from his learning when it becomes the product of a service profession and he becomes a consumer. . . . The more education an individ-

---

[31]Ivan Illich, *Tools for Conviviality* and *Shadow Work*. Michel Foucault, *The Order of Things: An Archaeology of the Human Sciences*.

ual consumes, the more "knowledge stock" he acquires and the higher he rises in the hierarchy of knowledge capitalists. Education thus defines a new class structure for society within which the large consumers of knowledge—those who have acquired greater quantities of knowledge stock—can claim to be of superior value to society. They represent gilt-edged securities in a society's portfolio of human capital, and access to the more powerful or scarcer tools of production is reserved to them.[32]

A person feels a need, that is, and immediately feels dependent— impotent. Each act of consumption decreases the possibility of a community of intimates. With the help of Madison Avenue, corporate America has transformed everything people *want,* like vernacular competence, into deep-seated *needs,* like literacy. To achieve their goal, corporations had to eradicate what might be called basic, vernacular feelings. People want transportation, to get from one place to another with a minimum of inconvenience, but they are made to feel that they need the fastest, sleekest automobile to accomplish that end. People want to feel good, but they have been convinced not to listen to their own bodies and not to take responsibility for their own diets and exercise. They believe that to reach that state called health—defined for them by the medical profession—they need to subscribe to something called a health delivery system. People want to feel refreshed and invigorated, and intellectually stimulated. Television, movies, and the publishing industry have made them feel the need to be entertained. People try to gratify desire by patronizing stores and consulting professionals.[33]

Values of self-awareness and self-reliance fall by the way.

---

[32]Ivan Illich, *Toward a History of Needs,* 71.

[33]William Leiss, *The Limits to Satisfaction,* is a good starting point for an inventory of the transformation of individual wants into needs through industrialization.

Friends and loved ones no longer hold the key to wisdom and knowledge. Only professionals possess that authority. And so people feel isolated, frustrated, and—most destructive of all— stupid. This radical shift in the West from wants to needs can be located before the advent of the industrial revolution in the reign of Charlemagne, during the late eighth through the ninth centuries.[34] That shift gives rise to the concept already mentioned, the *alma mater*—the nourishing, "alms-giving" mother—which found expression in the Taught Mother Tongue.

Through the efforts of Alcuin, an abbot at Tours who served as court adviser to Charlemagne, priests became pastors. Priests were men invested with the power to preach—*pre-dicare,* "to proclaim"—and to officiate at various church offices. But, then, from the eighth century on, priests began to define the needs of their parishioners for them. They then took the next "paternal" step. They took on the administrative responsibility for their parishioners' care. Lewis Mumford noticed many years ago that this shift—to pastoral care—ushered in a new age of welfare. In Mumford's view, the pastor should be seen as a precursor of the service professional—the social worker. Mumford invites his readers to make the following comparison: An indigent cannot receive a welfare payment without the intervention of a case worker; a medieval cannot attain salvation without the personal services of the institutionalized Church.[35]

The Church applied this same paternal attitude to language. The term *Mother Tongue* does not appear until the eleventh century. Up to that point, the laity spoke "people's language," *sermo vulgaris.* Quite suddenly, the sermons of the monks at a particular abbey, at Görz, not far from Verdun, raised the vernacular into the lofty realm of the universal maternity of the Virgin Mary,

---

[34]For a philosophical analysis of the commercialization of desire in the West, see Illich, *Toward a History of Needs.*

[35]Lewis Mumford, *The Culture of Cities,* passim, for the transformation of priests into pastors.

and the symbolic maternity of the Church, as a way of defending the vernacular, the monks argued, against defilement and debasement.[36] Language appeared to receive special consecration by this new alignment. As the idea of *materna*—motherhood—came into the domain of the clergy, the clergy, in effect, co-opted the basic connection between mother and child on behalf of the Church.

Translated into Low Latin as *materna lingua,* the term spread throughout Europe, and was applied to various forms of the vernacular in the fourteenth and fifteenth centuries. By making a category for people's speech, the Church could then define it so that, in a crucial, breathtaking move, men could take over the teaching of the Mother Tongue. Orality, once the domain of women, would now move under the control of men, who would teach a "cleaned-up," regularized version of it. Formal learning had always officially been consigned to the domain of men. Now, all aspects of literacy—including its oral, vernacular dimensions—were brought under the administration and custodianship of men. Whatever shreds of the vernacular remained with women were dismissed with the deprecating term *gossip.*[37]

The crucial step that converts the Mother Tongue into a precisely controllable artifact takes place in Spain in the fifteenth

---

[36]For centuries in France, the bear had stood as an emblem of the Church. For the Church licked its novitiates into shape, just as the sow did. Heathens have no shape; they act uncivilly and without boundaries. The monks at Görz did not pull off any radical trick. They only added to the many powers of the bear's tongue. I am indebted to Ivan Illich for this discussion of the *sermo vulgaris* and the Mother Tongue.

[37]For more on Church appropriation of speech, see Ivan Illich and Barry Sanders, *ABC: The Alphabetization of the Popular Mind,* 29–70.

century. In 1492, a Spaniard, Don Elio Antonio de Nebrija, makes such a strong case to Queen Isabella that he convinces the Crown to publish the first grammar in any European language. Nebrija dedicated his *Gramática Castellana* to his Queen, Isabel la Católica. The book perplexed her. A grammar certainly was a teaching tool, but how in God's name could the vernacular be taught? And why?

Nebrija answers her. We have sent our soldiers abroad to rule, he says to Isabella, to far-away places like Aragon, Navarre, and even to Italy. The Castillian language has followed them. But our men speak a diversity of tongues. Instead of a continually evolving vernacular, Nebrija wants a timeless language:

> To avoid these variegated changes I have decided to . . . turn the Castillian language into an artifact so that whatever shall be henceforth written in this language shall be of one standard coinage that can outlast the times. Greek and Latin have been governed by art and thus have kept their uniformity throughout the ages. Unless the like of this be done for our language, in vain your Majesty's chronicles . . . shall praise your deeds. Your labor will not outlast more than a few years and we shall continue to feed on Castillian translations of strange and foreign tales (about our own kings). Either your feats will fade with the language, or they will roam among aliens abroad, homeless without a dwelling in which they can settle.[38]

Nebrija claims something of immense significance here. He argues that real domination comes not through platoons of soldiers, but only when the Crown can congeal the profusion of tongues into one universal Taught Mother Tongue—into some-

[38]The *Gramática Castellana* was printed on August 18, 1492, in Salamanca, fifteen days after Columbus set sail. I quote the text here from Ivan Illich's "Taught Mother Tongue," in his *In the Mirror of the Past: Lectures and Addresses, 1978–1990,* 138.

thing solidly unchanging like an artifact. The time is now, Nebrija urges, for after Columbus returns "your Majesty shall have placed her yoke unto many barbarians who speak outlandish tongues, by your victory these shall stand in new needs: in need for the laws that the victor owes to the vanquished and in need of the language that we bring. My grammar shall serve to impart to them the Castilian tongues as we have taught Latin to our young."[39]

Nebrija turned the Mother Tongue into something formulaic, a commodity that could be regulated by governmental institutions, and prescribed by professionals.

Today, an *alma mater* refers to a graduate's college or university, especially when it serves as a repository for alumnae donations. The history of linguistic transformation of this term has been all but lost. And children today? They come into the world virtually dependent upon instruction administered by professionals outside the home—and they are totally dependent upon schools.

But young people show a tenacity, a struggle to keep the vernacular alive by any means necessary. Despite the enormous amount of scripted language that young people hear by the time they reach adolescence, their desire for a spirited vernacular makes itself heard in their practically insatiable appetite for linguistic play of all sorts. In particular, young children love to hear and love to make puns (in Latin, *paronomasia*): either in homophones (words that sound the same but have different meanings), homonyms (words with the same spelling but with different meanings), or polysemes (single words with different meanings). Puns are language's doppelgängers—double-entendres that

---

[39]Ibid., 139–40.

shimmer with one meaning one moment, and another meaning the next moment.[40]

Delia Chiaro, a scholar of language and linguistics, finds all three forms of punning a "duplicity . . . which is inherent in the language itself."[41] I prefer to see that "duplicity" as the inherently joking nature of language itself. People struggle to understand experience though a system called language, which can only function as a surrogate for experience and which therefore always provides a slightly disappointing facsimile of reality. Nevertheless, while language is an imprecise instrument, it alone makes possible the understanding of everyday experience. Language captures experience and at the same time falls short of holding it. Language teases and plays its practical joke: it seems to translate our sensory experience without filtering or distorting it—and yet betrays its true nature in those surprises called puns.

Linguistic legerdemain—now-you-see-it, now-you-don't, now-you-see-it-again—characterizes reality for young children, even for infants. The breast arrives, and leaves, and arrives back again. Parents leave and return again. The world itself disappears for the infant during sleep, and reappears every time he or she awakens. This may be why even the youngest infants squeal with delight playing peek-a-boo. That universal game captures the nature of their world. Peek-a-boo can also be construed as a very rudimentary miming of the spirit of puns: first the baby sees

---

[40]Scholarly work on children and wordplay all seems to rest on a basic Freudian notion that children treat words as real things. See Michael Mulkay, *On Humor: Its Nature and Its Place in Modern Society*, 109 ff.; Adam Phillips, *On Kissing, Tickling, and Being Bored: Psychoanalytic Essays on the Unexamined Life;* and D. W. Winnicott, *The Child, the Family, and the Outside World*, especially "Why Children Play" and "Stealing and Telling Lies." For the Freudian model, see *Jokes and Their Relation to the Unconscious*, 125 ff.

[41]Delia Chiaro, *The Language of Jokes: Analysing Verbal Play*, 43–45.

one meaning—physical presence—and seconds later another meaning—disappearance.⁴²

Peek-a-boo, as a way of framing or conceptualizing reality, works its way into the origins of literature. In Iran, the cradle of literacy, every fairy tale—ancient or modern—begins, as we have seen, with the same formula, "Yeki bud, yeki nabud" ("There was somebody, there was nobody; this happened, this did not happen"). The fairy tale plays hide-and-seek with reality. What you are about to hear, the formula announces, is a dramatized pun. "Once upon a time" translates that Persian image of liminal presence into the English equivalent dreamtime. Every fairy tale is a dream—a blinking on and off of meaning, a magical narrative that plays peek-a-boo with the child.⁴³

Reading participates in the same game. When Horace says of writing: *Litera scripta manet* ("The written word remains"), *manet* contains a Latin pun on *manes,* the remains of the dead—their shadows. Written words lie on the page, inert and dead, and return to life before the reader's eye, or more accurately, *because* of the reader's eye. Reading turns into a peek-a-boo game in

---

⁴²To find the definition of *peek-a-boo* in *The Oxford English Dictionary,* one must look under its earlier name, *Bo-peep:* "A nursery play with a young child, who is *kept in excitement* by the nurse or playmate alternately concealing herself (or her face), and peeping out for a moment at an unexpected place, to withdraw again with equal suddenness. Johnson says 'The act of looking out and then drawing back as if frightened, or with the purpose to fright some other' " (emphasis mine). To a very young child, the coming and going of reality does not so much baffle and frustrate as it surprises and excites. For that reason, games like peek-a-boo not only represent the pulse of experience but also provide a crucible for future, more complicated tasks, like reading. See also Jerome Bruner and V. Sherwood, "Early Rule Structure: The Case of Peekaboo," in Mary Gauvain and Michael Cole, eds., *Readings on the Development of Children,* 77–82. Disappearance and appearance figure prominently, of course, in the nursery rhyme "Little Bo-Peep," where the child continually loses her sheep.

⁴³For a discussion of "the dreaming" as a "poetic key to reality," see W. E. H. Stanner, "The Dreaming," in T. A. G. Hungerford, ed., *Australian Signpost,* 51–65.

which scenes and characters come startlingly alive, only to disappear again once the reader moves on or closes the book.

Such playful activity, reading—and writing, too—takes a playful form of give-and-take. Infants get a "taste" of it early on in nursing, and play it out in the nursery with versions of bo-peep or peek-a-boo games. They hear it in the form of fairy tales. And then most strikingly, they play the games on themselves, much to their delight, when they learn to read.

CHAPTER FOUR

Humboldt . . . said that real language is that speech which can only be fostered, never taught like mathematics. Only machines can communicate without any reference to vernacular roots. Their chatter in New York now takes up almost three quarters of the lines that the telephone company operates under a franchise that guarantees free intercourse to people. This is an obvious perversion of a public channel. But even more embarrassing than this abuse of a forum of free speech by robots is the incidence of robot-like stock phrases in the remaining part in which people address each other. A growing percentage of personal utterances has become predictable, not only in content but also in style. Language is degraded to "communication" as if it were nothing but the human variety of an exchange that also goes on between bees, whales, and computers. No doubt, a vernacular component always survives; all I say is that it withers. The American colloquial has become a composite made up of two kinds of language: a commodity-like, taught uniquack, and an impoverished vernacular that tries to survive.

—Ivan Illich, "Taught Mother Tongue,"
In the Mirror of the Past

have been arguing a position that would have been unthinkable at any other time in history. The "human being," a fairly
consistent creature these past few thousand years or so—since
the introduction, at any rate, of the alphabet—is disappearing
before our eyes. This is not a murder mystery; the body is not
missing. Rather, we are being forced to change the way we think
about human beings, about the creature that has been socially
created for centuries, because the innovations of technology are
now calling into being a radically different kind of person. Illich's
words on the degradation of language into communication
should be read as a warning. It takes us to the dark side of
Nadine Gordimer's encomium to language that I quoted at the
outset. We may not want to acknowledge the presence of this
new creature—this technological dybbuk—but the evidence is
now clear.

One might well ask, then, why has there been no outcry, no
front-page headlines screaming the truth to us? I believe that our
notion of what constitutes a human being has been changing so
rapidly and so radically that most people have not even been
able to assimilate it. Denial has been the protective response.

When I refer to the disappearance of human beings, I do not
write fancifully, or metaphorically. I mean the following: The
characteristically European, Western mental space that has been
shaped for nearly two thousand years by the alphabet is now
being displaced by a new perceptual space, one that has been

shaped by the computer. To cast this in other terms: One dominant metaphor—the alphabetic text—has collided head-on with
another—the computer screen. These two metaphors simply
cannot occupy the same space. I want to report on the casualties
that have resulted thus far from that head-on collision.

I have argued that guilt and conscience and self are possible
only in literacy. Human behavior looks very different once people no longer feel anchored by the metaphor of the text. We may
all be witness to that behavior; we may all be present in a living
science-fiction nightmare of the most colossal proportions. The
truest expressions of where our culture is headed may be found
in a generation of those young gangsters who rape and torture
and murder without constraint or remorse, without being able to
help themselves. We need to be able to imagine a nation peopled
with under-aged sociopaths.

Casualty reports from the effects of illiteracy appear every day
in the newspapers, but they pass undetected because they hardly
ever mention the word *illiteracy*. In one of those typical stories, the
New York Times reported on the rape and murder of two teenage
girls in Houston, Texas, by six young men. The girls, fourteen
and sixteen, had stumbled on to a gang initiation while they
made their way home in the White Oak Bayou area of the city.
The young men, aged fourteen to eighteen, belong to the new
category of post-illiterates I am describing. Houston residents
were not so much shocked by the murders, however brutal they
appeared, as they were by the reaction of the young men:

> . . . the absence of any coherent explanation for the killings and
> the suspects' apparently thorough lack of any remorse. The
> police account, which investigators say is based in part on state-
> ments made by the suspects, describes an almost unfathomably
> mindless act of violence."[1]

---

[1] "Houston Knows Murder, but This . . . ," *New York Times*, Friday, July 9, 1993,
A-7.

On a local television program on gangs that got broadcast the day before the killings, one of the suspects, who happened to be featured in that program, lifted a can of beer in a macabre toast and bragged, "Human life means nothing."

Nowhere does the news story specifically mention anything about illiteracy, except to say that several of the young men came from broken homes and met at reform schools. But the details of the murders most assuredly speak to the problems of the new illiteracy. The connection just needs to be made, the complete story needs to be told. Someone—beyond this single reporter— has to see this new youth as belonging to a new category. The facts are all there.

Our laws, our penal institutions, our hospitals and halfway houses are feeble in the face of this change. It matters very little how many cities respond with more arrests by more police in the streets. Arrest reports might reassure citizens that "At last, something's being done," but the problem defies statistics. The problem will continue to grow without any natural limit so long as politicians and school administrators insist that the root cause of illiteracy lies with the school system. That kind of thinking might have been correct several decades ago. In the 1950s, Americans mustered immediate sympathy for classrooms filled with too many students, and labs filled with too little equipment, and teachers filled with too many dull assignments. But once the technological revolution hit high gear—and I include TV, film, and video games, as well as personal computers—the parameters shifted radically. The problems changed. To correct problems of illiteracy one can no longer talk about revamping school programs, or even wresting administrative control from school boards. The voucher system will not touch the problem.

What Ivan Illich called for several decades ago, the "deschooling of society," has occurred, but not in the way he imagined.[2] Illich had hoped that youngsters would no longer feel that

---

[2]Ivan Illich, *Deschooling Society*.

everything they needed to know had to be learned in school. Certain skills in particular could be learned through apprenticeship. Young people, he hoped, would grasp their sense of confidence, their feelings of power, back from the schools. This has not happened. True, they have left school behind, but they have not decided to make the break out of a conscious decision. The computer has intervened. The school world seems dull compared with TV and movie and video-game images. There's more money in drug dealing than in fry cooking. This is not de-schooling, but dis-education. Illiteracy festers deeply inside young people today. The problem has to be addressed at the very beginning of their education, in the home, immediately after birth. Illiteracy is a shared problem—between infant, and mother and father.

It's easy to blame the schools, to cry it's all a failure of teachers. Then administrators can argue for salary raises and call for more training for teachers; schools can find grants to implement the latest reading strategy. Students can be trained, like seals, to perform well. With the right exercises, teachers will post substantial increases in their students' reading scores. Teachers can, as they say, "teach to the test." But finally no matter how successfully these measures turn out, every school administrator and every politician who wants to be seen as doing something serious will ultimately turn to technology to address the "decay of the school system."

Technology is no-nonsense; technology brings the enormous weight and seriousness of science to bear on every problem. Unfortunately, the solution misses the point. It sees illiteracy as a problem isolated in the classroom and assignable to the teachers. It treats students as lazy and poorly motivated. In virtually every school, the strategy sounds the same: Get students behind a computer screen with any one of a series of reading and writing programs, behind what are called interactive media programs. Advertisements for the Voyager Expanded Book, for instance, the latest in books on disc, proclaim a Revolution in Reading. Programs like Voyager's claim that individualized tailored instruction, in which students communicate directly with the screen, without the presence of a teacher, can bring them to literacy faster and more efficiently than teacher and classroom discussion can.

But calling in more computer power will only exacerbate the problem: locking students onto a screen, especially in the name of having them appreciate language's potential for power and play, destroys their literacy by robbing them of the internalized text as a psychosocial frame of reference. In the end the computer moves them closer and closer to illiteracy. It breaks the human connection and reinforces the broken connections at home. The social contract was not drafted on a word processor. It cannot be repaired with one.

If the dictionary kept record of deep social changes, we might find under the entry *human being* a startlingly new definition in the 1995 or 1996 edition of Webster's: "A hominid of the genus and species *Homo sapiens* which possesses the ability to recall, but lacks memory; which possesses the ability to react to stimuli, but not to respond; and which seems to behave without guilt, shame, embarrassment, or conscience. The young gather in packs or gangs, and appear to be driven by a primitive desire for revenge. They kill one another off at an astonishing rate." When people behave aberrantly, we call them criminals or insane and deal with them through the legal system or with psychiatric rehabilitation. Lawmakers use categories like "repeat offenders" or "hardened criminals" but rely on a belief in restitution and rehabilitation. Psychiatrists write off only the smallest number of patients—as sociopaths, or severe schizophrenics. But even that small fraction of the population—recidivists and psychopaths—remains human in most people's eyes. That is why some states still insist on the death penalty. Even the most hardened criminal, it is hoped, faces death with an awareness, with pain, with remorse and regret. Except in the rarest of cases, we do not think of altering our basic definition of human nature.

The basic category—human being—has a stable, consistent meaning that persists through most of Western history. We rely on that definition, fall in love, pass laws, educate—all based on its universal acceptance. Only recently have people even begun to break the tyranny of something as solid as sex differences by moving beyond biology to more socially constructed distinctions that separate *men* from *women*. Cultural and social historians for that reason prefer the term *gender*. Nevertheless, so persistent are the traditional categories that even such a formidable repository as the Oxford English Dictionary contains no entry for *human being*. *Human* is given a cursory, straightforward definition simply marking off mankind from God. Perhaps the editors assumed that, uniquely, humans exist outside any definition. But it has become crucial to understand how notions of humanness are constructed out of and through literacy from an amalgam of texts. My point is that we are witnessing a social catastrophe: the dissolution, at the deepest levels of consciousness, of that alphabetically constructed human being we have taken so much for granted that we ignore its nature and disregard its definition.

This disaster is fostered, not combated, by teaching reading and writing to young people who come to it unprepared. This disaster is compounded by employing computer technology to assist in trying to make young people literate. Illiteracy is a fallout from the collusion between pedagogy and technology. When a teacher asks a child to sit in front of a computer in grade school, that teacher has invoked the authority of a battery of screens—TV, movie, and video. Unwittingly, the teacher has plugged the child solidly into the anti-literate world of media.

That collusion has resulted in a paradox the effects of which threaten to tear apart the fabric of society. Literacy is under attack as much from modern methods of education as from modern forms of communication. We need to examine the implications of this paradox by paying close attention to the impact of electronic forms of communication. We need especially to understand the now dominant educational tool—the word processor. The computer, like all tools, has the power to bend individual perception to match its distinctive mode of operation. All tools behave as metaphors that affect the mind, the clock no less than the book. For thousands of years, the alphabet lay under the skin of a culture. It is now being replaced.

We face a historic shift every bit as explosive as the shift in the Middle Ages from orality to literacy. Over centuries of alphabetic literacy, people have internalized the model of the text and inscribed on it the story of their lives. The computer now acts to remove that internalized text and to replace it with the model of the screen. The switch has created the psychic environment that produces the unfeeling, uncaring youngsters for whom human life has become a cheap commodity.

A perverse medical analogy describes the state of education today, in which doctors administer poison to their patients. Teachers call on word processors to rescue their students from the clutches of illiteracy. But their patients grow sicker and sicker. Nearly seventy million Americans cannot read the warning label on a bottle of medicine, or make their way through a newspaper story. The majority of them are not black or Chicano or foreign; they are white, native-born Americans. While schools ask young people to read at earlier and earlier ages, by the time they reach the fourth grade the scores for most of them start slipping. Reading scores across the country have dropped each year for the past decade. More than 15 percent of the graduates from urban high schools cannot read above the sixth grade level. America ranks only 59th among the 158 members of the United Nations in percentage of the population that can read and write.[3] The number two killer of teenagers in this country is homicide: young children shoot each other down. (Death by automobile ranks number one.) In the summer of 1993, the Harvard School of Public Health commissioned a poll of some twenty-five hundred students who ranged from sixth graders to high school seniors. One in ten reported having been shot, or having shot at someone. Fifteen percent of them admitted to carrying a weapon to school in 1992. Thirty-five percent said they did not expect to live a long life: they expected to be shot. Forty percent said they felt threatened every day by guns. Sixty percent reported they could get a handgun if they wanted one; some bragged they could get it within a half hour. No one knows how many of today's youths are addicted to one powerful drug or another. The shopping malls, not the schools, have become the main arena of youth's acculturation to adulthood.[4]

In spite of these statistics, the race to plug every child into an Apple or an IBM computer continues apace. School boards want to get hold of as many government grants as possible. If they don't they will be perceived as not doing their jobs. The district will look like it's lagging behind or run the risk of looking backward. A certain giddiness sets in, a feeling of euphoria. The computer will solve it all. In their enthusiasm, teachers confuse technological innovation with progress and success. Here is a glimpse at the schools of the future, the near future as it turns out—the year 2000—from a book entitled *Educational Renaissance*. The introduction is by the former California superintendent of education, Bill Honig, long regarded as one of the most progressive educators in the country:

---

[3]These are the National Assessment of Education Progress figures from 1990.

[4]Figures reported in *Time* magazine, "A Boy and His Gun," August 2, 1993, and corroborated by the National Center for Health Statistics, and The National Education Association.

In the near future, American schools will have changed dramatically, and so will our relationship with them. On the outside, most will still be the same brick-and-glass structures—literally the same, half of them nearly seventy-five years old. But on the inside, the changes will be clear: Classrooms will be full of personal computers and other high-tech teaching aids. Teaching methods will have changed to reflect our growing understanding of the learning process.[5]

To solve the problem of growing illiteracy, the authors dream of more of the same: "A national literacy program provided direct to the home using computer-assisted instruction may make major inroads into this enormous problem." In another recent book, *Smart Schools, Smart Kids,* the phrase "smart schools" draws its meaning from "smart machines," computers that can receive new information and make adjustments to the overall flow of data. According to the author, the computer must now take over the classroom as the dominant educational tool if America ever expects schools to produce "smart citizens."[6]

I am concerned with something more fundamental than a generation of youngsters losing facility with letters. That should not take up our time and attention. People will either read or they will not read. Educators and politicians have already mustered enough arguments in favor of the book. Teaching someone to read and write can be done in any number of ways in a fairly short order. I am focusing here on what is eating away at the heart of literacy, like Blake's "invisible worm that flies in the night." In the name of defining the problem, well-intentioned

[5]Marvin Cetron and Margaret Gayle, *Educational Renaissance: Our Schools at the Turn of the Twenty-first Century,* 208.

[6]Edward B. Fiske, *Smart Schools, Smart Kids: Why Do Some Schools Work?*

educators like Cetron and Gayle become part of the problem. In the name of progress, they spoonfeed young people more of the wrong medicine.

We need a radical redefinition of literacy, one that includes a recognition of the vital importance that orality plays in shaping literacy. We need a radical redefinition of what it means for society to have all the appearances of literacy and yet to abandon the book as its dominant metaphor. We must understand what happens when the computer replaces the book as the prime metaphor for visualizing the self. I cannot argue the importance of this inner space, the dwelling place of the self, without showing how literacy has generated such an interiority. To do that, I must say something about the transformation in the Middle Ages of the manuscript—lines of writing on a piece of parchment—into a text, for that is what gets ingested—the internalized *gesture*—by readers.

Imagine the difference between a painting without vanishing point perspective and that same painting with it. The change from manuscript to text represents a shift of such volumetric proportions that it forces into existence the interior space of each literate or alphabetized person. Every person in a sense "fills out," moves from two-dimensionality to being fully rounded. It matters little if the person cannot read. For both literates and non-literates alike internalize the text and on it both inscribe the narrative of their lives. It is there that events get frozen into memory, there that deeds and misdeeds get judged by an internalized set of regulators called conscience and guilt. The author of that text is the self. And it is with that self that literate human beings—or alphabetized ones—carry on a silent dialogue.

Before the late seventh century, silent reading was an impossibility. Any inscription—on wax tablets, papyrus, parchment—consisted of an uninterrupted string of letters. The only way to make sense of a line—that is, to separate continuous sound into words—was to slowly speak each line out loud, hoping to chop the sounds into discernible units called words. Words constitute nothing more, after all, than segmented sounds. Sentences destined for a manuscript were dictated to a scribe in a classical rhythm called *cursus*. That same rhythm later provided penmanship with a certain elegance and speed—in *cursive* writing.[7]

With the introduction of word breaks—blank spaces—the production of manuscripts became an easier job. A monk still dictated to a scribe; but with spaces between words, scribes could now make copies in silence and by sight. Illiterate scribes made better copies because meaning did not get in the way of accuracy. A contemporary reader cannot conceive of the magnitude of this change. Like a highway that knifes through the countryside, slicing the landscape into one county and then another, these spaces worked their way through a string of letters, cutting off chunks into discernible words.

What sort of spaces are these? Not dead spaces certainly—empty and inert—but spaces that render words visible, and ideas understandable. Only by opening up such spaces on the page can reading take place as an individualized, rhythmic activity. Textual space ought to be seen as a dynamic, necessary emptiness. In contrast to speaking and listening, reading and writing can be formidably isolating experiences. What makes them exciting, in part, is the empty space that comes so dynamically alive inside each person, and in which a reader's consciousness, the self, comes into existence. The reader's relationship with the text is a complicated, interpenetrating one: as the reader enters the text by imagining its described world, the text—word *and* empty spaces—penetrates the inner being of the reader.

---

[7]Eric Havelock, *The Literate Revolution in Greece and Its Cultural Consequences*, 21, discusses the influence of Ionia in turning monumental letters into cursive. On the suggestion that music informed the rhythm of cursive writing, see Nancy G. Siraisi, "The Music of Pulse in the Writings of Italian Academic Physicians (Fourteenth and Fifteenth Centuries)."

In the twelfth century, several dozen manuscript innovations converge with the creation of words to make the text more visible by lending it more dimensionality. Monks assign titles, and then subtitles, to chapters to provide clues for reading. To make reference easier, they assign numbers to each chapter and to each verse; underline quotations in different colors so they stand out from the rest of the text; draw a horizontal stroke below the beginning of a line in which a break in sense occurs—hence the birth of paragraphs (*pará-graphos:* "By the side of what is written").

With the book divided up in this way, monks could provide an entrance into what was coming to be seen as subject matter[8] —a table of contents with reference to page numbers provides the front entrance. The back entrance comes about in a more interesting way. Monks who found an important passage in a manuscript would typically draw an index finger in the margin pointing to it so that subsequent readers would not miss anything of importance. (Such a practice also regulated a haphazard nature of reading.) In the twelfth century, monks collected those key passages, and arranged them alphabetically in the back of the book as a collection of index fingers, or simply an index. The book now had a head and a tail, a front and a back. Instead of reading through an entire book to find out what it contained, readers could now consult it at random. The new text became a useful tool, something that could be entered by readers, much as they entered holy space, browsing through it by following aisles and passageways created by specific kinds of spaces— between chapters, paragraphs, and finally, between words. By the seventeenth century, after books began rolling off the printing presses with some ease—in great volume—they had estab-

---

[8]The word *matter* looks curious sitting next to something as abstract as *subject*. But in the Middle Ages the manuscript evolves into a palpable text. In a mirror image, the reader's inner life begins to matter, as well, as it too becomes palpable by being textualized—inscribed.

lished such a recognizably architectonic shape that the word *volume* came to be applied not just to books but to the interiority of buildings as well.

In late Romanesque architecture, even the devil has begun to cash in on this new text. Sculptures show him recording the deeds and words and thoughts of every person. He has begun to capitalize on one of the key feelings that inhabits that new interiority—guilt. Perhaps he can buy a soul or two in exchange for some relief. At any rate, he has turned into a record keeper. The Church, too, began to keep more accurate accounts: In 1244, the Fourth Lateran Council commands every Christian to attend yearly auricular confession. Literacy creates a new, internal sense of memory that, like the book, can be consulted at will and recounted during confession. Call it a self, an invisible dictator, that holds the narrative of one's life. Call it a conscience, where the account of evil deeds, words, and thoughts have been stored. Whatever its name, this is the same text that Freud drew heavily upon in extracting the story of his patients' lives. This is the same text we moderns use in unexpected ways. Think about word associations, where one idea suddenly makes us think of something similar, as if we had somehow consulted an internalized index, or some other cross-referencing tool.

Let me repeat, I am not concerned that the computer—the word processor—is simply inhibiting full literacy. The degradation of language into "communication," including such phrases as "interfacing" with another person, or "accessing" some idea, represents only the most conventionalized aspects of a more serious problem. I am not concerned about what the word processor might be doing to erode writing styles in our young people, or how it might be helping to induce lazy habits. I warn about something that runs much deeper—about the collapse of an interior, alphabetized mental space. As we stand at this threshold, I raise the following question: What happens when the old space, whose architecture and codes of conduct and coherence are generated by encoded speech sounds, gets replaced by an electronic one ordered around the capacity for storing and manipulating information digitally in bytes—including sound bytes?

Some youngsters suffer badly. Soured on school, unable to write more than a few simple sentences, they start dropping out as early as the fifth or sixth grades. Without the critical, reflective thinking that literacy fosters, they are unable to filter anything out, moving through life as victims, prey to every image that rolls off the TV screen or out of the movie theater—images, in large part, of violence and sadism. The literates who are the audience for this book have yet to develop an adequate vocabulary for the new consciousness of illiteracy. It is important to remember that those who celebrate the intensities and discontinuities of post-modern electronic culture in print write from an advanced literacy. That literacy provides them the profound power of choosing their ideational repertoire. No such choice—or power—is available to the illiterate young person subjected to an endless stream of electronic images.

For young children who want to feel powerful, just as powerful as the adults around them, these images assume the status of cultural icons. After all, Dirty Harry and the Terminator Man get away "with murder." Unthinking, uncaring, many youngsters arm themselves, ingest the latest drug, and hang out in malls and congregate in video arcades. They have one aim in mind and that is excitement. They get a rush from unlocking those images that flash on and off in their imagination.

These children have disdain for books. They see literacy as an enemy, something used to control them by those in positions of power. In the past, illiterates knew there was another, higher level of competency, and felt stigmatized by their inability to master it. But a great many young people today have given up struggling with letters, or working their way through a sentence or a paragraph, let alone an intricate argument. They have abandoned the book. They have gone far beyond believing in the power and strength—the efficacy—of reading and writing.

The very desperate behave like young sociopaths, committing the nastiest sort of antisocial crimes without registering remorse or guilt. They get "jumped" into gangs, smoke crack with buddies, or "smoke" strangers in drive-bys; "jack-up" some store or driver; hassle and gang-bang; and wind up, a good many of them, strung out or dead.

These children should terrify us. But other casualties—those who hide their wounds—should disturb us just as much. We should feel no less terrified by the prospect of a child bored stiff every day in front of a teacher, and stiff as a board every night in front of a TV, his nighttime entertainment a subtle preparation for his daytime work. That child may have remained off the streets, but he or she has merely worked out a more acceptable, less visible, way of dropping out. Such children would rather be anywhere than where they find themselves. Fear, or will, or routine, keeps them going, keeps them in line. In the end, however, this kind of silent, smoldering dissatisfaction is just as destructive as the defiance of joining a gang. Illiteracy works its devastating effects on every level of society.[9]

As Western Europe moved into literacy in the twelfth century, everyone—those who could read and write and those who could not—became "alphabetized." Literate sentences, written testimony, charters, deeds, and contracts—all these shaped the perception of non-literates in the High Middle Ages. The alphabet changed social configurations dramatically. Trust, power, possession, as well as everyday transactions came to be functions of the alphabet. In oral cultures, oaths constituted an example of the word honestly given—"I give you my word." A man placed

---

[9]Ninety percent of New York City prison inmates are high school dropouts. See *New York Times*, May 22, 1990. See also Albert Shanker, "Where We Stand," *New York Times*, October 21, 1990.

his hand on his beard or his testicles, a woman placed her hand around her braids, and by uttering a formulaic phrase put the entire tribe or group at risk: "May lightning strike my people, may plague and famine wipe them all out, if I fail to fulfill my promise!" These oaths were replaced by documents that exerted tremendous legal force. Rather than implicating the entire group, the document became binding only when signed by an individual, who in so doing claimed responsibility solely as an individual for everything the document expressed.

Ideas of ownership also changed. No one actually owns anything in oral cultures. Instead, people possess some piece of land or some article of property—a kind of squatter's rights buried in the Latin verb *sedere*, "to sit," and hence to own by placing one's posterior on it. A person would typically hand over something of value, or perform some deed, for the privilege of possessing something of value, a plot of land for instance. In literacy, one could *hold* a piece of property because one could hold up a piece of paper—a deed—that represented the plot of land.

Non-literates got carried along in the new configuration, because literacy, like the force of a great river, washed over everything and took charge. The bedrock of orality remains, but literacy forces new and broader channels. Non-literates, for instance, had to learn to make some distinguishing mark on a piece of paper, a deed, to indicate they were signatories to it. Non-literates heard charters and ordinances read aloud to them, in the vernacular at times, in small groups—"textual communities"—by some professional reader. In short, non-literates became alphabetized. Literacy controlled their everyday lives.

Likewise, every man, woman, and child in this country—those who use computers every day and those who feel free of them—face the prospect of fast becoming "computerized." Which means that behavior adopts the "language" of computers; it tends toward the programmatic—experience devolves into either/or, stop/go choices. "Just Say No to Drugs" comes right out of that computerized mental space, as if that were all and

only all it took to stop addictive behavior—*just* to say "Just Say
No!" Simplistic responses of all kinds—wholesale acceptance of
the Gulf War, dismissal of AIDS victims—seem to replicate, in
an eerie and unsettling way, the binary system of PC programs:
complex problems reduced to simple choices.

Young men and women come to the computer with better
preparation than most youngsters bring to literacy. An appren-
tice system for using electronic gadgets has developed in this
country, no less thorough than if each household had a resident
master in electronics use.

Young people graduate to word processors out of that informal
training. Between the ages of six to eighteen, the average child will
have watched about 16,000 hours of television, spent an additional 4,000 hours listening to radio and CDs, and invested several
thousand more hours watching movies. That child will have
logged more hours with media than in the classroom or with his or
her parents. In less than two decades, daily television viewing by
youngsters from six to eighteen has increased over 70 percent,
from 2.8 hours per day in 1967, to 4.7 hours per day in 1983.[10] For
the child who reaches the age of seven, and who has been in school
for only a year or two, books and the classroom seem slightly alien.
Meanwhile, that same child has already developed a deep reverence for the screen. The youngster has not only become adept as a
viewer, but has grown comfortable as a voyeur—watching from a
safe distance as ghostly creatures appear, interact, and disappear.

Information comes to youngsters on the screen as sitcoms,
specials, or documentaries—as entertainment. Even the most
serious programs listed in *TV Guide,* as Neil Postman makes clear

---

[10]See Godfrey J. Ellis, "Youth in the Electronic Environment: An Introduction," *Youth and Society* 15, no. 1 (September 1983), 5.

in *Amusing Ourselves to Death,* take the form of entertainment.[11]
They have to. TV is image and spectacle. It has to satisfy too
many corporate executives and too many corporate sponsors.
The nature of the medium, as well, mitigates against very much
serious taking place. The screen flashes a new image, on the
average, every 3.5 seconds. For young children, that kind of
speed provides the rush of entertainment—action at the speed of
cartoons—no matter what the content of the program. TV does
not allow enough time for viewers to process the information that
passes in front of their eyes, or passes through their ears: 3.5
seconds is just too fast for intelligent comprehension. Argument
turns into banter, analysis into fatuous assertion.

Let me quote Postman: "What I am claiming here is not that
television is entertaining but that it has made entertainment itself
the natural format for the representation of an experience." No
matter what anyone is watching—sitcom, news, documentary,
state funeral, even a war—Postman goes on to say, "the over-
arching presumption is that it is there for our amusement and
pleasure."[12] The content of TV programs does not matter that
much. A "program" means what it says: an agenda apart from
its subject matter.

As soon as the child enters into electronic training—one that
begins with television viewing—without knowing it, he or she
has opted for a very specific cognitive track, with a complete set
of values, goals, and beliefs. The child has embraced a reality
simulated through pulsating light on a screen. In that reality,
emotions are not carried by characters who breathe and bleed,
but by representations of live human beings—tinier, more
brightly shining but nonetheless recognizable as actual human
beings.

---

[11]Neil Postman, *Amusing Ourselves to Death: Public Discourse in the Age of Show Business,* 87 ff.

[12]Ibid.

TV constitutes a virtual reality. From that decisive moment, the child will find it hard to return to the world of books. TV trains people to sit still and keep their mouths shut, to listen and to accept what they hear and see, passively, as they tune in on electronically produced, simulated human voices. The viewer cannot respond. He or she exercises control by pushing the buttons on a handheld "remote." A certain amount of power attaches to that activity—it's a taste of other, more lethal forms of handheld power.

Behavior at a distance does not disappear easily, because minute hand and finger activity constitutes choice these days— TV remotes, PC keyboards, video game controls. Soon, if a cable television company, Discovery Communications, has its way, a viewer will be able to select from close to five hundred channels. But even five hundred channels does not constitute a choice, for every program, Postman and other critics argue, repeats the same formula. Children come to believe that tuning a human being out requires no more effort, and carries no more significance, than turning a person off—switching his channel.

The nature of children's play has been profoundly altered in the last twenty years. A young child does not come to video games as a child used to come to play any backyard or sandlot game. In a vacant lot somewhere, a youngster might describe an idea on the spot, or make up rules of a game by playing the game or pass on a game learned from others. A democratic, egalitarian spirit informed most of these games. Indeed, in imaginative play nothing remains firm or fixed. Children choose up sides and struggle to make them fair—two tall guys to balance three short ones, two fast ones for four slow ones, and so on.

By the time a child turns on the power switch for Pac-Man, Robotron, Bad Dudes, Space Invaders, or Super Mario Brothers 2, that child puts into practice the role he or she has learned from sitting all those hours in front of the television. These children fulfill their longing to enter *into* that electronic world. They appear to be active participants—even "interactive" participants—but they are not. They have made a tacit agreement with a corporation 6,000 miles across the ocean to accept the rules that have been programmed into that game. (It's interesting that TV shows are called "programs," as if TV recognizes that the rules themselves are the real subject of every moment of every broadcast day. In this way, a TV show and a video game differ very little from each other.) A child behind a Nintendo game may be having fun with his machine—idly passing the time—but he or she is definitely not *playing*. A critical element is missing— the child's ability to define and control the conditions of playing for herself or himself. Every form of play turns into a game when rules are successfully negotiated, or when they get slightly relaxed, or fall away altogether. Nintendo rules dominate as thoroughly and as doggedly as any totalitarian regime.

Roger Caillois and Johann Huizinga, both of whom have written extensively on the social mechanisms of play, make clear that the computer represents the antithesis of play.[13] Following Plato, both Caillois and Huizinga assign play to the most exalted regions of the human spirit, equal to the rituals of religion. Huizinga in particular takes great pains to show how children situate play of all sorts in a consecrated space, so that no distinction exists between "marking out a space for a sacred purpose and marking it out for purposes of sheer play":

We found that one of the most important characteristics of play was its spatial separation from ordinary life. A closed space is marked out for it, either materially or ideally, hedged off from the everyday surroundings. Inside this space the play proceeds, inside it the rules obtain. Now, the marking out of some sacred spot is also the primary characteristic of every sacred act. This requirement of isolation for ritual, including magic and law, is

---

[13]Roger Caillois, "Man, Play, and Games" and "Riddles and Images," in *Game, Play, Literature,* ed. Jacques Ehrmann, 148–58; and Johann Huizinga, *Homo Ludens: A Study of the Play Elements in Culture.*

much more than merely spatial and temporal. Nearly all rites of consecration and initiation entail a certain artificial seclusion for the performers and those to be initiated. Whenever it is a question of taking a vow or being received into an Order or confraternity, or of oaths and secret societies, in one way or another there is always such a delimitation of room for play. The magician, the augur, the sacrificer begins his work by circumscribing his sacred space. Sacrament and mystery presuppose a hallowed spot.[14]

Huizinga's comments underscore the importance of internalized space and resonate with my argument that it forms a crucible for the introduction and development of literacy. Video games create the illusion of their own space, but in video playing the mystery that is generated by child's play shifts from the child to the machine. Like an electronic black hole, the computer game sucks up all the light, all the mystery, all the space, into itself.

To really enter into the video world, youngsters must abandon innovation and imagination. Eye/hand coordination, speed, ability to withstand violent outbursts of sound effects, and bright flashes of light—all these may be assets in racking up high scores. But in the world of Nintendo, imagination and innovation do not produce winners as they might in children's games. Nintendo does not want winners in that sense. The young boy or girl—and video gaming is essentially the domain of boys—does not even get to conjure his own images. These games exist outside the world of make-believe. The machine, supplying all the images in wave upon wave of repetition, takes over the activity and disrupts the intimacy of the child's own imagination.

We should not overlook the insidious sexist message that boys pick up from these games. In a sample of a hundred video arcade games, Terri Toles, a sociologist, determined that 92 percent of

---

[14]Huizinga, *Homo Ludens,* 19–20.

the games did not include any female roles, and that of the remaining eight games, six had females who assumed "damsels in distress" roles. Only two games out of one hundred showed females taking an active role. And even then, in the case of the two females who did take active roles, neither is human—one a mama kangaroo attempting to rescue her offspring, and the second a feminized blob, Ms. Pac-Man.[15]

Video games excite young children. So much so that in a 1984 study, when asked why they liked to play video games, 244 youngsters aged ten to fourteen responded that they found video characters, for the most part, more exciting and more fun than adults, and certainly more exciting than their parents.[16] Video characters can be manipulated, and they don't talk back. In the debate between nature and nurture, the terms need updating: the media now carry out a good deal of the job of nurturing. TV rivals parents in guiding children through the social, moral, and emotional gradations and nuances of the world. That shift from the human to the technical should jolt the attention of everyone. Do we want an electronic box that honors images of violence, and favors families in fatuous conversation, to serve as a monitor for children's moral, social, and spiritual growth?

Now, imagine the contemporary young person, *if* he or she does manage to stay in school—and recall that the odds are against that happening—as a freshman in college. This is a young person who has already drifted fairly far from books, fairly far from reading and writing. This same young person has already been accustomed to turning to the TV screen as a source of information, power, and probably as a reservoir of knowledge.

---

[15]Terri Toles, "Video Games and American Military Ideology," 207–23.

[16]G. W. Selnow, "Playing Videogames: The Electronic Friend." See also Eugene F. Provenzo, Sr., *Video Kids,* passim.

He or she has grown accustomed to looking to the TV screen as a source of entertainment. TV has taught him what to buy and with whom to associate—it has taught him to consume *without* thinking and *with* zeal. How is this young person encouraged to step through the scrim of late adolescence and into a broader, more exuberant, adult world of literacy?

Flipping on the personal computer, the young person again enters into an electronic world, one in which the rules are immutable and preestablished. Revising and editing *are* simplified with a PC, but what the student is doing is not writing in the truly literate sense. With or without features like Spell-Chek and Grammar-Chek, it would be impossible to compose *The Adventures of Huckleberry Finn* on a word processor.

But even if one could, I am concerned here with something more insidious, as I have said earlier, than "lazy" habits that the PC induces in its users. I want to call attention to the way the screen gets under the skin of the operator. A young person more than senses, he or she comes to know that authority, real knowledge, and skill, reside *in* the machine, dictated *by* an anonymous disembodied programmer. The rules have been irrefutably set by that anonymous expert, someone the student has never met, someone who resides far away in that mythical land, that fairy world of big bucks and big dreams, Silicon Valley. The computer program shapes reality like the invisible hand of God.

Authority resides in the book as well. But it is authority, not technological ukase. In a book, an author—a person—can be imagined: a live human being with a face and a history. We can look at photographs of that person, read biographies. On the page, we watch that author's mind in action, with all its starts and stops, the side trips and tentative conclusions. The reader enters into that meandering flow of ideas, not into a summary of rules. With a text, the reader winds up as the ultimate authority. With a PC, the anonymous programmer reigns supreme.

A mysterious presence inhabits the innards of our new, electronic Apples, a presence that, before the electronics revolution, used to emanate from the real objects of the world. These days, real aliveness as agency is ascribed to the machine. PCs sparkle with brilliance, performing in the realm of the remarkable—if we are to believe the ads. Most electronic pieces of gadgetry hum with a low level of electricity that continually runs through their circuitry—even when the switch is off. One can hear it pulsing from deep inside most machines. It's alluring, enticing in its promise of life. Is this phenomenon, too, somehow metaphoric, or even predictive—of those forever excitable, video game kids we call "hyper," those kids who always seem to be "on"? The world of real presences is fast fading. To recover it means to turn back to books.

The electronics industry pours millions of dollars into marketing research and sales strategies. Books cannot stand up against such a force. Even in grammar schools, with the most radically innovative ways of teaching reading and writing, literacy pales before the mesmerizing hold of the TV screen, the movie screen, the video screen. In some schools, the day begins with students watching the news, and listening to commercials, on Channel One, large-screen television. They start out the day with an electronic feast.

Literacy cannot be taught with a computer, with the machine that is robbing students of their ability to conceptualize language. The PC is not an illuminated manuscript page. It is a radically different tool from a book and it shapes perception differently, creating a world of youthful ghostwriters, both male and female, who shimmer with no more substantiality than those glowing letters on the PC screen.

In contemporary culture, where changes take place with great rapidity, the effects show up first most often in the popular media: in fashion, music, and film. And these days, even books have taken on the look and feel of popular entertainment. It

takes a while before significant change catches the attention of
the social or the cultural critics, before their statements get circulated in scholarly journals or in critical volumes. It took until
1991, for instance, for the philosopher William Gass to utter this
witty but chilling line: "Our previous definition of the human—
that we reason; that we reflect on ourselves; that we make tools;
we speak—is in the shop for micro-chip repairs."[17] Gass writes
in a consciously elliptical way, in a style counter to a computerized mentality. He, too, warns about the disappearance of
human beings, and he fingers the culprit as the computer, the
word processor.

The PC belongs to the family of popular entertainers, the
small-screen toys that begin with TV and run through video
games, home entertainment centers, and videotapes. Indeed,
studies show that the majority of people who own PCs use them
for playing games rather than for composing prose. How is this
change being presented in the popular media?

The popular media register change in immediate, direct
ways. They argue no theory. For them, bodies have indeed been
fast disappearing. The world of pop these days goes something
like this: A door has been flung wide open to the "other side,"
and swarms of invisible specters—ghosts and angels—have
rushed in to take over the popular imagination. Watch a movie,
or read a novel, or just pick up one of the slicker magazines—the
world seems to be haunted.

Blame it on Hollywood, for it discovered, sometime in the
eighties, that its magic rested on the one technological trick that
audiences seemed to love best, or that they seemed to feel most
comfortable with: transforming solid flesh into light. Hollywood
examined itself and found out what it was really doing—that it

---

[17]William H. Gass, "Human, All Too Human."

was in the business of manufacturing ghosts. Steven Spielberg took the lead in 1982 with a special-effects hit, *Poltergeist*. Two years later, the crew from *Saturday Night Live* spoofed this new haunting with *Ghostbusters*. The film seemed to suggest that the invasion of specters could not be easily dismissed. The opening scenes of the movie, prophetically enough, take place in the New York Public Library.

In 1988, after releasing films like *Poltergeist II* and *Hollywood Ghost Stories*, the studios let audiences choose from over a dozen ghostly features, from PG-13 films like *Beetlejuice*, *The Invisible Kid*, and *Poltergeist III*, to R-rated ones, like *Death Spa* and *Ghost Town*.

The following year, 1989, things began to change. *Ghostbusters II* looked tired and dated, a remnant of our nervous reaction to something so strange and unfamiliar as ghosts. Spielberg took a more serious foray into the other world, but he proceeded cautiously, by redoing a forties winner, *A Guy Named Joe*, which starred Spencer Tracy. In Spielberg's remake, titled, with very nice irony, *Always*, Richard Dreyfuss, a daredevil fighter pilot, dies in a crash and is sent back to earth as a ghost by an angel (Audrey Hepburn) to act as romantic guide for his former girlfriend.

That year, the blockbuster hit turned out to be *Field of Dreams*. That film exploited our national pastime—baseball, our national obsession—fame, and our national fear—death, and brought all three together in one image: an all-star team of ghosts. Set in the heart of the heart of the country, how could such a movie possibly miss? Indeed, the Academy of Motion Picture Arts and Sciences nominated *Field of Dreams* for Best Picture.

Suddenly, Hollywood smelled cash. In 1990, ghosts became big business. Why not exploit race? *Ghost Dad* offered family fun with Bill Cosby; *Heart Condition* offered blacks integrating the world of ghosts. The biggest surprise that year, even to its producers, was *Ghost*, a romantic fairy tale starring Patrick Swayze.

Publishers conspired with show business. In his final novel, *Mickelsson's Ghosts* (1983), John Gardner concocts a murder mystery about a haunted house inhabited by characters who themselves turn out to be haunted. The anthropologist Gregory Bateson put together his autobiography just before his death, which carried the working title *Angel's Fear* (1989). Death exerts such a strong force throughout the entire book that Bateson reserves the last chapter for a discussion of ghosts, ghostwritten by Bateson's daughter, Mary Catherine, from her father's notes. Lawrence Durrell digs up the haunted past in contemporary Provence, in a travel book he wrote just before his death, called *Caesar's Vast Ghost* (1990). But it's not just authors at the eleventh hour of their lives who see ghosts. Others did, too: Jerry Bosochio wrote a novel in 1990 called *Ghost*, followed by Laurence Thornton's *Ghost Woman*.

One of the Best Essays of 1990 was Sue Hubbell's "The Vicksburg Ghost," which first appeared in *The New Yorker*. The quintessential American novelist Norman Mailer gave us *Harlot's Ghost* in 1991, and the African novelist G. F. Michelsen gave us *To Sleep with Ghosts*. Random House published *A Collection of Contemporary Gothic Fiction* in 1991. Atlantic Monthly Press published a collection of contemporary ghost stories that same year, *The Literary Ghost*, whose table of contents includes a broad selection of well-known writers, from Donald Barthelme and Joyce Carol Oates, to Anne Sexton and M.F.K. Fisher. And John F. Blair and Company added *Mountain Ghost Stories*.

The list of ghosts and ghostlike presences saturating popular culture could be extended indefinitely. It is true that ghosts often preoccupy cultures at the turn of calendrical centuries, but the end of the century won't fully explain why they hang around these days in such numbers and with such pervasiveness. Today, they refuse to leave. Today, we have more on our hands than just the end of the century. God is dead. The author has passed away. The written page is being deconstructed. Word processors

have turned everyone into ghostwriters, so that technology, like
a hard-wired vampire, has sucked the very essence out of life.
Look around. Young people prowl the streets as if in mourning.
They dress entirely in black, like spectators waiting at any moment to be summoned to a funeral.

There is a bright side to all this, a reason to feel hopeful. It has
to do with a line that Jonathan Swift fell back on, in an age that
had developed population arithmetic, which reduced people to
masses, and individuals to statistics and averages. In its own way,
the eighteenth century experienced its own disappearance of
human beings. Swift wrote, "Vision is the art of seeing the
invisible." We have conjured all those ghosts and angels—those
evanescent spirits—out of the living, perdurable world of stones,
trees, animals, and humans. In the Middle Ages, those invisibles
gave proof that the world was teeming with life, every square
meter of it inhabited. They were taken for granted—as yet
another stratum of reality in the infinite gradations up and down
the Great Chain of Being. Today, when most things have been
drained of their invisible presence, ghosts and angels in popular
culture manifest a longing for a fully animated life, a spirited
existence. Every invisible creature assumes the character of a
holy ghost. As each new technological gadget gets under the skin
of our culture, and robs us of a bit of our essence, we suffer a
profound loss. We feel a great void. There must be life somewhere—a quintessence that can never be diminished or exhausted. Only by conjuring the most evanescent, fleeting
creatures can we conceive of the world as something solidly alive
and palpable. As the poet Seamus Heaney puts it, in a poem
wryly titled "Seeing Things," even "the stone's alive with what's
invisible." Out of desperation, we have reverted to acting like
little children who delight in seeing their breath on frosty morn-
ings. Ghosts and angels give us a firsthand look at our essence.

Man is "but breath and shadow," as Sophocles concluded, "nothing more."

We need to be reminded of that. It's what cannot be taped, measured, or documented—what refuses to give itself up to technological manipulation—that really constitutes life. It's the invisible, what George Steiner calls "real presences," that can never be destroyed. To realize that one's essence is only a shadow, a mere puff of breath, may be startling news, but we also know it's true. The most insubstantial, evanescent stuff—breath —is what keeps us alive, and what prompts us into aliveness. It should prompt a call for a radical return to orality.

Without that return, we will soon be living in a gothic novel. Very shortly, ghosts will outnumber the living. And it will do no good to call Ghostbusters. What a strange state of affairs, that in a world dominated by the most advanced technology, the warning about human salvation should be signaled by something so irrational, so invisible and so arcane, as the occult. On reflection, though, it may not be so strange. Maybe filmmakers and writers and musicians have been able to express what few social scientists have dared to undertake, the effects of technology on human nature.

I have argued that human beings, as we have known them— constructed out of a layering of texts—are fast disappearing. But popular writers and filmmakers have actually offered us a way of seeing our condition—through the *occult,* a word which itself refers to "seeing," as in *ocular. Specter,* too, refers to "seeing," and is cognate with both senses of *spectacle:* a "display" and the "glasses" used to see that display clearly.

Like pictures on a screen, the spectral images of recent popular culture allow people to look at their own condition more closely, and to reflect on it. The screen can act as mirror. This is the true meaning of vis-à-vis, to come face-to-face, *vis*ion-to-*vis*ion, with our visual echo. Like an echo, our beings reverberate meaning beyond our flesh-and-blood existence, beyond life even—each person a holy ghost. That ghostly image cannot be destroyed. To come to see that other is to "reflect" on ourselves. In a world that emphasizes the visual—television, video, and films—a survival mechanism has kicked in. We need to recover the art of seeing, vis-à-vis ghosts and angels. We yearn for true insight.

But even as ghosts and angels work as a warning, they serve to pull people out of a logical, literate world, to a world of orality where everything—including inanimate objects—percolates with life. For people who live in orality, ghosts and angels bear as much reality as the living. The literate mind—the scientific mind—tends to explain them away as mere optical illusions, hallucinations of one kind or another. In a sense, then, what has come drifting to us is not so much the world of ghosts and angels, as the re-creation of a world where such things signal unlimited possibilities, where nothing remains invisible. That is the world of orality. Only with a new immersion in that world can people ultimately achieve the solidity that literacy alone can bring.

Society trains us to look for outside help: to turn to technology, or professionals, or experts—to some "other" for a miraculous solution. We get used to punching keys on computers without having the foggiest notion what's going on inside those complicated machines. For most of us, they might as well be something superhuman, a deus *in* machina. We do not care how a PC works. All we know is that when we have a problem, we want a solution, and we want it fast. The computer is both ghost—where once was parchment and quill, paper and pencil—and angel—where once was labor and frustration. Apple and Macintosh and IBM stand ready to serve. User-friendly is their motto. But this time, they can only let us down. They don't have the right program.

So, we have a rash of ghosts and angels on our hands, a symptom of the dis-ease in the Body Social. Ghosts and angels: a spectral system. In some ways, they meet as polar opposites—death and hope, the earthly and the heavenly, the frightening and the reassuring. Ghosts come to spook, angels to help; ghosts

come to torment, angels to rescue. Ghosts hang out in the darkness of creaky, old houses, angels dramatically present in the
light of the Annunciation, and at the birth of Christ. One is
secular, the other religious. Ghosts begin life on this side and
cross over, shedding most of their particularity. Angels, on the
other side, develop a holy individuality. But they work well
together in our schizophrenic, modern time. From their separate
worlds, they come trailing meaning.

CHAPTER FIVE

The very fact that a kid is in a gang means that something is missing. So many of them are functioning illiterates. So many of them come from abusing backgrounds. The hardest cases were probably sexually molested or they were routinely beaten— probably both. Depends on what kind of father influence was around the house. If any. You find a gang member who comes from a complete nuclear family, a kid who has never been exposed to any kind of abuse, I'd like to meet him. Not a wannabe who's a Crip or a Blood because that's the thing to be in the 1990's, I mean a *real* gangbanger who comes from a happy, balanced home, who's got a good opinion of himself. I don't think that kid exists.

—A. C. Jones, Staff,
  Camp Kilpatrick Probation Facility,
  in Léon Bing, *Do or Die*

Hold one of the new death machines in your hands—an AK-47, or a Colt Python, or a Smith & Wesson Model 29, or the favorite of gangs in the eighties, the Cobray M11/9—and you hold the top of the line in technological innovations. Fabricated out of new space-age materials, many of these superweapons sight with laser technology and, in the case of the Cobray, can operate with the lightning speed of the most advanced computer chip, firing off thirty-two 9mm bullets in the blink of an eye— slaughter in just one and a half seconds. That translates to over a thousand rounds per minute, which the Cobray will fire in its automatic phase, a design modification done cheaply and easily on the street, and which places the Cobray in the category of submachine gun.[1] But referring to this gun as a "machine" is as silly as referring to a word processor as an advanced typing machine, or a Boeing 727 as an advanced flying machine. The higher levels of technological innovation have transformed every tool—the gun included.

Not intended for hunting or even self-defense, these stepped-up Saturday night specials have been designed so that crooks, drug dealers, and gang-bangers can lay down a wall of bloody fire with maximum effect and, perhaps more important, maximum show. Officials at the Bureau of Alcohol, Tobacco and Firearms even call many of these semiautomatics "ugly guns": to hold a fierce-looking weapon is to take on the image of fierceness. Manufacturers know that, and tailor these guns to the special needs of their clientele.

Like their personal computer cousins, these super-high-tech weapons can boast their own perverse version of user-friendliness. The Cobray cannot be used for something as precise as target shooting: It's a two-fisted weapon that's too heavy, and unbalanced; it rocks up and down when fired. Its two-inch barrel defies accuracy. Shooting the Cobray requires a special technique, something like watering a lawn with just a bit of lethal overspray. On automatic, one simply holds the trigger down and waves the barrel in front of whatever happens to come into view. It's an untidy way to go about killing, but it is the way to make

---

[1]Submachine guns are machine guns that fire handgun, as opposed to rifle, ammunition.

a splash gangster-style. Here's an assessment of the Cobray in its standard, semiautomatic mode, from a colonel in the Maryland Police Department: " . . . hold it someplace in front of you, pull the trigger as fast as you can, put as many bullets out as you can, and hope like hell they'll hit something. Now, that may be nice on a battlefield. It isn't so nice in an urban environment, where that bullet may go through your bedroom into your child's bedroom or into your neighbor's bedroom, or may go outside and kill a passerby."[2] The *New York Times* describes a recent drive-by that used such a weapon: "A steamy night in August [1992] saw one of the most ferocious gun battles on a New York City street in recent times. A car drove up to an apartment building at 871 Lingwood Avenue in Hunts Point, sprayed gun-fire all over the street and left 12 people wounded." In no more time than it took to pause in front of that apartment house, sixty bullets, according to police reports, ripped into a group of people gathered in small clumps, strolling and talking on the sidewalk. The horror of the scene prompted one police official to ask in astonishment: "Who was here, the U.S. Army?" The *Times* writer himself could find no more accurate verb than a garden-ing one, "sprayed," to convey the leisurely but lethal attitude that weapons like the Cobray engender.

Such weapons eliminate any premeditation, or plotting, or for that matter, any planning or practicing. No need to even take careful aim and draw a bead. In the Hunts Point incident, as with every drive-by, the car sets the pace. To talk about marks-manship with such weapons is absurd. To talk about a gang-banger making his mark with one is not absurd. As IBM and Apple like to say, anyone, even a child, can operate one. And they do.

Hold the Cobray M11/9 in both hands, and you hold brute power, an instrument that enables a young gang-banger to kill without ever touching the flesh of another human being with his

[2]Erik Larson, "The Story of a Gun," 51.

own flesh, or without ever approaching close enough to make eye contact. The Cobray offers—and encourages—anonymity. It is one of the most terrifying remote devices imaginable. Like the remote that switches channels or turns an unwelcome image completely off, it can erase a person instantaneously and from a fairly distant range. These death toys offer the possibility of remote behavior at the extreme. Handheld destruction comes in many forms: with a channel changer, a video game, or a gun. But only a gun, as one enthusiast exclaims, "makes remote destruction a dynamite rush!"[3]

Grabbing onto an AK-47 or a Cobray M11/9 is like holding the guts of a computer in both hands. Ambiguity drops away the instant one points the barrel in the direction of a group and pulls the trigger. One moment that group of people exists, and the next they're gone. This is the binary system with a blast. There is no doubt about the effect: the gun goes off with ear-splitting sound and blinding light. If a problem arises in the form of another person, an enemy, a score of enemies, the Cobray provides a solution perfectly suited for a computerized culture: simply eliminate them. Every young person who gets "jumped into" the Crips swears his allegiance—"Do or die!"—in either/or terms which mirror the no-nonsense blast that comes out of the barrel of one of those handguns. Translated into street terms, "Do or die!" means only one thing—"Kill or get killed!" An estimated 100,000 young people in Los Angeles County, some as young as eight or nine years old, have sworn similar oaths, a horrible distortion of formulaic bits of speech that once bound oral cultures together.[4] Nevertheless, "Do or die!" seals a person's fate with no less finality than an oath sworn by a peasant in the ninth or tenth century. The social logic governing the two acts of oath taking is, however, radically different.

---

[3]Ibid., 57.

[4]Figures compiled by Los Angeles Police Department and cited in Léon Bing, *Do or Die*.

Guns offer a way into gang mentality. They stand out as the instrument connecting the dark, hidden world of gang operations with activity broadcast in the light of day. In gangs, the gun is the most solid point of contact between internal life and the outside world, a conduit through which understanding can pass back and forth. The gun is actually an object of hope—one of the few signs of hope—in gang life.

Just as the definition of human being has changed, so has the definition of the gun. When a gun-toting gang-banger no longer operates out of a sense of self, when he no longer subscribes to ideas of murder, or conscience or regret, then what he holds in his hands—a gun—also takes on a different social construction. For young people who can boast that "human life means nothing," the gun has lost its deadly mystique and mystery. No longer something exotic and taboo out of the world of crooks and old-style gangsters, the Cobray enters the neighborhood as a tool—more advanced than others—but nothing more than a specialized utensil to be used for eliminating people. The gun is still a death instrument, but it is not something revered in a special category. A Cobray earns respect from gang-bangers not because it's a gun, but for its capacity to fire fast. Its owner, on the other hand, commands instant respect for his ability to score such a prize.

Guns do something else for gang-bangers that is usually overlooked. They make a moment real. Firing at someone fuses the young gangster to the present moment in a way that nothing else possibly can. Rock (crystallized cocaine) and heroin pull him out of time altogether, but firing a gun blasts that moment wide open, an adrenaline rush of sound and light and final solution. Killing brings the world alive for an orgasmic few seconds. But it's a feeling that disappears just as fast, because no remorse or guilt envelops the act, animating the young person's conscience and recalling the deed to memory. Lots of young murderers confess to not remembering the gruesome details of their actions. Gang members use one another as corroborative witnesses to death in order to feel alive. The event gets passed around as a collective memory, growing to mythic proportions and binding street life together.[5]

Guns do something else even more important. Guns say to other people—to those outside the group—in no uncertain terms, "Stay the hell away." A gun is an electrified fence, an explosive border separating gangland from everything and everyone else. An armed camp is difficult, if not impossible, to penetrate. A gang member wants to remain private, protected, unassailable, and yet he needs to create a loud and noisy presence. He needs to be seen and heard to be taken seriously. But the noise and the light are all surface: the gun remains unconnected to any inner life. Every gun, in a sense, fires automatically.

Young gang members cannot afford to abandon themselves to literacy because that would "disarm" them in every sense of the word. Reading and writing would blow apart that space they so fervently guard, and force them to enter a new, metaphoric space where they would have to confront who they are, and ponder what they are doing. A gun keeps them powerfully in control by holding the other at bay—or eliminating the other altogether. But no matter the caliber, the gun fails to eliminate that pervasive, most powerful enemy—literacy. Brandishing a gun says, "Leave me alone, don't ask me any questions. I want my own impenetrable solitude." Children need solitude in which they can confront their real desires. Adolescents need solitude as well, in order to make serious decisions—about career interests, relationships, sexuality, and other adult matters. But gang solitude is in fact social isolation, a secession from the community of

---

[5]*Gang* can be a misleading term. Chicano gangs and black gangs differ in behavior, and differ from state to state. Even sets within the same gang differ greatly. Asians organize themselves differently from the others. I try to maintain distinctions in this chapter by referring to actual gangs by name and to actual gang-bangers by their street names.

readers and writers. A gun-enforced solitude is a truncated, distorted one. It forecloses the possibility of the pleasure and excitement that accompanies self-discovery. The solitude of literacy requires the risk an illiterate cannot take—that of meeting an internalized self.

Those who stand at the opposite end of the barrel—those who live outside gang life—perceive the gun as an increasingly frightening instrument these days. The gun has become so commonplace, it has come to signal the collapse of social order. Gang-bangers see the gun as just another piece of personal property, like a penknife or a credit card, that gets whipped out and used. A threat is a thing of the past. Young people back up their words with deeds. In a world skewed by violence and drugs, deeds often turn out to be lethal.

In gang life image means everything. Handguns promote the illusion of power. A journalist writing in the *New York Times* notes that so-called ugly guns "can't be tucked discreetly in a waistband or shoulder holster. But they confer upon their bearers, commonly drug dealers, an aura of big-time criminality, evoking images of terrorists or Colombian cocaine cartels."[6] That brief description uncovers a fundamental truth about guns. A gang-banger fully intends to put his weapon on open and blatant display whenever he uses it. He needs to, for in gangster terms, to be seen is already to be heard. The trigger is always just about to be squeezed. Image and action merge. With his gun in his hands, the gangster continually threatens to explode. The disenfranchised illiterate speaks through his own effective instrumentality, just as I am speaking through mine on this page.

Seeing one of those weapons inspires terror. Holding a cheap, tiny Saturday night special in the palm of the hand, on the contrary—a Raven MP-24, of small caliber (.22 or .25)—smacks of wimpiness. Costing about twenty dollars to manufacture, these "junk guns" wind up in the hands of small-time dealers and

---

[6]David C. Anderson, "Street Guns," 21.

on high school playgrounds. No self-respecting gang-banger would own one. They do not look ugly or bad. Even an assault rifle, like the Uzi submachine gun, has a wire stock that can be folded back to make it look "ugly."

Gang-bangers accompany each act of killing with a tall tale, fueled by the emotional charge of the moment. Léon Bing records the following conversation in her book on gangs, *Do or Die*, between two fourteen-year-old gang-bangers, Sidewinder and Bopete. Bopete begins:

> "In my 'hood, in the Jungle, it ain't like a gang. It's more like a nation, everybody all together as one. Other kids, as long as they ain't my enemies, I can be cool with 'em." Bopete lapses into silence. "I'll tell you though—if I didn't have no worst enemy to fight with, I'd probably find somebody."
>
> "Okay, look, I'm so high"—Sidewinder holds up his hand to indicate his height when he is standing—"And killin' somebody, that make you higher. 'Cause you got enough heart to kill somebody, then, like you got the heart to destroy. Make you tall."[7]

Handguns make a deafening racket; they explode; they speak power.

The handgun has become nearly as ubiquitous as the camera in urban America. The use of the handgun has risen to astonishing levels in just the past five years. Since 1990, 60,000 people in this country have been killed by handguns, more than all the Americans who lost their lives in Vietnam. Los Angeles County alone accounts for over 8,000 of those deaths, a county where two youngsters die each day in gang-related shootings. Over

---

[7]Bing, *Do or Die*, 49.

22,000 people die each year in Los Angeles County staring down the barrel of a semiautomatic "ugly gun." As of 1989, 66.7 million handguns were in circulation in the United States—over 200 million firearms in all shapes and sizes and categories! The latest census places the population somewhere near 250 million in this country—including men, women, *and* a sizable number of children—which means that lots of people clearly own more than one or two firearms. Some of them own arsenals. With close to 250,000 federally licensed gun shops in this country—one for roughly every 1,000 persons—no one has to wait in line. There are only 22,000 public high schools in this country.[8]

How could the United States *not* stand so far ahead of every other country in the world in homicides? Or so far behind a good many of them in literacy? Homicides and illiteracy are related. Fostering a lack of remorse and guilt, illiteracy makes it easier to pull the trigger. The handgun is the writing instrument of illiteracy.

Not only does the number of homicides seem alarming, but so does the trend. In 1960, in New York City, 19 percent of the crimes involved handguns; in 1988, that percentage jumped to 69 percent. One out of every five high school students now walks onto the school grounds armed with a weapon, many of which are high-powered handguns. Airport metal detectors have been installed in several high schools in Philadelphia, New York, and Washington, D.C. Security guards now use handheld metal detectors at more than fifty Los Angeles County junior and senior high schools.

In this land of opportunity and freedom, why should any young child in the school system feel the need to arm himself or herself? Who's the enemy? Certainly not some fellow student, and certainly not an innocent bystander, or even another gang

---

[8]Sources: Office of Juvenile Justice and Delinquency Prevention, U.S. Justice Department, and the FBI. Handgun statistics from Bureau of Alcohol, Tobacco and Firearms.

member—even though gangsters like Bopete and Sidewinder hate each other as sworn enemies.[9]

The real enemy is invisible and too powerful to be eradicated by an automatic weapon. That enemy consists of that which drains these youngsters, day after day, of substance and reality. The enemy has been rendered so indistinct and diffuse, one might as well spray away at everything in sight. You're bound to hit something; and that will do. If you don't get anything in your life right, hitting something, some person, will suffice. If you feel like a cipher, a nothing, a gun provides power. If you feel frightened by virtually everything around you, a gun can keep the world at bay. If you feel like the Invisible Man, a spectral presence, then a gun offers the possibility of substance. The opposite of a ghost, or even an angel, is something with heft—something with density, like iron. That's one of the gang phrases "packing iron"—for carrying a gun. An Uzi assault rifle or an AK-47 can increase the bulk of the average teenager several-hundred-fold. A young person can put on much more bulk by packing iron than by pumping it.

Gang members are not alone in their desire to feel more substantial. The whole world wants more heft. Gang children have just found a lethally immediate way of trying to obtain it. The race is on in this country to feel like some beefed-up marvel. Sylvester Stallone, Arnold Schwarzenegger, and Jean-Claude

---

[9]Increased violence is quite clearly tied to more powerful weapons. Joan W. Moore interviewed Chicano gang members in East Los Angeles—both young ones and veterans—and concluded: "The most common explanation offered by residents for increased violence concerned weapons. Not only were more 'real' guns available in the 1970s compared with the homemade zip guns of the 1950s, but guns were used now for hurting people—aiming at the body, rather than just scaring them by shooting in the air or at legs. An older White Fence woman commented wryly: 'You know it's easier for kids to get ahold of guns and other weapons to fight with. Pulling the trigger is now called gang fighting.' Younger cliques—both male and female—were more likely to mention guns and older ones to mention fistfights" (*Going Down to the Barrio: Homeboys and Homegirls in Change*).

Van Damme are fully realized terminators representing the new, pumped-up ideal of human agency as interpreted by popular culture. They represent socially acceptable, larger-than-life gang-bangers.

In wealthy enclaves like Beverly Hills, California, firing ranges do a lively business these days, not with police cadets in training, but with affluent men and women. Professionals pass pleasant evenings at these firing ranges the way they used to hang out at fancy restaurants or sports bars. The new, improved version of the firing range serves fine food and alcohol. Friends socialize in the gun boutique, a conspicuous part of these well-guarded sports palaces. Actors and agents, lawyers and CEOs, all bring their 357 Magnums, or Sphinx AT-2000s, or their SIG-Sauer P-226s for an evening workout. According to a 1993 *New York Times* article, these new sports enthusiasts confess to enjoying the rush of firing at pop-up targets, imitating the action of *Starsky and Hutch* or *LA Law*, like no other high, including drugs, that they have ever tried. "Everybody in LA has a gun," admits one shooter, a medical professional, described as wearing a "raw-silk shirt under a Gaultier jacket and carrying a Sphinx AT-2000 semiautomatic pistol, which he caressed much as one might fondle the lunging beast on the hood of a new Jaguar." The article goes on to characterize this new gun culture as "the dirty little secret in the liberal closet."[10]

The man in the expensive jacket has lots of company. The *Times* article notes the jarring images of a young man firing a 357 Magnum in an Armani suit, a young woman standing next to him in gold lamé trousers sighting down the barrel of a LadySmith, a small .38 caliber Smith & Wesson revolver, and another fashionably dressed woman holding the slightly larger Smith & Wesson Model 49 with hammer bobbed, to prevent it from getting caught on something in her tiny purse. The gun of choice at ranges is the "nines," 9mm revolvers or semiautomatic

[10]Molly O'Neill, "Arming the Armani Set," 6.

pistols. Gang-bangers also make the 9mm—the caliber of the Cobray—their preferred weapon size.[11] Since 1987, the number of 9mm guns used in crimes of all kinds has doubled. In the 9mm category, the top-of-the-line status on the street and on the ranges belongs to the SIG-Sauer, which sells for close to $1,000. Like a Mercedes or a BMW or a Jaguar, the "SIG" confers enormous and instant status.

In Hollywood, where fantasies come true in theme parks and on the screen, the firing range serves as a movie set for the frustrated. Pop-up targets can be pictured as a boss, landlord, or business rival. The firing range suggests one wild step beyond the bland simulation of a video game. The range fills with real sounds and real smells. Excitement hangs in the air. The gun culture's euphemism for firing a machine gun on full automatic is "rock and roll."[12]

In fairly traditional terms, these young adults on the firing range have made it. Or, they have it made. But do they? Deeper, more subtle issues are at work here. Gangster images appeal to this upper-crust clientele for reasons that are not immediately obvious. Even with all that financial and social security, these young professionals feel a sense of emptiness, of unfulfillment— not on the same level, necessarily, as inner-city youngsters, but an emptiness all the same.

For anyone, the gun makes the hand as lethal as a super- hero's. Inside a firing range, one can sense danger. Those are real bullets after all. What prevents a young executive from turning his carefully polished SIG-Sauer on the other patrons? No one has done that—not yet, but one of these days, one of them might. Perhaps that contributes to the excitement—the excitement they suspect must be going on out on the streets. In

---

[11]According to a study conducted by the Bureau of Alcohol, Tobacco and Firearms in 1987.

[12]Larson, "The Story of a Gun," 52.

the name of protection and safety, they arm themselves, preparing to kill the very people they superficially imitate—and, through their clothes and jewelry and stance—even emulate.

So when we think about describing today's young gangsters who find themselves in gangs without ever knowing exactly how it all happened, we should be on guard against falling into easy blame or horrified dismissal. The truth is that many of us are pale versions of gang members without knowing it—carrying out our daily, acceptable forms of behavior, feeling powerless and overwhelmed, afraid to leave our neighborhoods and willing to defend our homes with high-velocity rifles.

However diverse their perspectives, sociologists and enforcement officials consistently mention one fact about young gangbangers: They cannot read or write. A. C. Jones, who deals with these young gangsters on intimate terms, says it flatly: "So many of them are functioning illiterates." We are so used to the phrase "functioning illiterate" that we fail to realize that it no longer describes these children's fate accurately. In fact, it belongs to another time, to people under entirely different conditions. Stripped of literacy *and* orality, these youngsters have gone beyond illiteracy. They function in wholly new but quite predictable patterns. If we hope to have a society less marked by violence, then lawmakers, teachers, and parents need to learn to understand these young people in new ways. These youngsters are not "willful" in the moral sense often attributed to them for their behavior—shooting guns and taking drugs. The truth is they have no choice. In fact, to escape from their lives of craziness on the streets, they need to exercise will. But their complete lack of literacy constrains them. Their broken homes constrain them.

They live in a world where everyone wants to make his or her own mark. That is a metaphor, of course, which refers to a deep impression left through an act or deed. It has its origins in writing, with a pen's impression on papyrus or paper. But no longer. These days, making a mark, a real, lasting impression, entails violence. Writing won't do it anymore. Which may be why Chicano gangs call graffiti "writing." As a pastime, "writing" on walls is acceptable, but it is not considered *real* gang-banging. For that, you need a gun in your hand.

Being in a gang is not the most dramatic thing that has happened to this underclass of young people. Gang membership is only the most visible symptom—a solution, really—to a much deeper problem. It is a problem that almost defies comprehension for anyone reading this book. But we have to imagine it, before more and more young people—in our inner cities, as well as in our suburbs—turn to violence and drugs as solutions to despair. Deep inside these fourteen-, and seventeen-, and eighteen-year-old young people, where others tap easily into conscience and a sense of guilt, these youngsters find nothing. Their entire structure of internal, social regulation has been erased. Nothing, not a single sentence of the social contract has inscribed itself on that historically constructed, internalized text of the self. Conscience no longer guides their behavior. With few exceptions, gang-bangers can describe in gruesome detail how they shoot down enemies, or total strangers, or even innocent bystanders, without expressing one shred of remorse. Bopete, the Crip we heard earlier, responds in terms that typify the behavior of gang members:

> "While you don' it . . . it's like" . . . he giggles and shrugs . . . "it ain't no thing. Don't make no difference even if it's a kid like you. While you shootin' 'em, it don't make no difference."

One young man, a member of a Pasadena gang called the Vipers, talks in the most matter-of-fact terms about tossing one of his rivals into an enemy's territory: "I guess they killed him or something. I don't know." The interviewer comments that the young man maintains the same tone of indifference throughout the entire interview, no matter the subject. Bopete's sidekick, Sidewinder, describes gang-banging and killing in much the same way:

> "*I'd* find somebody. 'Cause if they ain't nobody to fight, it ain't no gangs. It ain't no life. I don't know . . . it ain't no . . ."
>
> "It ain't no fun." [Bopete]
>
> "Yeah! Ain't no fun just sittin' there. Anybody can just sit around, just drink, smoke a little Thai. But that ain't fun like shootin' guns and stabbin' people. *That's* fun. Like, see . . . people you kill . . ."[13]

To kill without expressing remorse obviously means that the young gangster does what he does unfeelingly. But it also suggests something else. It suggests that a gang member does not view what he does as killing, at least not in the way that structures the moral sense of most people and organizes the social contract of most societies. To kill someone, to truly wipe him or her out, to erase that other person, means perceiving that that other person has a personality, a self—a life informed by his or her *own* unique set of feelings and responses. It implies that there is something deeply interesting to know about that other person, and that presupposes, in turn, the means and ethical value of "getting close" to him or her. But drive-by shootings exemplify and enact what gang members already believe with their whole beings—that everyone is really anonymous.

In an earlier chapter, I described the way in which the computer, in getting under the skin of a culture, has ousted the text from its psychosocial role in founding the coherence of the self.

---

[13]Bing, *Do or Die*, 49.

Of all of America's youth, gang members have been most severely "computerized." Even though they own no PCs, they have developed a reverence for the screen that takes on fundamental and frightening dimensions. Not only have they passed through the normal technological development, from TV and CDs, to video games and movies, but they act out those electronic images on the streets. They merge with them. The comments of one Crip named Racketeer make him sound like a movie critic from some nightmarish universe: "The movies we looking at are killing movies. Like gang movies. I don't know their names, but we be liking the killing movies where, like, people's heads is cut off. Because they letting you know what you can do to people, like sneaking up on somebody, you know?"[14] Story line matters little. Image is all. The screen shimmers with a compelling reality—as if it were an army training film.

For most young people—not just gang members—the screen has so thoroughly replaced the text that their world has turned into a virtual reality. A glimpse of just how virtual virtual reality can become is provided by the story of one young man who spent most of his time in what hackers call "cyberspace," the long-distance never-never land where one computer terminal interfaces with another computer terminal. The journalist Philip Elmer-Dewitt writes: "The WELL, one of the hippest virtual communities on the Internet, was shaken 2 1/2 years ago when one of its most active participants ran a computer program that erased every message he had ever left—thousands of postings, some running for many pages. It was an act that amounted to virtual suicide. A few weeks later, he committed suicide for real."[15]

---

[14]Interview with Léon Bing, "Confessions from the Crossfire," *L.A. Weekly*, May 6–12, 1988, 26. Racketeer is thirty-four years old, a high school dropout who lives with his mother, and who reads and writes with great difficulty. "When he speaks it is without passion or urgency; he simply states facts."

[15]Philip Elmer-Dewitt, "Cyberpunk!", 60.

Like cyberspace commandos, gang-bangers no longer believe they are killing real people. That is how altered cognitive reality has become. Gang-bangers' victims are only the street version of corpses they have seen keeling over in hundreds of violent TV episodes and hundreds of even more violent films. Dead people in films remain casualties in a gigantic light show playing in the mind. Erik Larson indicts the media in the most sweeping terms:

> America's entertainment media provide the last ingredient in the perverse and lethal roux that keeps the body count climbing even as the domestic arms industry shrinks. Just as *McQ* promoted the Ingram [a powerful automatic], *Dirty Harry* promoted the Smith and Wesson Model 29 and *Miami Vice* such assault weapons as the Uzi, Bren 10, and members of the Ingram family. Park Dietz, a California forensic psychiatrist, studied the effect of *Miami Vice* on gun prices and demand, and found that the appearance of the Bren 10 in the hands of Sonny Crockett (Don Johnson) in early episodes of the show immediately boosted demand for the weapon. Dietz told the Cox Newspapers that *Miami Vice* "was the major determinant of assault-gun fashion for the 1980s."[16]

Sidewinder, in a moment of recollection, confirms this analysis: " 'Hey, remember that movie we saw on TV? Where the guy shot the lamppost and made a big ole hole? Well, I wanna get me one of them.'

" 'I don't remember what kinda bullets they was. The long kind.'

" 'Yeah, and fat.'

"Bopete snaps his fingers, grinning hard all over his face. 'Oh wait! I got it—thirty-thirty! Went *boom!* Man, them booms made you happy. *Boom! Boom!*' "[17]

---

[16]Larson, "The Story of a Gun," 74. *McQ* is a 1974 movie starring John Wayne.

[17]Bing, *Do or Die,* 60. A light image—movies—broadcast as an electronic image—TV—makes reality even more virtual.

Even the space that gang members occupy and describe and love—the neighborhood—resembles more the space of "cybertown" than that of a traditional community. Gangs have charged the 'hood with meaning far beyond what anyone might expect, far beyond what anyone could ever hope from an old-fashioned meaning of *neighborhood*. Some well-defined series of blocks of course exist on the ground for those gangsters, but they have dreamed up and romanticized their meaning and value. They have created a substitute home where "homies" dwell, a projection that constitutes the *only* space where they feel safe. For most of us, if we had a neighborhood as children, it was a place where we played, a spot where we met our friends who lived nearby. But its boundaries were loose, so loose one had a hard time noticing where one neighborhood slid into the next. We never dreamed of defending it with our lives. Neighborhoods serve a different purpose today, as if a child felt that his own being, his identity, could expand to become as large as the territory he's able to imagine in his mind or defend with his gun.

The name "Eight-Tray Gangster Crips" refers to the kind of vast, constructed territory I mean. The Eight-Tray rule in Los Angeles from Sixty-seventh to Century Boulevard on the north and south; from Vermont to Western on the east and west, then across Eighteenth Street to Eighty-third (Eight-Tray), from Vermont to Van Ness Boulevard. That covers so much ground it can hardly be called, at least not in the strict sense, a neighborhood. It more resembles a domain, a fiefdom. More important, the area describes an emotional and psychological map, an area that the Eight-Tray prowl and patrol, sniffing out any unwanted intruders from other "'hoods" who might have penetrated into theirs.

Gang youth have redesigned their streetscape by investing it with new mythologies, new strengths, and capacities. Stories begin and end in the streets. So do lives. Right there on the cement and blacktop and on the street corners a person can hear and see and feel life in all its rush and excitement—one immediately vital presence. Within that new mythologized space, life teems: One can hear it in gang slang, rap music, and loud greetings. One can see it in peculiar walks and particular gestures. Although violence and despair dominate their lives, Crips and Bloods come close to living at a vernacular level: they move out in the streets defining their own boundaries, deciding on their own friends, establishing their own set of rules—and inventing their own language.[18] They survive by taking life into their own hands and shaping it, even though the solutions, more often than not, end in disaster.

By vernacular solutions, I mean that gangs constitute the only kind of social arrangement that makes sense for many in the middle of the hopelessly chaotic life of the inner city. Gang kids do not fit into any standard categories: they have fallen so far out of the traditional social units that they are in a position to form new ones. The media call them gangs. The teenagers call themselves gangsters. But that designation doesn't capture their actual social position. These young people form themselves into startlingly new but historically familiar configurations. Their arrangements are tribal.

The reasons for this particular kind of configuration lie close at hand, and mirror the logic of the tribal arrangements of pre- or non-literates. The family no longer serves as the basic unit for most of these children. The substitute family is constructed on the street, peopled mainly by boys from the 'hood. The virtual neighborhood turns into an actual piece of describable turf, bounded by local streets and avenues, punctuated by landmark buildings and hangouts. Individuals squat on an even smaller piece of it and so possess it, a style of ownership from a

---

[18]Crips and Bloods constitute the two dominant black gangs in South Central Los Angeles.

pre-literate time. But that's all they own. And they will defend it with their lives. Because it *is* their lives. They are their neighborhoods.

When gang members walk out of their houses, they leave behind their old identities. The gang offers the possibility of a new identity, conveyed through a form of naming reminiscent of pre-literate, tribal times. Names highlight singular characteristics and thus dictate carefully prescribed modes of behavior. This one acts crazy and picks up his gang moniker "Loco"; that one impresses everyone with his large lips and so gets dubbed "Duck." Gang members, like tribal members, have their names conferred on them: a person never chooses his own name. Gang names offer a glimpse into a member's behavior as witnessed by the entire group *and* as accepted by them. A gang name embraces and reassures. In the end, not much separates the way character gets communicated in a name like "Loco" from a name like Sitting Bull in more traditional groups.

These may look like forced connections—the similarities between the old and the new tribes. But one can find many close affinities. Instead of territory, gangs hold on to turf; they wear colors instead of costumes; use hand signs instead of hand gestures; display tattoos and piercings instead of tribal markings. Graffiti replaces tribal art. "Jumping in" approximates the physical ordeals of what anthropologists have termed "initiation rituals," in which young men become full-fledged members of the tribe. The improvised sound of rap resembles, in an almost uncanny way, the formulaic method of musical composition found in oral cultures. And finally, though their goals diverge dramatically, both groups share a desire to reach altered states of consciousness through drugs.

The behavior that captures public attention, for both old tribes and new, is revenge and retaliation, two modes of dealing with experience that require decisive action and little thought. They can be carried out best without feeling. They arise naturally from a pre-literate warrior society, where groups of men

take on new names that usually stand for some broad, characteristic features (in some sense, a cruder form of what moderns call
a *personality*). In Anglo-Saxon England, warriors broadcast their
skill and prowess by declaiming their bravery through a traditional form of boasting called a *Beat.* Gang members, too, in their
sworn fealty to "do or die," pledge their lives if they should ever
back down from a fight, or refuse to announce—"claim"—what
set they belong to, particularly to a rival gang member. To
dummy up or to turn tail and run is called "busting," and can
result in death, or even worse, in expulsion from the gang, a
"jumping out," which usually involves a near-death beating.

   Not much literature has come out of gang culture.[19] When it
does, the story usually gets dictated to a journalist. For the
most part, news in gang culture travels by word-of-mouth. In
their new tribal settings, gangsters have reinvigorated storytelling. In a recent book about a Crip set in San Diego, entitled
Baby Insane and the Buddha, the author/recorder returns time and
again to a street practice that binds gang members together:
"Crips tell each other stories. That's how they pass on skills
and wisdom and validate their lives. Some of the stories are
he-said, she-said gossip. Others are told and retold, polished
and honed into legend. The legends begin to shape the character of the gang, and the gang shapes the character of the community."[20] This sounds very much like the storytelling sessions
in oral cultures, in which vital information necessary for the
survival of the village gets inculcated in every tribal member.
Both in tribal settings and in gangs, stories achieve the status of
myth, and provide the warp and woof out of which the social
fabric gets woven.

---

[19]*Always Running,* a novel by Luis J. Rodriguez, is a notable exception. But
even Monster Kody's new book has been dictated to a journalist. Kody was
recruited into the Crips at age eleven; he's currently serving time in a maxi-
mum-security prison.

[20]Bob Sipchen, *Baby Insane and the Buddha,* 5.

Young gang members have worked out patterns of behavior
that provide for their survival at a most basic level. Most of these
young people, whether they are blacks, Chicanos, or Asians, feel
like outsiders in the most fundamental way—because of their
inability to read or write. Job prospects are grim, and when they
do appear, only pay the minimum wage. A good many inner-city
kids find work only at fast-food restaurants like McDonald's and
Jack-in-the-Box. Such jobs debilitate young people even further
by convincing them that that's all they are good for. Typically,
these jobs require no facility with reading or writing, except to
fill out the application. They actually reinforce illiteracy. Punching in sales on the cash register used in these places, for instance,
short-circuits abstract thought. In place of prices, the keys have
pictures of every food item pasted over them, similar to Fisher-
Price toys designed to teach children a rudimentary facility with
object recognition. Push the brown malt for chocolate, the red
one for strawberry. Given these deadly conditions, it is not surprising that these young people turn to drug-dealing, a job which
certainly pays much more, and provides the additional attrac-
tions of excitement and prestige.

And then there is the attraction of killing. Gang-bangers who
get arrested have scores of newspaper reporters and television
cameras descend on them to get the latest interviews and the
exclusive stories. Once gang youths become "media stars," they
immediately and dispassionately talk about the number of rivals
and enemies they have maimed or murdered, either "head-
up"—face-to-face—or in drive-bys. Some sets declare continual
war against other sets, making particular neighborhoods sound
like battle zones, or territories under siege. These are the voices

we hear, and on the basis of these stories the country constructs its opinion of every gang member and every neighborhood. Americans rightly respond with shock to all that shooting and killing they see on the late news, and read about in newspapers. They bar their windows and double-lock their doors, or move into gated, guarded communities.

The statistics don't help to disabuse the public of its image of gangs. Gang-related homicides set a new record in 1992 in Los Angeles County, as they have every year for the past five years. But examining the information and the numbers more closely cast a completely different light on these killings. In 1992, eight hundred people died from gang shootings in Los Angeles County. The Los Angeles Police Department Gang Division estimates the number of young people in gangs in the County at a hundred thousand. While eight hundred is a shockingly high figure, it certainly does not come close to what we have been conditioned to expect. Only a tiny fraction of gang members pulls the triggers. The rest boast and brag and talk a tough tribal game.

The explanation for this discrepancy between real numbers and image actually comes as a bit of good news. The youngsters who get arrested are by-and-large those who have committed crimes—burglaries, rapes, and killings. The media pay attention to them. They sell well. The other gang-bangers feed off the power of the most vocal members of the gang by striking the same poses, speaking the same language. They either own guns and don't pull the triggers or they exploit the image of an "ugly gun" to the hilt without actually possessing one. They own a gun in their imaginations, and shoot their mouths off. The idea of power has captured their imagination. They cannot bring themselves to fire the gun, though they stand in desperate need of expressing its violent power.

Those who do kill experience killing as tribal members once did and not as literacy-constructed selves. To even contemplate extinguishing someone else's life involves the violation of layer upon layer of social constraints that contemporary society hardly ever questions because they are so much taken for granted. Today, the suspension of those internalized constraints in such a large segment of the population should demand the attention of every one of us. It is the nexus between person and person, between one person's life and another's that literacy most powerfully enables and constructs. It is the transformation of that nexus into an anonymous killing zone that defines the real significance of gangs. One gets the sense, after hearing enough gang members, that they have no life except as it maps onto gang activity. A Crip behaves like a Crip, a Blood like a Blood. For a gang member to recognize an "outside," individual, and personalized life, he must first be able to recognize it in himself or herself. Oral cultures do not operate with the same concept of "murder" as literate ones. One cannot "take" someone else's life, because a demarcated, fully articulated internalized life exists only in literacy. A fully individualized, autonomous self guides only literate, or only alphabetized lives. And here is where gangs and tribes meet most closely. It is here that we can discern the widest tear in the social fabric. Without the reliability and assurance of the self, a person cannot be expected to act with anything but aberrant behavior.

Gang-bangers can kill so easily because they operate without the real concept of murder. They do not perceive another life at the end of the gun. In fact, they hardly ever use the term "murder," but speak instead of "dusting," or "wasting," or "blowing away." They can kill without feeling because guilt and conscience no longer inform their lives. That is the terrifying side of the ease with which they can participate in tribal organization. Not only are they bereft of conscience and guilt, but more important, they are devoid of that very crucial construct that animates a conscience—a self. Thus, where others derive power and strength, urban gangsters feel only emptiness. How to fill up that hole? How to feel powerful, if only for the moment? Join up with other young people in the same desperate, frightened condition. And then the group—the gang—can fire itself up with guns and drugs and stories to fabricate a "collective self," which finds expression not in pondering ideas, but in committing crimes. Violence and drug addiction are the fallout from that kind of illiterate society. Given enough time, everyone will eventually behave like gangsters. The new human being will dominate. Gang behavior will describe a larger and larger segment of the population. Literacy creates a community of individual selves, each directed by conscience, and driven by purpose. Reading and writing force people to imagine the lives of others. Reading and writing demand reflection. Literate people question and question again. They reflect critically. Young gang-bangers act—without reflection.

Most illiterates know that another, more complicated level of competency exists, and feel stigmatized by their inability to master it. But many of today's youngsters have given up struggling with letters. They have abandoned the book but do not enjoy any of the advantages of pre-literates. They derive no inner strength from orality. History has never been witness to such a phenomenon: an entire generation dispossessed of language—both oral and written.

This strange return to tribal times, like the gun itself, however, can also be read, paradoxically, as a hopeful sign. Gang-bangers react out of instinct. They have not read books about tribes and oral cultures. Yet they know that what they need can be found only at the vernacular level. In spite of all the odds, and as odd as it appears, they have found their own unique voice—dramatically separated from the Taught Mother Tongue—and have inscribed their own behavior on the streets. They have started over, because without literacy they cannot find a way to move forward.

Even jail sentences and Youth Authority Camps provide young gang-bangers with what they need. Punishment makes their lives more real. For only a flesh-and-blood person, not a ghost, can be convicted and then confined in a jail cell. Cops and courts, at least, take them seriously. They catch on quickly: they come alive by being a nuisance and a menace. The one sentence that sticks to them comes from a judge's mouth and takes the entire machinery of the penal system—from public defender to probation officer—to implement. Punishment is essential to a gang-banger. Even being searched attests to his substantiality: getting "patted down" for weapons or drugs takes on a bizarre quality of intimacy.

In addition, gang-bangers who go off to jail become local heroes for those outside: Myths and stories grow up in their absence. Fighting breaks out in defense of their reputations. When parolees return to the neighborhood, they bring back stories of the exotic world of the prison that fuel gang imagination. Typically, membership in gangs increases on their return to the neighborhood.[21]

Punishment will not reduce violence or drug addiction, though that seems to be the major response from authorities. From 1984 to 1987, the California State Legislature busily passed eighty-three bills designed to suppress gang activity.[22] Much to lawmakers' consternation, gang violence increased in each of those years. In 1989, the state senate passed a law permitting random stops of cars by police officers to search for firearms. That same year, the district attorney, also convinced of the need to step up legislation, declared that he would no longer permit plea bargaining for any offense involving gang members.

---

[21]The sociologist Malcolm Klein argues that gang workers make the idea of gangs more attractive to the neighborhood kids by focusing attention on members. Parolees do the same thing. (Malcolm Klein, *Street Gangs and Street Workers.*) Martín Sánchez Jankowski says that the presence of parolees in a neighborhood—indeed, the whole judicial process—has "the unintended consequence of strengthening both the defiant individualist character of gang members and group solidarity" (Jankowski, *Islands in the Street: Gangs and American Urban Society,* 283).

[22]Figures cited in Joan W. Moore, *Going Down to the Barrio: Homeboys and Homegirls in Change,* 5.

The more gang members behind bars, he reasoned, the safer the streets. President Clinton seems to think the same way: in his first address to Congress, he called for one hundred thousand more police officers in the streets to fight violence.

But it is time to put illiteracy and the contemporary epidemic of youth violence in long-term historical perspective if we truly want to get at the connections at the deepest level. Recall that rigorous instruction in writing was carried out principally by the universities, and exclusively for men, over an extended period of time—from the seventh all the way through the seventeenth centuries. Universities, in effect, posted signs across their doors that announced: "Women not welcome!" For a thousand years, standards of correctness in language, including grammar, syntax, usage, and construction—the world of rhetoric—remained solidly in the control of men, and got passed along by men. Vernacular discourse, on the other hand, with its utter disregard for rules and correctness, and its life of rhythm, pace, suspense, and emotion—the world of narration—lay with women, and got transmitted particularly through a mother's intimate, fleshly connection to her child. Both sides provided nourishment.

Literacy, born of a close interaction between speaking and writing, integrates these two, traditionally gendered domains. Historically, men have come to be associated with authority and rule making, with assertion through government and corporate enterprise. Historically, women have come to be associated with the emotional life-world, expressed through a lively kind of free and easy discourse. I am caricaturing here through the broadest of generalizations. But in the most general terms, those two opposing parts of the social agenda—writing and speaking— merge in literacy to create what might be termed a linguistic androgyny. Learning to become literate means learning to recognize and to appreciate the tension between rule and play. But more than that, it means internalizing their fundamental interaction. It may in fact quite literally "inform" a person's life in a way that no other paradigm can ever hope to, for the tension between rule and freedom characterizes so much of adult, socialized life. This is what parents teach, how to give just enough free rein to a playful, joyous spirit, to make it fit comfortably within the bounds of civility. Literacy continually reinforces that dual, parental role.

A young child grows into maturity, in part, by orchestrating the tension between the twin poles of play and authority. Whatever the subject, life forces always lie on the side of play. A young person engaged in the act of reading and writing is always engaged in the deepest, most serious form of play. A young dropout has not only dropped out of school—elementary or secondary—he or she has also dropped out of the most immediate forms of mastery that literacy has to offer. What a gang member misses in literacy—the fun of engagement with experience—he tries to get on the street. That's where lots of gang youth also work out their relationship to authority—on the street. The street hands out the hardest of knocks and the toughest of grades.

In an abstract, "informing" way literacy "civilizes"—makes individuals into consenting members of the body politic. Rules of grammar hold sentences together the way physical laws hold the natural world together, and constitutional laws hold society together. A beginning writer learns to pay to grammatical rules the same respect a scientist pays to the laws of gravity. Writers can achieve variety—interest—only within the restrictions imposed by grammar. Good writers continually test the possibilities of expression by pressing against whatever the rules will allow. In successful writers, that struggle produces sentences marked by innovation and invention. Such an attitude—the exploration of variety within boundaries—gradually shapes a writer's perception of the world. Learning to read and write instills a cognitive practice *and* an attitude that a young person internalizes and that begins to inform his or her behavior.

Compliance and rebellion—that is, a delicately balanced dance of political and social responsibility—begins in literacy. What takes place inside sentences finds expression in the contours of the real world. The arrangement of words in the Constitution of the United States is there not just to describe the constitution of its citizens, but to call that constitution into being. To comprehend literacy is to move beyond letters. Learning to read and write is metaphoric activity: a person *ingests* the shape of literacy and so gets shaped by it. Letters offer the soul its most nourishing food.

A side benefit arises from writing sentences: Every child—boy *or* girl—will come, unconsciously, to appreciate the fluidity of the female principle, while learning to respect the limits of the male principle. To make sentences requires a marriage between matter—sounds and a pattern—grammar and syntax. Everything in the world requires these two elements, *matter* and *pattern,* which derive, respectively, from Latin *mater, pater:* "mother" and "father." Mother, as we have seen earlier, encourages fluidity through baby talk and play. Father brings authority and rules into the house from the outside world. Just as biological creation takes place through sexual intercourse, civic life comes into being through social intercourse. A sentence is no less the creative offspring of words than the child is the offspring of parents. Each—sentence and child—has a new, independent existence of its own, once it has come into the world.

Parental influence flows into a child's sentences as if the child were a conduit keeping the process running smoothly. When a child loses one of its parental guides—the father suddenly disappears, or the mother becomes an addict (whatever the disabling circumstance, including the family's spiral into welfare)—parental incompleteness affects the child's ability to remain open to literacy. It has to. Not many gang members come out of a

complete nuclear family. Instead of working out playful relationships with authority on paper with sentences, and having them
reinforced and shaped through the presence of mother and father, many young people take their experiments to the streets—
where the stakes run much higher. On the streets, play and
authority become totalized and turn into explosive, deadly
polarities that collapse in upon each other. Killing *is* fun—one
and the same thing—and breaking the law *is* excitement. On the
streets, erasure spells death: one is simply "rubbed out." Street
life offers no time for revision.

What is being expressed on the streets is a twisted, deformed
version of the basic drive toward literacy. A young man or
woman is trying to inscribe his or her new life in the 'hood. He
or she is *writing* in the wildest, most unorthodox way, in an
attempt to compensate for what has been so lethally absent in
daily life, the linguistic dialectic between play and rule. On the
street, a gun makes sense, produces awesome fun, and becomes
a toy that delivers the absolute kick of authority.

As deformed as the growing up of these youngsters might be,
they persist in finding substitute forms for their broken lives.
They have worked out a way to survive—both physically *and*
emotionally, by creating their own families, complete with loyal-
ties and allegiances and attachments at the deepest levels. Even
those youngsters without conscience and guilt, but who possess
the smallest shred of a self—even those at the margins, that is,
can still talk about something they call love: a testament to the
human spirit. As a reporter in a recent *New York Times* article on
gangs delights in noticing: "Boys who will kill without remorse
use the word love to describe their bonds with their street
friends."[23] Some of those "boys" have given their lives defending
close relationships. Although these street "families" consist solely
of men, they nonetheless provide a structure and an organization

[23]Erik Eckholm, "Teen-Age Gangs Are Inflicting Lethal Violence on Small
Cities," 16.

through which young gang-bangers can reconstitute a sociality of sorts, however destructive. Gangs may be one of the few positive signs of inner-city life, in that they at least represent some form of social cohesiveness, a desperate statement about the desperate need to belong.

I hope I can now make the following claim convincingly: The fact that gang-bangers cannot read or write very well does not mean much, unless we are prepared to understand and act on our understanding—that gang life is itself constructed from a struggle with literacy, as I have been using the term. To be illiterate in a literate society is to feel both outside the system and at the same time to feel persecuted by it. As schools teach reading and writing today, young people treat literacy both as something irrelevant, and as an insurmountable obstacle. They have a hard time seeing literacy as a playful activity, because most young children have missed their time in orality, a time when a desire for linguistic play begins to develop. Without that experience of delight and joy in language, learning to write looks like learning so many rules—and reading gets reduced to cracking an impossibly difficult code. As a result, young people feel that they stand outside a social system that they perceive as both authoritarian and unfair.

Some of those outsiders gather together for identity and protection, to form a distinct outsider group, whose members all feel they belong—at least to one another. They mime larger society with distinctive forms of orality and literacy. Rap music, initially an inner-city black phenomenon, gives the impression of free and easy improvisation—puns and clever rhymes—played out against a carefully prescribed, regular beat. Rap music sounds very much like a modification of the "dozens"—improvised insults in contests of spontaneous cleverness—performed on street corners in black neighborhoods. In practice, most rap songs get worked out on paper, with a rhyming dictionary and a thesaurus, and have little to do with oral composition.

If reading can be described as "cracking a code," then graffiti writing has incorporated that idea into the script itself. Deciphering "tags" requires a kind of specialized literacy. It privileges the small group who can read its message, just the way conventional writing makes of literates an elite class. Graffiti closes the door to literates as solidly as literacy shuts out most inner-city youngsters.

To set a young person back on the path toward literacy—an admittedly painstaking and difficult task—is to return that child to a social matrix that has failed him or her in the past. It is to return that child back home. If that young person has grown up in a broken home—which indeed describes most of them—the Taught Mother Tongue will seem especially alien. It makes no sense. Only the vernacular of the gang can provide comfort and reassurance.

But for youngsters who have not yet been officially jumped in, or who have not actually dropped out, there is hope. The fulfillment of that hope will entail elementary and secondary schools recognizing that they have an entirely new role to fulfill, that they must promote the matrix of love and nurturing that is fundamentally embedded in orality. Elementary schools must provide those two poles of playfulness and authority in their reading and writing programs. In particular, as mothers move into the workforce, or drop out, or find themselves in need of welfare for their family's survival, schools have to pay more attention, in the child's critical, formative years, to that motherly connection.[24] As children turn to *la vida loca* (gang life), schools will have to turn more and more to *in loco parentes* (in place of parents). The matrix I name is anathema to bureaucracy and budget. It demands radical shifts in perspective and attitude. I advocate a far-reaching return, all the way back to orality, as the alma mater of literacy.

---

[24]As of 1992, 10.1 million families in America were headed by a single parent, usually the mother. This works out to be about one-third of all families with children in this country, and represents a 300 percent increase since 1970. Demographers predict that by the turn of the century, half the children in this country will grow up in single-parent families (reported in *Chicago Tribune*, April 23, 1992).

CHAPTER SIX

This decay of sovereignty over the tongue and its vernacular domains appears clearly in the way people speak about teaching. Were I lecturing, I would be speaking *to* you, and I could, if we were together, speak *with* you. But neither then, nor now, do I have any intention of teaching. . . . Much less am I educating you. I do not want to have anything to do with the kind of task for which nature did not give me the appropriate organs. *Educatio prolis* is a term that in Latin grammar calls for a female subject. It designates the feeding and nurturing in which mothers engage, be they bitch, sow, or woman. Among humans only women educate. And they educate only infants, which etymologically means those who are yet without speech. To educate has etymologically nothing to do with "drawing out," as pedagogical folklore would have it. Pestalozzi should have heeded Cicero: *educit obstetrix—educat nutrix:* the midwife draws—the nurse nurtures. Men do neither in Latin. They engage in *docentia* (teaching) and *instructio* (instruction). The first men who attributed to themselves educational functions were early bishops who led their flocks to the *alma ubera* (milk-brimming breasts) of Mother Church from which they were

never to be weaned. This is why they, like
their secular successors, call the faithful
alumni—which means sucklings or suckers
and nothing else.

> —Ivan Illich,
> "Vernacular Values and Education,"
> in Bruce Bain, ed., *The Sociogenesis
> of Language in Human Conduct*

A lot of teaching takes place these days—on every subject
imaginable, from business takeovers to cosmetic makeovers—
but very little, if any, education finds its way into young people's
lives. One can even select from a wide range of volumes at the
local bookstore on some strange activity called *parenting*, which I
take to be education in the sense in which Illich refers to it—
rearing a child in the home. I once told an old woman in a
Mexican village that such books were commonly available and,
indeed, quite popular in America. She was shocked by the skills
and common sense missing in grown people in the United States.
Why should anyone, let alone a mother, need a handbook for the
care of an infant—a guide to the nature of human nature itself?
She had heard that owner's manuals came with new pieces of
farm machinery or with new cars, but certainly not with newborn infants. She laughed at the absurdity of it all—at the silli-
ness of anyone needing lessons on how to raise a child.

The old Mexican woman began the education of her offspring in the only way it could begin—at her breast. While
nursing, she held the infant close and talked or sang to it. All five
senses in the infant came alive simultaneously, as that tiny crea-

ture remained in fleshly attachment to the *alma mater*, ingesting milk and the metamorphic extensions of milk: fluidity, rhythm, and language. Slowly, as the infant settled in as an alumnus, the infant acquired his or her voice.

That Mexican woman knew a fundamental truth, that literacy begins at the nipple—not just in the child's ability to speak, but in its propensity to listen in a rythmical way as a result of the mother's heartbeat and breathing impressing themselves on the infant's consciousness.[1] One of the curious and too little discussed facts about growing up, of course, is that inside the home no one ever teaches language to an infant. An infant learns by listening to the articulation of sounds. Being in close contact with the mother's heart, the infant hears the most essential sound being articulated. The mother's words and sentences get under the infant's skin. Each time the mother utters something, the infant mirrors those sounds by flexing facial muscles, primitive tics that will eventually enable the infant to utter its own sounds.[2]

A particular sound—a phoneme—induces a particular response, which seems to vary in kind and location from infant to infant. It has been found, according to one specialist, that "infants born to deaf-mute mothers have no repertoire of muscular

---

[1] See R. G. Patton and L. I. Gardner, *Growth Failure in Maternal Deprivation,* who established that babies deprived of maternal contact experienced physical and mental growth retardation (cited in Jeremy Rifkin, *Biosphere Politics*). See also C. Hoefer and M. C. Hardy, "Later Development of Breast Fed and Artificially Fed Infants," which concludes that infants "breast fed for four to nine months advance more quickly mentally, learning to talk and walk at an earlier age." See also Marcelle Geber, "The Psycho-Motor Development of African Children in the First Year and the Influence of Maternal Behavior," who claims that Ugandan children were developmentally far ahead of their American counterparts because of the close maternal contact of African mothers.

[2] See William Condon and Louis Sander, "Neonate Movement Is Synchronized with Adult Speech: Interactional Participation and Language Acquisition."

movements to speech, and make no such movements until there is prolonged and close contact with a speaking person or persons."[3]

Breast-feeding, then, provides much more than an initial ingredient in the development of an infant's diet. Breast milk more closely resembles what the early Middle Ages knew as *licour*, a life-affirming liquid that quickened all of nature, both human and animal. Certainly, milk starts the child growing, but just as important, it calls into being the child's emotional and physical life. At the mother's breast, the infant drinks in a tiny stream of consciousness. This is what the medieval clerics and monks meant by *educatio proles* (*educatio:* "to rear," "to bring up," and *proles:* "offspring," "posterity"), and from which we derive the word *education*. *Education* is first used in English in the early seventeenth century to refer to rearing children by paying attention to their physical needs—in the earliest years of the child's life this meant attention to nursing. By mid-century, in the heart of the scientific revolution, the word had expanded to include habits, manners, and intellectual concerns. (It is in this period that education seems to have taken on some of the urgency exemplified in modern times by the outcry in the 1950s in this country when Sputnik was sent aloft, and schools reacted by emphasizing science in elementary and secondary curricula.) But even with that new, modernized sense of education, initiated in the seventeenth century, it was still the mother who carried out education, and in the home.

Not until the middle of the nineteenth century does the word refer to some activity that takes place, without a touching relationship with the mother, outside the home—to schooling. As the mother increasingly moves out of the home, institutions

---

[3]Joseph Chilton Pearce, *Evolution's End: Claiming the Potential of Our Intelligence*, 20. *Infant* derives from the Latin *infans*, "unable to speak." Etymologically, the movement from infancy into childhood is a movement from wordlessness into a fuller orality.

gradually take over her role. By the late nineteenth century, for instance, a kindergarten movement is already in full swing in this country. A second round of pre-school activity takes place during the time of World War II. In both periods, mothers left home for the workplace, a departure that spelled disaster for literacy. With the mother gone from the home, a disastrous break occurs. A crucial nexus connecting the child to its ultimate development in literacy falls apart. A long historical perspective emphasizing a developmental emphasis on the child's relationship to the world compels the following stark question: How could a teacher and a bottle possibly replace the mother and the breast?

The medical profession coupled with commercial interests eased women out of the home by altering the way mothers fed their infants.[4] In the middle of the nineteenth century, most infants in this country were being breast-fed. By the middle of twentieth century, the majority were bottle-fed. That shift provides evidence of a profound break, a fissure separating mother and infant. That break resulted from the commercialization of both mothers and infants.

In the early nineteenth century, mothers who did not, or who could not, nurse their babies depended on wet nurses, or on

---

[4]One study concludes that the amount of time parents have to spend with their children has decreased about 40 percent since World War II. Between 1960 and 1986, the potential time with parents for white children dropped by ten hours a week, and by twelve hours for black children due to increases in mothers' employment, in fathers' increased working hours, and in the incidence of single-parent households (Victor Fuchs, *Women's Quest for Economic Equality,* 111).

On the history of education, see John Williams Jenkins, "Infant Schools and the Development of Public Primary Schools in Selected American Cities Before the Civil War"; Carl F. Kaestle and Maris A. Vinovskis, *Education and Social Change in Nineteenth-Century Massachusetts;* and Alan R. Pence, "Infant Schools in North America, 1825–1840," in *Advances in Early Education and Day Care,* 1–25.

alternative foods they concocted out of cow's milk. During the second half of that century, physicians attributed an unusually high rate of infant mortality to inadequate infant nutrition— either at the breast, or from cow's milk. Physicians scared women into believing their milk no longer contained the proper nutrients. Gabrielle Palmer, in her book *The Politics of Breastfeeding,* points out the economic link between the medical profession and the milk industry:

> It is not a coincidence that the decline of breastfeeding acceler-
> ated as the predominantly male, medical profession took over
> the management of childbirth and infant feeding. Nor was it
> chance that led to the expansion of the baby milk industry during
> the late nineteenth and early twentieth centuries when mechani-
> sation of the dairy industries had resulted in large whey sur-
> pluses. When a manufacturer has a waste product his first
> business instinct is to search for a way of marketing that product,
> and the development of baby milk has been a marketing success
> story, not least in the skill with which the competing product has
> been destroyed.[5]

With the endorsement of research physicians, commercial firms began marketing standardized, sterilized (the first ads claim "irradiation") infant-food formulas. The medical historian Rima Apple summarizes the nutritional state of affairs at that historical moment: "Mothers' changing perceptions coupled with develop-ments in medical practice, the growth of infant-food manufac-ture, and scientific research resulted in American mothers typically bottle feeding their infants under medical supervision."[6] Magazine advertising, medical brochures, endorsements all con-

---

[5]Gabrielle Palmer, *The Politics of Breastfeeding,* 3.

[6]Rima D. Apple, *Mothers and Medicine: A Social History of Infant Feeding, 1890–1950,* 5.

vinced mothers that "medically directed artificial infant feeding was equal to, if not better than, breast feeding."[7]

The earliest commercial infant food products came from Germany, at exactly the same time that German educators began developing theories of early childhood education. These two areas—early education and formula feeding—reinforced each other, and represent a collusion of events that ultimately helped to undermine literacy. In the early 1860s, Baron Justus von Liebig, a German chemist, announced that he had developed the perfect infant formula: wheat flour, some cow's milk (pasteurized), malt flour, with a dash of bicarbonate of potash to reduce acidity. As early as 1869, mothers could buy Baron von Liebig's "Soluble Food," at one dollar a bottle, at the local druggist's in America.

Other companies, including Nestlé, Mellin, and Horlick's, followed with similar products. Over the next several decades, as more and more doctors recommended these products, the preference for bottle-feeding increased. Rima Apple hints at a radical perceptual shift in mothers that enabled them to turn so easily away from breast-feeding: "In their desire to provide the best care for their children, American mothers relied increasingly on experts. A combination of sophisticated advertising techniques, the aura of scientific motherhood, and the vaunted expertise of the medical profession—an interplay of ideology and material factors—created an atmosphere that motivated many women to seek out commercial products and medical advice."[8] In that period of greater and greater reliance on scientific expertise—not just in the area of medicine but in education as well—obstetricians and pediatricians turned infants into objects of study, and then turned them over to the world of manufacturing and commerce as tiny consumers.

---

[7] Ibid.

[8] Ibid., 19.

With the introduction of formula feeding, a mother can both be present in the home and at the same time take back her autonomy: she does not have to be at the beck and call of her hungry offspring. Moreover, the bottle makes it easier for her to leave the home altogether. In either case, the bottle changes the infant's relationship to the world around him or her, for the bottle cannot replace the breast. A child can hold the bottle anywhere; it requires no human connection, and little if any supervision. The bottle smells of rubber, of plastic; it stays warm only a short time; it runs out. True, a breast runs dry, too, but the mother can switch her infant from one side to the other. Abundance comes from the right, abundance comes from the left, in a glorious display of ambidextrousness. How this aids in future skills, like writing and reading, we can only conjecture. But it might just promote the flexibility necessary for scanning a page or following an argument. The side-to-side switch surely broadens an infant's perspective, as he or she gets to see the world from different points of view.

An infant draining formula from a bottle is no longer being educated. He or she has begun to be schooled. Milk—fluidity—has become a commodity, disembedded from the intimate context of mother and child, and delivered back to that tiny consumer in carefully measured parts of this ingredient and that ingredient. Every mother's milk varies in percentages of fat, protein, and other vitamins and minerals. Indeed, breast milk changes taste and content depending on the mother's diet on a particular day. Infants nursed on Nestlé's, say, ingest the same precise formula each and every day. After a time, the infant comes to expect this sameness, perhaps developing in that tiny creature an initial preference for chain food—for uniformity and consistency. As a mother's breast milk changes, the infant responds with different sounds, prompting different sounds from the mother, too. In this way, a complicated oral interaction builds up day after day, a sophisticated code based on satisfaction and pleasure *and* change.[9] As the psychoanalyst Stephen Mitchell says, "The infant is almost oblivious to the mother as a person; she 'brings the world' to the infant and is the invisible agent of his needs."[10]

Sucking on the bottle, a baby receives an initial lesson in manipulating precious cargo. A bottle will go places a breast would never fit. In some cases, the bottle even seems to be an extension of the infant itself; it rarely leaves the infant's mouth. A mother is not a container for holding milk; a mother is a provider. Her breasts belong to her. An infant has to be placed on them, and removed from them. With a bottle, an infant has a much harder time internalizing the pulse and beat of the mother, its first truly *linguistic* (tongue) contact. Separated from the breast, the infant feeding itself with a bottle, or even being held by the mother and fed from a bottle, has missed out on the fundamental, kinesthetic connection to literacy because he or she has been snatched, in a specific, physiological way, from its mooring to orality.

Bottles weaken the newborn's ability to breathe: An infant sucks less vigorously from a bottle than it does from a mother's nipple, causing reduced or restricted breathing in general, which later affects its performance in orality—in the rhythms and patterns and pitches of speaking and listening. Studies have shown, for example, that compared with breast-fed babies, those fed by bottle contracted "four times as many respiratory infections . . . twenty-one times more asthma, and twenty-seven times more

---

[9]Researchers have recently discovered that a hormone, an opiumlike substance many times stronger than morphine, is released by the pancreas of both mother and infant during breast-feeding. This chemical connection of pleasure between mother and her charge may foster an additional layer of intimacy.

[10]Stephen Mitchell, *Relational Concepts in Psychoanalysis*, 32. See also Humberto R. Maturana and Francisco J. Varela, *The Tree of Knowledge: The Biological Roots of Human Understanding*, for their concept of "Structural Coupling."

hayfever."[11] The research concluded that vigorous sucking on a breast was actually necessary to promote proper breathing habits in babies, especially in its earliest days of life: "In the first few weeks after birth, infant breathing is generally shallow and unstable. Vigorous breast sucking stimulates respiration."[12]

But nursing does not merely provide pulmonary exercise. Nursing also means intimate touching. What can happen when the baby literally loses touch with its mother was demonstrated graphically in the last century. Infant mortality rates rose to frighteningly high levels during the Industrial Revolution. More than half the babies born in the nineteenth century mysteriously died of an illness that went under the equally mysterious name of *marasmus,* what doctors could only describe as a "wasting away of the body." In some orphanages nearly 100 percent of the infants died. Still, doctors could not isolate the specific cause, hence the elusive name they gave it. Finally, however, an explanation surfaced in the most accidental way. Jeremy Rifkin, exploring the catastrophic results of separating the infant from its mother, summarizes this important piece of medical history:

> The mystery of the fatal illness was solved just before World War I when a Boston doctor, Fritz Talbot, visited the children's clinic in Düsseldorf. The American physician noticed a large woman carrying a sick baby and inquired about her presence in the wards. His host replied, "Oh, that's old Anna. When we have done everything we can medically for a baby, and it's still not doing well, we turn it over to old Anna, and she is always successful."

> This chance encounter helped change infant care practice in the United States and Europe. In the 1920's, pediatricians in the U.S. began introducing a regular regime of "mothering" in the

---

[11]Ashley Montagu, *Touching: The Human Significance of Skin,* 70, 72.

[12]Jeremy Rifkin, *Biosphere Politics,* 222.

wards. Some hospitals required that every baby be "picked up, and carried around, and mothered several times a day." In New York's Bellevue Hospital, infant mortality dropped from 35 percent to under 10 percent in the first few years of "mothering" on the wards.[13]

One can only wonder if the technological management of the lives of infants had gone too far when doctors advised against breast-feeding as an annoying and inconvenient business. The name of Luther Emmett has faded from history. But in the late nineteenth century, Emmett, a physician, wrote numerous how-to books on infant care. His story makes clear just how minutely doctors were willing to manage the lives of infants. He campaigned for infants freed from dependence on their mothers, freedom from the breast. To that end, he recommended taking the infant out of the cradle, a device that enabled a mother to maintain some contact with her baby while she did other things, like sewing, knitting, or reading, and imprisoning the tiny creature. Breast-feeding created an unwanted dependence, and rocking the baby, Emmett argued, only tied the infant to the mother with an additional knot. Crusading for the autonomy of infants, Emmett created the crib, an innovative piece of nursery furniture that embodied that newly found independence. But autonomy in a modernized, commercialized sense first brought into being in America in the nineteenth century meant that some institution—in this case, the profession of medicine—had the power and license to define autonomy, and then prescribe what the "autonomous" infant needed. Commercial enterprises could then satisfy those needs. Indeed, now only commerce could bring satisfaction.[14]

---

[13]Ibid., 223.

[14]In the nineteenth century, service professionals began to invent needs, thereby creating a demand for commodities that they slowly came to monopolize. On this transformation, see Burton J. Bledstein, *The Culture of Professional-*

How did such a wide chasm open, such a vast canyon separating the wisdom of a traditional Mexican woman from all those how-to books on the shelves of every bookstore, from the nineteenth century into the twentieth? The change did not come about deliberately or maliciously. It began as a way of mitigating the loss of the mother from the home as she began to enter the workplace during the Industrial Revolution. As the mother's presence diminished, the care and comfort she once provided became institutionalized and professionalized in the name of trying to protect the young child from abandonment.

Sometime during the Industrial Revolution in this country, the definition of what constituted an infant began to change rapidly. That tiny creature animated by a "vital spark," as D. W. Winnicott says, "with the urge toward life and growth and development"—that tiny intelligence the medical profession transformed into a tiny bundle of needs. Winnicott describes even the newest of the newborn as a "going concern," that is, a being in business for itself. But it is also a being concerned with everybody and every thing—a consciousness whose goal is establishing the *with*-ness of living.

I have described young people moving into that broadening *con*-sciousness in the early phase called orality, through play, fairy tale, and song. This is an experience essential for literacy later in life. In one of the oddest strokes of history, the profession most devoted to the care and well-being of people, the medical profession, interrupted that movement into literacy by warning

---

ism. See also Christopher Lasch's untitled review in the *New York Review of Books*. "Professionals played on public fears of disorder and disease, adopted deliberately mystifying jargon, ridiculed popular traditions of self-help as backward and unscientific, and in this way created or intensified a demand for their services." See also Ivan Illich, *Medical Nemesis*.

mothers about the dangers of polluting their infants with breast milk. They broke the infant's connection to literacy at the most fundamental level. From that point on, mothers found it easy to question their own instincts, their own body wisdom, about the proper and natural way to raise their offspring.

Educators, in their pastoral concern, took on the responsibility for mothers' fears. Instead of being perceived as "going concerns," with their own innate abilities, two- and three-year-olds were viewed by professional educators as ignorant, helpless things, who, if they were ever going to survive, would require heavy doses of teaching over long periods of time. They would have to be taught a lesson on a daily basis. By the time children reached three, sometimes even two years of age, these professional educators, all with the best intentions, plucked them out of their homes—out of the cradles—and resettled them in schools—into cribs. Even with the aid of physicians, those two- and three-year-olds had entered a system that would keep them constantly hungry, in need of more and more of whatever the curriculum determined they lacked. Professionals in both education and medicine had opened a new market for goods and services—mothers and their infants—amidst the general euphoria of the Industrial Revolution.

So while children themselves did not disappear, they got caught up and redefined as tiny consumers—things to be managed—in the nineteenth-century revolution in technology. They moved from being educated in the old, traditional sense to being schooled, in the sense that Ivan Illich has so brilliantly described. Education believes in the innate abilities of pupils and recognizes their place in that historical continuity of human development. Education believes in the inherent wisdom of even the tiniest infants. Schooling wrenches each child out of history and treats each one as a blank, ignorant slate, in need of that one scarce and elusive commodity—knowledge. Schools presented reading and writing in the same way that schools today teach computer skills. Everyone needs to know how to manipulate a computer, the argument goes, because every job requires one. But very few people need to know how to program, and certainly very few, if any, need to know how the machine actually works.

Schools treat reading and writing the same way, as a tool that first has to be mastered for successful entry into the world of jobs, a tool that can be manipulated in the same mechanical way as a personal computer. Push a button marked RULES OF GRAMMAR AND SPELLING, and become literate. The nuances of programming remain locked away inside the machine, and the mysteries of language locked away inside the heart of sentences. In both cases, the student simply needs to learn a set of do's and don'ts—the rest is of no concern. The connection between literacy with the rest of the world of orality has, for the most part, evaporated. What children once experienced as their first taste of literacy—the intimate, tactile connection of mother and infant—has already been lost to most of them. Schools do not view literacy as a process—one that begins at the nipple and carries a person to the very core of experience. They view it as an isolable, definable subject, that with enough diligence and attention to detail can be learned just like any other subject.

This points out the critical difference between understanding literacy as inseparable from the cognitive development of the self and literacy as an externally measured set of skills—a commodity that can be quantified, packaged, and delivered by professionals. Reading and writing turn into literacy by measuring them through statistics—levels of reading skills, rates of comprehension, and so on. Reading and writing are being lost as activities that transform a person into an entirely different creature, a person who has the capability of making continual discoveries about himself or herself. They are being lost as activities through which one finds constant surprises in sentences—both written *and* spoken—and in the self.

Literacy, as a commodity, can be achieved without regard to orality. But true reading and writing have deep, telluric connections that run back to speaking and listening. Reading and writing never end. They are gerunds that designate activities that continue to carry a person through life by enabling selves to create the stories they tell in internalized, silent, and protracted conversations. Reading and writing charge language with enough life to keep it changing. They ensure that the person will not get locked into just one story. The word *gerund,* used three sentences ago, is itself interesting in this regard. It comes from the familiar Latin root *gero-,* "to carry," out of which arises a long string of words associated with textual activity: *author, actor, gesture, ingestion,* and ultimately, *story.* More than fifty years ago now, Walter Benjamin noticed the consequences of treating reading and writing as vehicles for the commodification of knowledge as "information." He wrote, "If the art of storytelling has become rare, the dissemination of information has had a decisive share in this state of affairs. Every morning brings us the news of the globe, and yet we are poor in noteworthy stories. This is because no event any longer comes to us without already being shot through with explanation. In other words, by now almost nothing that happens benefits storytelling; almost everything benefits information. Actually, it is half the art of storytelling to keep a story free from explanation as one reproduces it."[15]

Infancy radically changed in the nineteenth century. Baron Justus von Liebig, a German chemist, and Friedrich Froebel figure prominently in this cultural divide. I have already discussed how Von Liebig's formula changed the idea of infancy. The views of Froebel, a pupil of the famous educator Johann Heinrich Pestalozzi, revolutionized childhood education in the United States. The influence of the ideas of Jean-Jacques Rousseau and the conception of harmonious development led Froebel to make the discovery that too many children stumble into ado-

---

[15]Walter Benjamin, *Illuminations: Essays and Reflections,* 89.

lescence with little or no maternal care. Too many of them, he
said, spent the day with nannies or with wet nurses. To solve the
problem, he advocated taking children out of the home during
preschool age. This was now feasible, he argued, since his col-
league had devised a way to free them from the breast. He
advocated providing education for them in a preschool setting he
quite deliberately called a *kindergarten*, a "children's garden."
Man and nature, he believed, proceeded from the same ultimate
source, and must, therefore, be governed by the same laws of
growth and development. Children needed to be removed from
their beds, where they were not thriving, and transplanted to
these new gardens, whose curriculum more closely followed the
principles of natural science. Froebel attempted to heal an "illness" he had diagnosed in the lives of children. In doing so, he
in fact exaggerated the disruption in the natural order of their
growing up.

He further argued that the care for these children, who
ranged in ages from three to five and six, be given over to a
woman—a professional educator. Froebel warned against teaching or giving instruction in anything in particular to these youngsters. Kindergarten must be involved solely with nourishment of
the soul. That meant that groups of infants were to be gathered
together in small communities for the sole purpose of playing
together. Responsibility for the garden would rest in the hands
of the gardener, who would tend her plants and watch them
unfold according to some inborn plan that was not possible to
fully understand. Basically, the teacher only guided and encouraged, cultivated and augmented when necessary. She lent a
helping hand, but she certainly did not teach. After all, the rose
needed no lessons to bloom correctly. What could be more
benevolent than to characterize education through gentle nurturing and care? What could be more traditional?

Kindergartens caught on in this country just at a time when
technology began a revolution so powerful that it not only for-

ever altered modes of production, it also rearranged the way people lived. Increased factory production required a workforce. More and more people were displaced from the land, and thrown together in large urban areas, like Chicago, Saint Louis, and Detroit. Traditional families splintered into smaller and smaller units, and local community life in most instances faded or disappeared. People worked long hours separated from relations and friends, sometimes by great distances. But while the revolution in technology destroyed traditional forms of community life, it spawned its own, more specialized groups. One historian, Ronald J. Zboray, for example, argues that technological advances enabled companies to produce cheaper books, stronger incandescent bulbs, and finer corrective lenses, all of which combined to create a new community, in a sense, of individual readers across certain parts of the country, who learned about the latest books in cheap newspapers and national magazines. Indeed, statistics gathered in 1884 tell an interesting story of reading habits:

The records of American publications, for the twelve years ending in 1842, show an aggregate of 1,115 different works. Of these, 623 were original, and 429 were reprinted from foreign books. The full list of reprints would show nearly the same number as the originals, viz.: an average of 52 each per annum. In the year 1853, there were some 733 works published in the United States; of which 278 were reprints of English works, 35 were translations of foreign authors, and 420 (a large preponderance) were original American works—thus showing an increase of about 800 percent in less than twenty years. As the average increase in the population of the United States in the same time,—great as it was—scarcely reached 80 percent, it appears that literature and the bulk of the book trade advanced ten times faster than the population. If we compare the numbers printed of each edition, the growth is still greater; for 20 years who *imagined* editions of 100,000 or 75,000 or 30,000, or even the now common number of 10,000.[16]

Technological innovation effected a new, radically different configuration of families in general. It also reached down into each family, especially in urban areas. It moved women into the workplace in unprecedented numbers beginning in the years just prior to the Civil War. As technological innovation gradually escalated, the social changes associated with that trend included a marked increase in the rate at which women turned their time and talents to earn incomes in the workplace. That rate continued to rise over time in the nineteenth century. Between 1880 and 1910, the labor force grew at a rate never again matched, the proportion of women who were employed increasing from 14.7 to 24.8 percent.[17]

As one response to the familial disruption, working mothers could send their children to carefully controlled, little neighborhood communities called kindergartens, which, in turn, provided additional jobs for women as teachers. Kindergartens became popular because they answered a need, but also because they mimicked what, in fact, was being destroyed, the presence of an extended family as a vital source of human interaction.

As Susan Sontag reveals in *On Photography,* the camera in this period moved very rapidly from being an instrument of art to a plaything of mass culture because it served so effectively to document the disappearance of the extended family. By the 1850s,

---

[16]Cited by Ronald J. Zboray, "Antebellum Reading and the Ironies of Technological Innovation," 180–81. Already in this account from 1884, we can see literacy being transformed from a self-revealing activity in the medieval sense into an agent of commodification, both in the book itself as commercial object and in the dissemination of a newly structured world organized as information and professional administration.

[17]W. Elliot Brownlee and Mary M. Brownlee, *Women in the American Economy: A Documentary History, 1675 to 1929.*

people other than studio photographers were shooting each other with this new technology in new ways. Families that had not seen one another for a time would come together on Christmas or Easter, crowding in front of the big box camera and smiling as if the idea of the extended family had not changed, as if all year long scores of relatives had been living in mutual, close, and harmonious contact.

Larger communities broke into smaller ones; extended families divided into smaller units: the atomizing of America went on almost everywhere. The camera enabled people to hang on to the idea of the extended family, long after it had passed.

The desire for the old traditional forms charged kindergartens with a special life, each kindergarten bringing dozens of children into close contact as if they were siblings. The model came from the old, extended family, where children from various branches of the same family occupied the same house, brothers and sisters and cousins all playing with one another for long, uninterrupted stretches of time. Rooms might be filled with a dozen or more women—some aunts, some nieces, a grandmother perhaps, a couple of mothers. Kindergarten, those "little bright rooms," exploited the desire for the extended family as ruthlessly as the camera. Coming together from disparate families—but from a local neighborhood—children would congregate around the *alma ubera* and would be made to feel like they belonged to one, large extended family. Kindergartens even promoted their own form of Mater Familias—the teacher. But the kindergarten teacher could never exercise authority quite like a mother. A mother has ultimate authority over the child, ultimate responsibility for its control and direction. As skillful as a teacher might be, her authority extends no further than the confines of the playground, and no longer than the clang of the last bell.

Parents took great delight in Froebel's plan. For one thing, he presented kindergarten as something other than school—something closer to the extension of the home. A child could expect to find there a nurturing environment filled with objects for

fanciful play. By constructing such a world, Froebel harked back
to the medieval idea of *educandus*—back to the abundant breast.

Froebel's idea of the kindergarten stood in solid opposition to
another educational movement in America, one that had come
into being some twenty years earlier, called Infant Schools.
These schools intended to bring poor or otherwise disadvan-
taged children of preschool age into the school experience early
on, to cut down on crime by providing youth proper moral and
character training. Infant Schools also served a much more
practical goal: to free poor mothers to earn a living. In a sense,
Infant Schools operated as the Head Start programs of the early
nineteenth century. Maris A. Vinovskis, who serves as research
advisor for the U.S. Department of Education, and who has
probably written more on the subject of Infant Schools than
anyone else, outlines the reasons why these schools were established:

> Most of the proponents were eager to provide early education
> for the children of the poor. Their rationale was both to relieve
> the poor mother of child care so that she could earn a living and
> to provide proper socialization for her children that middle-class
> reformers feared were being brought up without proper moral
> guidance. Some reformers also believed that infant schools
> would help prepare children from disadvantaged homes to do
> better in the regular public schools. A few, like William Russell
> who edited the influential *American Journal of Education*, saw in
> infant schools an opportunity to reform early education alto-
> gether by introducing more effective, Pestalozzian methods of
> teaching into the public schools.[18]

---

[18]Maris A. Vinovskis, "Early Childhood Education: Then and Now," 155.

Vinovskis goes on to say that while American reformers did not believe that crime in this country was as bad as in Great Britain, "they feared that unless immediate, corrective steps were now undertaken, the quality of life in American cities would rapidly deteriorate."[19] For educational reformers, corrective steps meant learning to read and write. In most Infant Schools, it appears, teaching literacy turned out to be the best baby-sitting plan, for literacy forced a young person to internalize rule and authority—in a sense, to spy on himself or herself.

Infant Schools varied, however, in how they instructed their pupils. Many of these schools emphasized only literacy. In Boston, schools employed rote memorization and stressed severe classroom discipline. Vinovskis again: "Some infant schools stressed play and de-emphasized intellectual pursuits while others immediately tried to teach the alphabet and reading. Often it was the parents who insisted that infant schools stress rigid classroom discipline and teach their children how to read."[20] In these schools, the classroom was not a way of meeting educational needs but a way of moving students more efficiently through an intellectual process known familiarly as "the school system."

Froebel, of course, believed in an entirely different kind of experience—called education—by which he meant something very close to the medieval idea of nurture. And he definitely changed the course of Infant Schools. Once Froebel introduced his kindergarten system devoted to play, parents and educators alike began to question the wisdom of three-year-olds learning to read and write. Froebel's philosophy of harmonious development encouraged parents to think seriously about the delicate balance among intellectual, physical, and emotional growth.

---

[19]Ibid.

[20]Ibid., 156.

Too much attention paid to cognitive development might result in socially maladaptive kids. By the time of the Civil War, Infant Schools had fairly well been dismissed as an interesting but failed experiment.

But the desire to teach reading and writing to preschool children never really died out. Periodically, the idea would be tried in one experiment or another. It surfaced most strongly in the middle of the twentieth century. One hundred years after the closing of the last Infant School, as a part of President Johnson's massive war on poverty, the Office of Economic Opportunity, under the direction of Sargent Shriver, launched Project Head Start in late 1964. Head Start emphasized a wide range of ideas, from health and psychological services to athletics and education. Designers of the program included reading and writing in their curriculum, but chose not to focus on literacy, thereby creating the illusion of a strongly academic program. Still, policy makers continually argued the cognitive benefits of early intellectual training, and so, like Infant Schools, the Head Start program became identified with reading and writing. Hoping to increase the brain power of their children, middle-class families in the nineteenth century wanted a chance to participate in their own version of Infant Schools. Middle-class parents had the same reaction in the 1970s with the Head Start program. Educated parents became frightened lest their children be outstripped by poor black children becoming the advanced scholars of the future. Wealthy white mothers and fathers had no intention of being left behind, and so they pressed Froebel's idea back into service—with a vengeance.

Popular interest in preschool education was low in the 1950s and early 1960s. But as more and more child psychologists began arguing that intelligence could indeed be increased through early childhood education, parents bought the idea.[21] By the 1980s,

---

[21]See Edward Zigler and Jeanette Valentine, eds., *Project Head Start: A Legacy of the War on Poverty,* and especially 3–19.

parental demand for preschool education was in full swing. At
the same time, more mothers had entered the workforce, which
also increased the demand for child care. Parents were willing to
pay to keep their kids off the streets, and away from so much TV.
Among social workers and educators, a consensus began to
emerge that *quality* day-care programs may not be detrimental to
older children and may in fact benefit poor children.[22] And here
began a curious, paradoxical history: the more attention is paid
to literacy and instruction, the more reading scores dip and the
more young children drop out of school.

Kindergartens reappeared in a new, more vigorous form in
the 1970s, infused with the spirit of both Infant Schools and
Project Head Start. Play took a secondary role in these new
preschools. Parents wanted their children, age three years old, to
learn to read and write, because literacy seemed to offer the most
promising road to success. That strategy swept through the popular imagination. In 1965, 59.5 percent of five-year-olds attended kindergartens. By 1990, that number had swelled to an
astonishing 79.5 percent. When we consider that some children
receive home schooling, that number reflects practically universal attendance in preschools.

The unit of instruction in schools in this country, as early as
colonial days, consisted almost entirely of reading and writing.
Grammar schools, Dame Schools, Infant Schools, and Head
Start all reinforced the importance of teaching young children to
read and write. Once students' performances could be measured, through diagnostic testing, they could be categorized.
Thus, in 1883, two years before Mark Twain published *The
Adventures of Huckleberry Finn*, the *New England Journal of Education*
had created a new category of citizen by coining the word

[22]See Alison Clarke-Stewart, "Infant Day Care: Maligned or Malignant?"

literacy.[23] By 1885, the *Journal* was already conducting surveys to determine levels of literacy in Cambridge, Massachusetts. Early childhood education had spread rapidly throughout much of the United States and, by 1840, approximately 40 percent of all three-year-olds in a literacy-conscious state like Massachusetts were attending school. By 1885, the *New England Journal of Education* wanted to find out how those students were performing.

It is only a century ago that the New England school system transformed the complicated interconnection between an innate ability to speak and a learned facility to read and write, into something called literacy. Suddenly literacy headed the list of items in a category called subject matter that could be studied, analyzed, and passed on. Hornbooks, readers, and grammars all prescribed correct grammar and syntax through a carefully worked-out set of rules. Those rules turned sloppy and playful oral discourse into precise, correct sentences on the page. Educators correlated sloppy speech with slovenly, loose standards of behavior, and conversely, sentences written to exact standards of correctness reflected an upright, moral outlook. Illiterates and literates were divided not only into categories based on skills of reading and writing but on degrees of moral lassitude and rigor.

That idea of high moral standards lies at the heart of literacy. *Elite* is, in itself, a word derived from *legere,* the Latin root for "reading," and has the word *literacy* buried in it. When a student learns to read and write, those rules of correctness become an integral part of a new, literate perception. A literate person can't help but "read" the entirety of experience through the grid of right and wrong, correct and incorrect. In nineteenth-century

---

[23]Notice the way the word, from the beginning, is used to draw class and ethnic lines: "Massachusetts is the first State in the Union in literacy in its native population, and the nineteenth only from its Irish and French-Canadian illiteracy," unsigned article titled "First Fruits of Butler's Inaugural," *The New England Journal of Education*, XVII, 54.

America, literacy and illiteracy reinforced distinctions of class and color. In a literate world, illiterate people of color are vulnerable to the constant risk of being cast out as morally reprehensible.

Writers like Thoreau and Twain, Melville and Emerson all recognized literacy as the great wall separating classes and peoples of colors in nineteenth-century America. A hundred-year-cycle had come full circle: Kindergartens had removed children from their mothers, and in the process had also disembedded education from the home. Over that hundred-year-period, from roughly 1760 to 1860, education gradually gave way to schooling. The idea that literacy begins at the breast, in the home, had vanished long before. Instead, literacy had been made into a commodity off a production line, shaped into a form that could easily and systematically be consumed. Educators began to emphasize literacy's potential, first articulated in the days of Infant Schools, for reforming young people and bringing them to a moral uprightness.

Nowhere does this trajectory hit home more forcefully than in *The Adventures of Huckleberry Finn,* the novel from which, Ernest Hemingway said, all modern American literature descends. The early 1880s can be seen as a watershed for literacy, characterized by both the coining of the word and the literary creation of the semi-literate character, Huck Finn. Through Huck, Twain dramatized the political implications of literacy by revealing its relationship both to orality and to the social and racial ordering of American democracy.

Huckleberry Finn offers the strongest indictment I know of the imposition of standards of literate correctness by an outside, central authority. Not only does the novel lay out the various levels of literacy in nineteenth-century America—the literate Widow Douglas; the semiliterate Huck; the non-literate (illiterate) Jim—it also exposes the political bias in those levels of literacy. Twain explored quite openly an issue that the *New England Journal of Education* could only mention in the most hushed academic terms—that the ability to read and write correlated to the color of one's skin: levels of literacy with shades of white, and levels of illiteracy with shades of black.

Huck Finn is a semiliterate who speaks funny lines, which the reader sees on the page as even funnier sentences. Twain makes it plain that the young man will have a difficult time reaching literacy, by offering us some crucial clues about his home life. Indeed, Huck comes from one of the most broken families in American literature. He seems to be without a mother, and the novel remains conspicuously silent on the subject. His father, who disappears mysteriously some time before the novel opens, reappears suddenly as the action unfolds. But Pap turns out to be a drunken sot. Huck receives no physical nurturing that we can observe, no education that the reader can discern in the course of Huck's story.

It is quite clear, however, that Huckleberry Finn was not fed on formula from a bottle. His sentences, filled with puns and wild constructions, betray the time spent at his mother's breast. By talking and laughing with him, and by giving him huge doses of nonsensical baby talk, someone—I suggest the most logical person, the mother—has brought Huck so deeply into language he revels in it. That's apparent in the way he loves to tell his story, to digress and describe, to talk about every prank and pratfall. He knows the rhythm of suspenseful prose; he can create amazing drama just by describing the sun rising on the Mississippi. Huck Finn can flex a complex array of facial muscles.

Mother's milk, that tiny stream of consciousness, runs underneath an infant's sentences, just as the Mississippi River runs beneath Huck's meandering prose. Huck's sentences flow like the Mississippi. They wander from idea to idea without regard to grammar or spelling. Twain doesn't have to mention Huck's mother because her presence has been so decisively incorporated into a boy's playful, spirited sentences, sentences that have not been crippled by some demanding set of rules and standards. Huck Finn embodies vernacular talk.

Some time before the novel opens, his mother takes him on a river ride, a trip down a metaphoric river, where Huck finds his own "fluency." Psycholinguists have suddenly begun to pay attention to the sophisticated linguistic and cultural encoding in the sentences that pass back and forth between mothers and their infants.[24] To much of the world, those sentences seem devoid of meaning. In fact, sharp changes in pitch and intonation, and rapid shifts in rhythm, can signal everything from hunger to love to anger. Questions sound different from statements, demands different from desires, and complaining different from fatigue. The psycholinguist Breyne Arlene Moskowitz maintains that the infant's "random string of babbled sounds" are absolutely necessary for language acquisition:

At an even earlier stage, before a child has uttered any words, she is accomplishing a great deal of linguistic learning, working with a unit of phonological organization even more primitive than the syllable. That unit can be defined in terms of pitch contours. By the late babbling period children already control the intonation, or pitch modulation, contours of the language they are learning. At that stage the child sounds as if she is uttering reasonably long sentences, and adult listeners may have

---

[24]Daniel N. Stern, *The First Relationship: Infant and Mother,* maintains that perspective and voice in speech is handled quite early. Perspective is also carried by affective expressions, like laughing and crying, along with stress level and similar prosodic features in early speech, rather than by either lexical or grammatical means.

See also Catherine E. Snow and Charles A. Ferguson, eds., *Talking to Children: Language Input and Acquisition;* Ann Fernald et al., "A Cross-Language Study of Prosodic Modifications in Mothers' and Fathers' Speech to Preverbal Infants"; and Jerome Bruner, *Child's Talk: Learning to Use Language* and "The Ontogenesis of Speech Acts."

the impression they are not quite catching the child's words. There are no words to catch, only random strings of babbled sounds with recognizable, correctly produced question or statement intonation contours. The sounds may accidentally be similar to some of those found in adult English . . . the intonation contours are carried over from the babbling stage into the later period.[25]

As playful, and as clever, and as animated as Huck's sentences might appear, the reader immediately recognizes that they come from a person who has not passed into literacy. They violate rules of spelling, grammar, even syntax. Huck uses too many "ain'ts," he ends too many sentences with prepositions, he confuses *good* and *well*. He could not care less about literacy and its rules. Huck doesn't "break" the rules, because he doesn't know them. The authority figure in his life, his father, Pap, has fed him pap. And, according to the Widow Douglas's plan, a lesson in literacy for Huck amounts to little more than a lesson in morality. So Huck's attitude toward language carries one of the themes of the novel—to hell with authority.

Like today's gang members, Huck is a survivor. He knows that at a fundamental level he functions without a sense of internalized authority. He's a scofflaw, disinterested in those fine distinctions between right and wrong. The social fabric has not wrapped itself around Huck. No matter: he wants to have a good time; he craves action. But he also knows that his life has been broken, and so he founds his own family: Huck joins a gang. Led by his best friend, Tom Sawyer, the gang swears to fight for one another to the death; they pass messages back and forth in secret code; they shake hands with special grips. They own a knife and a gun, which they pass around at opportune times. They go off on adventures and make up their own rules and work out their

---

[25]Breyne Arlene Moskowitz, "The Acquisition of Language," 147.

own punishments. Most nights, they never go home, for they have no place to which they can go home.

But outside forces work on Huck to try to bring him back into society, to have him "make" something of himself. That can be accomplished, Twain sees, only through literacy. But he clearly has mixed feelings about the process. And so the Widow Douglas and her sister, Aunt Polly, set out to teach Huck how to spell correctly and how to read the Bible intelligently. They also expect Huck to dress up in "Sunday clothes" to look like a civilized young man. In literacy, lots of things can be "read," even a person's clothing. Huck can't stand any of it: reading and writing bore him. Bible stories make no sense to him. And what Huck cannot stand, like any good gang youngster, he turns his back on.

So Huck sets off down the Mississippi River on a raft, eventually meeting up with the illiterate outsider Jim. With Jim, he exchanges elaborate stories, listens to Jim's legends and myths of the wandering river, learns what to expect in dreams and what they mean, and how to play practical jokes and how to tell "white lies." Huck forgets the world of spelling for the world of spells. Jim also gives Huck a sense of boundaries and limits. But he does it not by presenting a set of abstract rules—something possible only in literacy—but through moral questions situated in a particular event or circumstance. Jim makes morality concrete.

In one episode on the river, which occurs in chapter fifteen, Jim plays the role of gentle father to Huck. It may be the most morally charged episode in the entire novel. Huck and Jim become separated one night in the fog—Huck in a canoe, Jim on the raft. A raging Mississippi turns their flimsy crafts this way and that, generally disorienting both of them. As the fog clears, Huck sights the raft with Jim on it, who, exhausted by fright and fatigue, has fallen asleep.

Huck lies down next to Jim and when Jim awakens, filled with

joy to see someone he thought had died in the storm, Jim tells
him the entire harrowing story of trying unsuccessfully to find
Huck and finally crying himself to sleep. Huck looks shocked—
he convinces Jim that he must have been dreaming. Jim then
proceeds to assign significance to the dream. For the non-literate,
oral mind, things like fog and storms reverberate with meaning
of mythic proportions. Suddenly feeling superior, Huck decides
to hit Jim with the punchline: He asks Jim what all the debris—
leaves and twigs and logs—that has blown onto the raft means.
Those leaves are real, not dream stuff. Jim stops. He feels humiliated; Huck has tricked him into playing the fool by taking advantage of their friendship. Jim's response turns Huck's words into
a nasty deed. He makes Huck aware of what power he can wield
with just his voice:

> "What do dey stan' for? I's gwyne to tell you. When I got all
> wore out wid work, en wid de callin' for you, en went to sleep,
> my heart wuz mos' broke bekase you wuz los', en I didn' k'yer
> no mo' what become er me and de raf'. En when I wake up en
> fine you back again, all safe and soun', de tears come en I could
> a got down on my knees en kiss yo' foot I's so thankful. En all
> you wuz thinkin' 'bout wuz how you could make a fool uv ole
> Jim wid a lie. Dat truck dah is *trash;* en trash is what people is dat
> puts dirt on de head er dey fren's en makes 'em ashamed."[26]

Huck senses that only a deed can now redeem their friendship, only an act can recharge his words with truth. Otherwise,
virtually everything he says Jim can take as lies. Huck faces the
problem of making his words believable again, of reestablishing
Jim's faith in him. He has reached the heart of orality: "It made
me feel so mean I could almost kissed *his* foot to get him to take
it back." It takes Huck some time, but that's what he does: "It
was fifteen minutes before I could work myself up to go and

----

[26]Mark Twain, *The Adventures of Huckleberry Finn*, 94–95.

humble myself to a nigger—but I done it, and I warn't ever sorry
for it afterwards, neither. I didn't do him no more mean tricks,
and I wouldn't done that one if I'd a knowed it would make him
feel that way."

Jim teaches Huck a powerful lesson—Huck must always take
responsibility for his words. He has to think seriously about every
word. They can hurt; and a joke can backfire. Jim, the illiterate,
has given Huck an inkling of the literate world where right and
wrong, good and bad, inform every sentence. Jim of course does
not know how to read or write. He's far from literacy. Rules and
regulations do not guide his behavior. But in his black, oral
world, stories and myths teach the same kinds of truth: a person
does not treat others in mean and nasty ways. Who should know
better than a slave, who has been robbed of his right to the self
he possesses, and robbed of his wife and daughter?

By the end of the novel, Huck knows he has to make a choice.
If he stays with Aunt Polly and the Widow Douglas, he will be
able to rely less and less on his tongue. As he grows older, he will
have to learn to read and write. In 1885, when *Huck Finn* was
published, with industrialization in full swing, success—money
and position—required literacy. The business world, that is to
say the white, managerial world, demands literates. The *New
England Journal of Education* is breathing down Huck's neck. If he
stays with the Widow Douglas, he will have to assume authority
for his actions, which will involve the most radical shift in his
young life. He will have to become literate. That will be the
means of establishing his membership in the white world. But
Huck can only see it as enslavement—to a constricting books-
and-Bible, spelling-and-Sunday-school world. Huck loves his
freedom, but it is an adolescent version, measured by freedom
from all rules, and not by a freedom to make choices, or to
understand complex issues. It's a freedom that equates broad,
open spaces with liberation, and disregards the vastness of the
soul. So Huck turns his back on it all and decides to "light out
for the territory."

Change the time, put a weapon in his hands, a little rougher language in his mouth, and Huck could pass for a dropout like Bopete or Sidewinder. More likely, though, once in the territory Huck would see the light, return to school, struggle with literacy, and land a decent job. Jim has no such options, and as generation after generation of Jims drifted into ghettos and the slums in the inner cities, downcast and cast out, they became raw recruits for new, more frustrated, more violent gangs. In that sense, then, the novel is about Jim, whose troubles really begin when the novel ends and his owners have set him "free." But free to do what? What jobs can he land? Huck's freedom to leave must be set against Jim's enslavement to stay put. What Huck sees as slavery, Jim can only perceive as freedom. Huck can of course enjoy the luxury of staying put and finding freedom through reading and writing.

But Huck never takes his sentences into literacy, for he refuses to deal with authority. Twain has made that virtually impossible. Huck has no mother and a drunken father; Jim has lost his wife and daughter; Aunt Polly is a spinster; Miss Douglas has lost her husband; and Tom Sawyer grew up in an orphanage.

So even though we read a magnificent novel by a brilliant writer, Huck can only come off as a magician, not an author. If he expects to be an author, he must himself have a sense of authority. As Huck recedes into the background in the telling of this story, Mark Twain comes forward as the real author, the real literate genius. The moment for Huck to become truly literate seems to have passed him by. Twain implies this when Huck conflates spoken sounds with the written word. What we read on the page is some transfiguration of Huck's speech, made visible through the miracle of typesetting. It is as if some photograph of his speech had been taken with a magic camera. (Twain was born in 1835, the same year the first kindergarten opened in

Europe and the camera was invented.) Linguistics, of course, recognizes two languages: the one we speak, and the other, orthographically and grammatically correct, that appears on the printed page. They are radically different in what they convey.

Huck has been stopped short. He cannot make the transition from orality to serious reading and writing. However mysterious the link between orality and literacy, it involves an ability to abide by an absolutely strict set of rules of grammar and syntax and spelling. Rule and regulation serve as the bridge from orality to literacy. To travel to the literate side, a person must accept authority. Traditionally that acceptance comes easily in an infant's life through the father.

Twain shows us just how desperately Huck needs that connection in the turning point of the novel. Huck faces the choice of turning Jim in to the authorities as a runaway slave. When he finally decides not to turn Jim in to Miss Watson, he makes his choice about his new father—about a dear friend. Mulling over the decision in his mind, Huck remembers that crucial moral moment in his life, and how glad Jim "was when I come back out of the fog." He wrestles with the idea of sending Jim back into slavery, and struggles to write a note to Miss Watson:

> Miss Watson your runaway nigger Jim is down here two mile below Pikesville and Mr Phelps has got him and he will give him up for the reward if you send.
>
>   Huck Finn

The note is curious. It violates grammar—number and agreement, "two mile"—and disregards all punctuation, except for one final period. He has managed to scrawl one meandering stream of prose. The note, written to an authority, itself carries no trace of authority. Huck stares at it, this alien object, struggles with the idea and finally tears it up: he decides to trick the authorities about Jim instead. But he not only tears up this single note, he tears up—rips forever—his connection to letters, to that "other" world, to literate authority. Huck turns his back at that moment on the civilized world, and faces the territory.

How can Huck act any other way? Pap, his own father, has abused him both physically and verbally. His newfound father, Jim, has been enslaved, and bought and sold as an object. Huck escapes the tyranny of his own father through a trick, and secures Jim's freedom by a trick as well. Without a sense of authority, like today's young dropouts, Huck relies on tricks and devious schemes to deal with tough choices.

Even writing a novel about him can only be pulled off with a trick, a practical joke. For that's what *The Adventures of Huckleberry Finn* remains—a trick, a sleight-of-hand transcription. Huck has put his speech patterns on a piece of paper, a mark left like a lipstick blot. But he has not written a prose that adheres to or even recognizes rules of grammar, punctuation, or spelling.

In the nineteenth century, literacy began to stand out as something that divided classes and races. It began to stand out in such bold relief, in fact, that by 1883, it was necessary to coin the term *literacy*. In the midst of this development, Twain puts Huck on display as a model of orality. It would be difficult to imagine any character conjuring a more interesting story. But Twain also shows us that Huck's education has fallen short: semiliteracy lands· him in a limbo. He needs to complete his education if he hopes to succeed, and get counted in that new category of literate citizens. Otherwise, he can rise no higher than Jim. That is the sad truth of the period, and that is what parents were responding to when they made the decision to send their young sons and daughters off to kindergarten, and that is the decision that parents of poor black children made when they sent their sons and daughters off to Infant Schools. How shocking for Twain's readers that Huck, in a sense, has opted to be black.

Twain, the real literate, has to impress Huck's words on us. With the barest ability to read and write, Huck must rely on an amanuensis. But this is only part of Twain's practical joke. Trickster that he is, Twain pits us, the readers of the novel, against Huck, the speaker of the text. And here, the second part of Twain's trick goes off smack in our faces. As we read, we correct Huck's misspellings, and gaffes of grammar, acting both as readers and editors at the same time. We read and correct each sentence, feeling superior in the process to the semiliterate Huck. Twain neatly turns each and every reader into an Aunt Polly or a Widow Douglas. When Huck lights out for the territory, he is also lighting out from us, the readers, who try to put him into his tight-fitting suit of grammar and spelling. That won't do: Huck won't move into literacy by having someone correct his every utterance. By correcting that benighted, barely literate young man, we automatically feel superior to him. But by turning his speech into prose, we silence him, make him dumb. In essence, we turn him back into an infant—a creature without sound. As readers, we become elite authorities. Or, perhaps more accurately, our elite attitude is revealed through our deep commitment to literacy.

Twain wants to make us understand the incompleteness of an incomplete family by forcing us to complete the family *for* Huck. That's the task the Widow Douglas takes on for herself, and after Huck rejects her, Twain forces us to do the job. He makes us put Huck's play within bounds. Even if we don't think we believe that should happen, he still forces our hand. In the end, Huck would have to "light" from "us," just as fast as he wants to bolt from the Widow Douglas and Aunt Polly—because as readers we impose the same kind of smothering, correcting, authoritarian brand of literacy on Huck. As readers, we know the rules, and Huck does not. We're right, and Huck's not. But rules simply won't work to bring Huck back into literacy. In fact, the rules—authority itself—shuts the door to literacy. That's just the problem—Huck's problem and society's problem today—when the path to literacy has been blocked by broken homes, rules and authority present fierce obstacles, enemies to elude or eliminate.

Huck would first have to learn to read his *own* novel, and

come to recognize the differences between his spoken *lines* and written *sentences*. For better or worse, he has to see that once his sentences touch paper, they are riddled with mistakes. He may speak some vernacular dialect—Twain claims to use a number of them: Mississippi Negro, the extremest form of backwoods South-Western, the ordinary Pike County, and forms of it—but literacy knows *one* and *only one* standard of writing. Even harder for Huck, he has to understand that his errors arise from violating hard-and-fast rules. And if he wants to reach literacy, he has to accept those rules—without question. They will not budge for him, they make no accommodation. Writing adheres to such strict rules precisely as an instrumentality of uniformity and control. Nebrija makes that the basis for his political argument to the Queen, urging her to print, as the most powerful political expression of the Crown, a book of rules for Castillian grammar.

The printing press, one of the earliest precursors of the Industrial Revolution, cranks out uniform bits of knowledge. It makes literacy the perfect mate for nineteenth-century, assembly-line production in America, and so writers understandably pay lots of attention to it during the period. Literacy would make Huck, as it makes everyone, a part of that "machinery." Huck's experiences with Jim down the Mississippi have made him see the way literacy dominates through its insistence on uniformity and rule. That will always hold true: Someone like Monster Kody feels no less victimized by literacy today than Jim—or Huck.

But Twain embodies the other, equally powerful side of literacy. It empowers a person by affording a tool for critical analysis and judgment. Twain, not Huck, has written one of the greatest pieces of fiction in the history of American literature. Precisely because it creates self-reflective individuals, however—a powerful elite—that power can be used to oppress those who are less literate, or who stand outside of literacy altogether. Jim is enslaved with a piece of paper that the Widow Douglas holds; he is likewise set free by another piece of paper, the Emancipation Proclamation.

Reluctantly and sadly, readers have to let Huck light out, because as readers we, just like the Widow Douglas, have tried to enslave him by forcing on him correct rules of spelling and grammar and syntax. The Widow Douglas "owns" Jim but she also makes her strong claim on Huck—through literacy. Huck lights out for the territory, just as Jim fled down the Mississippi to the territory, for his freedom.

When the novel ends, every reader should feel compelled to reexamine his or her own literacy: How did I get here? How did I acquire such a powerful sense of authority? Why am I making all these judgments about such a young boy? In the end, Huck should not run off in our minds as a single youth. He represents scores of young people just like him, who feel frightened and oppressed by literacy, instead of feeling empowered by it. Once a person faces literacy as an enemy, it is hard to ever give its other side, its ability to empower, a real chance.

It comes as a surprise, I think, that a novel filled with such adventures and tricks and fun should turn on a knotty moral issue. At the climax of the novel, Huck decides he would rather burn in everlasting fire than turn Jim back to the authorities: "All right, then, I'll *go* to hell." But Huck has a terrible time deciding what is right, and what is wrong. It's his love for Jim, finally, that makes up his mind. He can only decide, like A. R. Luria's non-literate peasants, situation by situation. But literacy releases people from that kind of concreteness, a concreteness that ties thinking to events. Rather, literacy fosters a critical ability, a capacity for reflective thinking, that enables each person to decide, to think abstractly, about right and wrong. Literacy creates absolute categories, including moral categories of right and wrong.

A literate person meets experience with the idea of correctness. A student can learn a second language by listening and trying to speak it, by living in that country and trying to fend for himself. But that second language called writing can be learned only by first assimilating rules of correctness, and can be practiced only by writing sentences and having them corrected.

The result is that literate people always judge and analyze; literate people always criticize and correct. As part of the process, the literate person feels superior to those who speak in local dialects and write poorly—superior both intellectually and morally. That idea of moral superiority, a feeling that Twain draws out of each reader, as he or she reads *Huck Finn,* shaped the curriculum of teachers' schools in this country throughout the nineteenth century.

Teachers' schools in this country, called Normal Schools, took their name from the French *école normale. Normal* is an odd word, especially when applied to education. No student wants a normal grade—the average C. No child wants to have a normal mind or normal ideas. In its earliest sense, it doesn't describe behavior: *Norma* is a Latin word that means "a carpenter's square," an instrument that carpenters used in the distant past to lay out perpendicular lines and right angles. Only much later did the word get transferred to human behavior. But the transfer makes sense. Being normal prepares one for the geometry of life: keeping on the straight and narrow, standing tall, living on the up-and-up, staying in line, learning to be morally upright. Being normal means not being a slouch. Living at right angles to the world means adopting the right posture and assuming the right attitude. If one is headed in the *right* direction (*recto* means "right"), chances are things will turn out correctly *(recto)*. At least, one won't be *left* out. Being graduated—moving up a degree or two—fits into this geometric scheme. So does climbing the ladder of success, or moving up the corporate ladder.[27]

---

[27]Deviants who fall outside the straight lines of this grid get reputations as "crooked" or turn into "crooks," or act in "kinky" ways. Straights lock onto this grid; gays move off it.

The adept carpenter must hammer his ideals into foundations, walls, and roofs. Through much of history, poets and philosophers compared raising children with raising the most majestic of buildings—churches and cathedrals. Philosophers recognized the profound similarity between enshrining God's breath in a cathedral, and ensouling a child's breath in its body. So that, if one wants to know what the early Church Fathers had to say about education, one must look under the heading *edifice* and *edification*.

All teachers need a carpenter's square—to provide their students with a solid foundation, to make certain they are set securely on the ground, that no wind or storm will tear them apart. Teaching schools in this country were once called "normal schools" because they hoped to graduate upright, solid citizens—pillars of the community. Teachers were the professionals who would ultimately take charge of those poor, slovenly kids in the Infant Schools. Teachers were being schooled in normalcy so they could eventually normalize their charges. This is where the systemic part of the school system narrows. In the best sense, teachers claimed to be architects of the soul. Like magic or miracle, the secular always turns holy when a pupil stands in the midst of wisdom.

The shortest distance between two points, mathematics and common sense tell us, is a straight line. The world musters up all its authority as it tries to apply that bit of geometric wisdom to young people's lives. Teachers and parents urge young kids to get ahead, to get on with their lives, to get it down, or get it done, or get it said, without fooling *around*. While the argument sounds good and looks efficient—a perfect measure of the normal—it may represent only one half of the model for a fully satisfying life. Sometimes it makes sense to take the long way around, to wander in what seems like an aimless way. Huck gains great wisdom and insight by playing and sporting his way down the meandering Mississippi.

In this grid of rule and authority and direction that is laid over every person's life—literacy in its most ruthless form—the most productive path looks like the well-beaten, well-worn one, the one that stares straight and directly ahead: *todo derecho,* as they say in Spanish, "totally right." The ideal way of arriving at the truth in the Middle Ages required getting lost. In the twelfth century, just at the confluence of orality and literacy, following the straight and narrow would have, indeed, been a dangerous choice. For tradition had it that the devil could travel in a straight line only. Which meant that the Prince of Deception *himself* remained most vulnerable to deception and trickery and lies. A zigzag could give him the slip. Mazes gave people practice in labyrinthine thinking and, as a side benefit, practice in out-maneuvering that arch villain. Struggling to make the exit demanded trial and error, hit or miss. The hope was that losing oneself in the center of the maze would not induce panic, but amazement; that working one's way through the entire mazelike process—developing a strategy that could be changed on the spot—would eventually inspire quick thinking and confidence.[28]

Reading a book is like walking through a maze. Readers even talk about losing themselves in an interesting novel. Each sentence, especially those that come from great writers like Mark Twain, takes us on a mazelike journey. We work our way through a line, periodically backing up to regain meaning, until we reach the pleasure of the final period. Literature teaches that the shortest distance—the straight line—does not always yield

---

[28]Daedalus, the artificer and craftsman—and writer—built the Cretan labyrinth for King Minos. Theseus killed the Minotaur, who lived at the center of the labyrinth. Minos' daughter, Ariadne, left a thread in the labyrinth—a narrative thread—for Theseus to find his way out. "Poetical labyrinths" is a name given to a whole body of literature that dates back to Augustan Rome.

the greatest pleasure. Successful storytelling takes a lot of wandering off the beaten path; joke telling, too. To make errors is to be *errant,* to wander—hardly the stuff of morality. Unless—a large word here—*unless* we can find forgiveness after committing an error, in just the way Jim embraces Huck after his practical joke.

So, in a sense, literacy does promote morality, but not always in the normal, geometric way. Wandering might cause a person to wind up back on the grid. A child without literacy who has dropped out of school today, and whom we call "lost," can only be *amazed* in the most damaging, punishing way. He or she is not lost or wandering, in the beneficial way I am describing, but cast adrift—rudderless and without a goal. The child's confusion should alert us to a serious need.

When the *New England Journal of Education* coined the term *literacy,* it set into motion an attitude toward literacy that schools have promulgated, up to the present day. Literacy is presented as a required tool of advancement—one that can enable a person to fill out this form or to complete that contract. Instead of being used to liberate people, to set them off on their adventures, literacy places them more solidly on the geometric grid of an administered world. Most teachers, overwhelmed by the sheer number of students, by hours of meetings and endless paperwork, find that aspect of literacy attractive. They simplify their lives by keeping their students occupied and quiet, by assigning mostly rote tasks—busywork that can be handled without elaborate instruction.

Class discussions, the vibrant heart of literacy, eat into a very busy schedule. When parents complain that their children cannot read or write very well, teachers respond by piling on more work—time-consuming, tedious chores that students dutifully slog their way through. They memorize rules of correct grammar and punctuation, they try to figure out where to place the apostrophe of missing letters and the apostrophe of possession. Students absorb their lessons passively, much the way they sit and soak up information from the TV. The result is that literacy programs are put in place that ultimately degrade young people into consumers—of goods and images. Medical workers and manufacturers define their needs when they are young, and educators when they get older.

As soon as I begin to describe the classroom experience, I walk into a trap. I act as if problems with learning to read and write can be fixed solely in the classroom, and I assign the problem to the "school system." I give the illusion that the problem can be repaired with money or tinkering, or a skillful combination of the two. Far worse, I make it seem that the problem that is running rampant throughout this country is something that newspapers and books and educators call *illiteracy*. As soon as I take the problem out of the home and place it in the classroom, I turn my attention from education and focus on schooling. The shift is a dramatically decisive one. Once the student adopts the mentality of schooling, he or she comes to realize that anything that can be learned must be taught. That is, it must be delivered by a teacher. Schooling assumes that students are ignorant, and if they pay the right attention and the right amount of tuition, they can learn to be literate and smart.

But as I have tried to suggest in this chapter, the problem is *not* that young people have a difficult time becoming literate. They have a difficult time becoming literate when things fall apart—the connections to family, the connection to voice, the connection to play. Their difficulty is compounded by schools that treat literacy as a commodity and use a delivery system to satisfy its consumers, and diagnostic testing to measure overall success. Instead of treating reading and writing as dynamic processes that evolve out of orality, institutionalized delivery systems reduce reading and writing to a credential called "literacy." Such an attitude enables teachers to deliver literacy to passive

recipients called students. Most parents and educators exacerbate the problem by taking for granted that all learning necessarily results from teaching—that learning is class activity in all
senses, in which authority hands down information. The *con* of
consciousness, the "withness" I have pointed to that emanates
out of group orality, usually does not inform the classroom
beyond the earliest years of schooling.

Sometimes the process of teaching in a classroom trips upon
itself and illuminates the truth in an instant. Such moments allow
a glimpse, as it were, backstage, behind all the painted scenery.
I was fortunate to have a student who enabled me to see into the
formation of a literate mind. This vision came in a most peculiar
way—through someone who stood so far outside the traditional
system that he opened a crack the rest of us might do well to peer
through.

This young college student of mine—I will call him Maxwell—was all but given up by the school system. He suffered
from such severe reading disorders that his high school counselor
cautioned him not to think about college. Nevertheless, his parents badgered and bothered him until he sent off for a few college
applications. Because of his poor grades and low board scores, he
got rejected everywhere. After interviewing Maxwell, the Claremont colleges agreed to admit him as a special student. This
meant that he would have to maintain a grade point average of
2.5 or better for the first year, and that he could not have any
incompletes on his record for that first year. He would have to
complete each class—no matter how rough things got for him.
His parents urged him on. His friends rallied around him.

He did remarkably well. But in four years of college, he had
not read one book. In the strictest sense, he had not written one
paper. Instead, he had worked out an ingenious way of bringing
books to life. Friends read chapters out loud to him. He would

then retell the argument in his own words to see if he had gotten it right. The group would discuss his responses, and move on. When it came time to turn in papers, Maxwell would dictate them to a friend, who would type them out in rough draft. The friend would read each page out loud slowly to see if Maxwell wanted anything revised. In his Senior Seminar, he received an A + . At graduation, he strode across the stage, holding his diploma high over his head, proud and happy. And triumphant.

I must call Maxwell a literate young man. His sentences sparkle. He can hear a clunker because he's so finely tuned to rhythm. He delights in that sense of pleasure as an argument nears its inevitable conclusion. In class, he fired off witty wisecracks that brought discussions into focus. His friends called him The Punster. He claims Puck and Huck as distant cousins. He is as articulate and wonderfully devilish as Huck. His dyslexia had permitted him to drop out of the competition without irritating his parents. On the contrary, he got lots of attention. He became a well-mannered gang of one.

Why did Maxwell, so seemingly cut off from reading and writing, turn out such brilliant work? How could that young man, so dyslexic that he found it painful to read a single sentence, serve as a model of what we want from our students? Despite the odds, something clicked for Maxwell. He became more curious about ideas during college and increasingly eager to see his oral utterances turn into permanent marks on the page.

I gradually came to see that Maxwell and his friends, out of mutual concern, had formed a close-knit community. Unknowingly, they had replicated that medieval phenomenon that has been called by historians "textual communities."[29] One member of the community, who knew how to read and write, would gather around him interested members of the larger group and read slowly and deliberately from a text. They would

---

[29]Brian Stock, *The Implications of Literacy.*

all discuss the passages together. In this way, the group became
alphabetized and more tightly connected. While they themselves were not literate, their own perceptions came to be
shaped by literate sentences. I have called this process alphabetization.[30]

In groups of this kind, it is not just Maxwell, let's say, who
benefits from the discussion. Since everyone explores ideas together, as a collective, every person learns something. Most
important, because problems with reading and writing often
involve problems with authority, in Maxwell's solution authority
becomes decentralized. Learning is probably the activity that
least needs manipulation from others. Which means that in
Maxwell's community each and every person has not only the
opportunity but the incentive to take responsibility for himself or
herself. No one treats Maxwell as an inferior illiterate. The words
have been freed from the page and turned back into orality so
that everyone in the group can more equally hear and understand. Maxwell in particular had to approach people with an
openness and an unusual trust. He came to others for whatever
knowledge they had accumulated. For him, people were living
books. Most students know what to expect from other people
because they have all been schooled the same way. But in Maxwell's case, he really stood outside the main corridors of instruction. The world really remained fresh and new to him, and so did
people. He had managed to turn schooling back into education.
He had learned to nurture himself.

Think about Maxwell's dyslexia not as a disorder but as an
internalization of something that went wrong at home. Think of
him as more or less the way that most young men and women
come to school these days. In that sense, he is representative.

---

[30]The practice continued in preindustrial America: "It was a common practice
in shops still tied to preindustrial work rhythms for someone to be hired to read
the newspaper aloud while workers performed their tasks" (Zboray, "Antebellum Reading and the Ironies of Technological Innovation," 194).

And his solution might be taken as a representative model, as well. For if we take away Maxwell's dyslexia, his educational experience more closely resembles that of most schools several decades ago. Before the era of electronic mass culture, elementary and high school classrooms used to be textual communities of the sort that Maxwell, by necessity, re-created with his friends out of the need for sheer survival. (We can usually rely on the wisdom of young people to find solutions to their problems, even if those solutions sometimes seem radical and antisocial.)

Teachers used to be able to transport children to fabulous lands by recounting a fairy tale or a myth. The room filled with mystery and suspense through the magic of one simple instrument: the teacher's voice. Most of the time, there was not even a book in plain view; the teacher knew the story by heart, or enough of the details to keep the yarn spinning. The children chattered. They acted out the stories, they took turns retelling them. They interrupted, asked questions, begged for more. Sometimes, they even learned a poem or two by heart. When the bell rang, they hurried home to act out their own fantasies. When they got bored, they had no TV to switch on. They were compelled to make up their own games.

The greatest gift we can give, not only to each young generation, but to teachers, is to reinvigorate the classroom by filling it once again with human voices. To do that, the present stranglehold of reading instruction has got to be broken. We need to take a lesson from my student Maxwell. Just as we miss the real problem by referring to young people as *illiterates,* we look past the solution by focusing sharply on that narrowly defined term *literacy,* as if the key to reading and writing were found solely in letters—as if literacy were to be unlocked by opening books.

In the last half century there has been a
great increase in awareness of the value of
the home. (It cannot be helped if this
awareness came first out of an understanding of the effect of the bad home.) We
know something of the reasons why this
long and exacting task, the parents' job of
seeing their children through, is a job
worth doing; and, in fact, we believe that
it provides the only real basis for society,
and the only factory for the democratic
tendency in a country's social system. . . .

I am concerned with the mother's relation to her baby just before the birth and
in the first weeks and months after birth. I
am trying to draw attention to the immense contribution to the individual and
to society that the ordinary good mother
with her husband in support makes at the
beginning, and which she does simply
through being devoted to her infant. . . .

[We must strive] to give moral support
to the ordinary good mother, educated or
uneducated, clever or limited, rich or
poor, and to protect her from everyone
and everything that gets between her baby
and herself. We all join forces in enabling
the emotional relationship between the
mother and her new baby to start and to
develop naturally. This collective task is an

> extension of the job of the father, of the
> father's job at the beginning, at the time
> when his wife is carrying, bearing and
> suckling his infant; in the period before the
> infant can make use of him in other ways.
>
> —D. W. Winnicott, "A Mother's Contribution
> to Society," *Home Is Where We Start From*

Every literate person reads through a book like this one with a growing anticipation—that the last chapter will eventually reach some climax, preferably a satisfying solution. I have no solution to offer. After spending countless hours with the subject, I can only conclude the following: No solution to what has commonly come to be called the literacy problem *can* be, or ought to be, attempted. By definition, literacy is not something isolable that can be attended to, repaired, and made whole, in the classroom or in the workshop. Literacy is the raw material out of which we have fashioned our culture; it informs every social relationship and institution. America's growing problem with literacy announces a radical fissure, a shifting of the very bedrock of culture. Anything short of a wholesale revision of the way we live our lives constitutes a tinkering with literacy and can only end in frustration and a further exacerbation of the problem. I am not being polemical here, or trying to shock through exaggeration. I can only bring news of the enormity of the change required to bring literacy back into the mainstream of life. A solution is simply impossible except in that word's fundamental and radical sense. Everyone concerned—citizens, educators, politicians, parents, anyone who has a stake in the survival of this democracy—must decide that literacy is worth saving, and make a firm resolve to create the conditions for a healthy literacy to flourish. Whatever it takes, however huge the undertaking, we must all be willing to sit down in small groups and discuss how to halt the horrible and inevitable deterioration of our young people under current conditions. Whatever has gotten in the way of literacy over the years must be rooted out by each and every one of us.

Teaching reading and writing in America, in 1994, is different from teaching those subjects at any other time in this country. Reading and writing Received Standard English have become highly charged political activities. Many young people of color equate English with the dominant culture; to speak "white talk" is to surrender, to lose ethnic identity, synonymous for them with giving up their ethnic solidarity. Many of these young people have consciously chosen to turn away from the classroom because they have concluded it has nothing of value to offer. "School is corny," one New York teenager defiantly announces to a *New York Times* reporter, and confesses that he walked out of school at age nine.[1] (He's been dealing drugs for the past seven years, been shot at several times, and imprisoned twice.) He had entered into a conspiracy, unwittingly, unknowingly, and unconsciously, with his teachers, in dropping out. The youngster looks stupid in class; the teacher piles on more work. The child rebels. The teacher throws up her hands. Why stay in school when there are no worthwhile jobs anyway? Why try to learn when it all seems so boring? The combination is lethal. The street has become the school of last resort. The money is better, and the hours are certainly shorter.

The result of this state of affairs is the fragmentation and retreat into violence that now plague most cities and many small

---

[1] Erik Eckholm, "Teen-Age Gangs," 16.

towns in this country. To safeguard their political and physical isolation, street youths have contrived their own language, marked by slang, jargon, made-up words, abbreviations, and a large amount of swearing. These languages bestow power on their speakers through exclusivity. They speak to no one else in the world but a small cadre of homies. Anyone outside the group needs an informer or a translator to break into the inner circles.

In these street argots, power coalesces around what Henry Louis Gates calls "identity politics," a cover for racial or group solidarity. These vernacular lingos occupy the counter-position to Taught Learned Latin, in that they are always spoken and never taught. Power passes through word-of-mouth; learning to speak is in itself a rite of passage, permitting entrance into the inner sanctum of the group or gang. A child cannot be a gang-ster—even if he owns all the right clothes—unless he can sound like a gangster. In street terms, he's got to walk his talk.

No one from what is perceived as the dominant culture, no one, that is, who speaks and writes elevated English, can ever hope to break through that linguistically constructed barricade. It is too solidly built at too fundamental a level. Moreover, this linguistic artifact has spread from the inner cities to other, more affluent young people. Tough talk and jerry-rigged grammar have become stylish. The only way to induce young people to move into the forbidding world of literacy is by radically redefin-ing literacy so that it does not begin when a child begins to learn the letters of the alphabet. It must begin, and be understood to begin, much earlier: in the infant's first attempts at regular and rhythmic breathing. That means it begins as far back as sucking at a breast, and includes all the forms of baby talk and baby listening imaginable—nonsense syllables, giggling, rhymes, peek-a-boo games, word games, and on and on.

The task is both simple and impossibly difficult. An entire government mobilized behind the cause of illiteracy cannot pry the problem loose from its moorings. Even the school system, with all of its bureaucratic weightiness, has only made matters worse. Such a fundamental move can only begin with each person, in each family, inside each neighborhood.

I am not proposing a recovery program, or a self-help program in self-esteem for young people. The obstacles to literacy are not dropouts who tote guns and shoot drugs, but a consumer culture that breeds economic inequality and racial suspicion and hatred. It is too easy to confuse low esteem and lack of self-confidence with loss of literacy. When people have no jobs, no hope, no chances in life, they can have no self-esteem—even if they write like angels. Pop psychology, the culture of self-love, can provide no help with those who have turned away from the alphabet. No quick fix can turn them around. Twelve-step community programs only exacerbate the problem and generate more enemies who pass themselves off as gang gurus.

I have described in this book the historical and traditional way that people journey into literacy without leaving their early familiarity with orality behind. I have also tried to show that the traditional route has been destroyed, and the borders closed to future travel. I have outlined the detours that young people have taken into gangs and violence and drugs, in their attempts to claim a voice. Without proper immersion in orality, however, no one can really hope to set out on that journey, let alone reach a destination in literacy.

I use the passages from D. W. Winnicott as an epigraph to this chapter to emphasize that the process of literacy starts with the baby's mouth working the mother's breast. Illiterates show up in the classroom; dropouts show up on the streets. But they represent no more than the symptoms, the results, of a much deeper, more profound relational problem that begins in the home. What educators describe as illiteracy is a response by young people—an attempt at reorganization for survival—to a break in the normal ordering of their lives—at their schools, in the economy, with authority. But it begins with a break in the home. To mend that break, we must first recognize the enormous importance of the mother as her influence works its way through the everyday life of a youngster, as well as through the rest of that young person's life.

When parents and educators complain about a problem with literacy in this country, they unknowingly point to that systemic movement of fluidity and fluency *(in-fluence)* that flows from mother to child. *Fluidity* and *fluency* resonate in the study of literacy with powerful metaphoric meaning. The infant listens to sounds and learns to speak in association with that tiny stream of milk. That fluency begins at the mother's breast, and the headwaters have been dammed. The breast, in all of its implications and reverberations, has been excised from the household. It is one thing to reject the milk of human kindness (the milk, that is, that creates humankind), it is quite another to deliberately cut it out of a culture. However different the impulse, the results remain the same.

In a previous chapter, I pointed out that when the early medieval Church took up the business of education, it also took on a new identity as the alma mater, nursing its novitiates from a socially constructed *alma ubera,* or milk-brimming breast. The young entered the Church to be educated (nursed) by priests who were often described as having breasts.[2] The inside of a cathedral spoke of interiority. By entering the holy building, the young took into their very beings this life-giving solution that mothering Christianity had to offer. So fundamental was this maternal connection, so integral to the life of the congregation, that cathedrals posted warnings, in the form of grotesque carvings affixed to the exterior of the buildings, against rejecting that relationship. First recorded in a building document of 1295, these gargoyles, in

---

[2]Christ, too, is often depicted in the late twelfth and early thirteenth centuries with breasts.

the shape of hideous animals or deformed humans, projected straight out from the gutters of ecclesiastical buildings (and, later, from town houses) and were used to direct rainwater away from the walls of buildings and onto passersby strolling below.

The word *gargoyle* derives from the Latin *gurgulio*, "gullet" or "windpipe," and becomes, in Early French, *gargouille*, "throat," and *gargouiller*, "to gargle." Gargoyles put on public display the idea of disgorging. If the priests inside the buildings were giving suck to their congregation, gargoyles represented the opposite movement on the outside of the buildings in their inability to take anything in. Medieval artists designed these monsters as huge gaping gullets, which, in the right season, spurted a continual stream of water, creating a deliberate nuisance for anyone walking below. Through these gruesome technological innovations, architects managed to redirect rainwater from the surface of the building and, in the process, to broadcast an important theological message.

Gargoyles have been variously interpreted. But in one view, they make graphically plain how the rejection of the alma mater could turn a Christian into the most monstrous and devilish character imaginable. They enact the topos of nourishment inside the cathedral transmogrified on the outside of the building into elimination and rejection—growth and change in the interior became a frozen horror on the exterior. The gargoyle flies from the face of the building virtually all head with little body, an inchoate and incomplete creature. The gargoyle knows one solution only—water—which will sustain life for a time, but will not nourish it. Their beady eyes stare off into the distance, situated too high up on any Gothic structure for the viewer to make eye contact, constant reminders to everyone of the awful consequence—the disfiguring, technological consequence—of rejecting the true nourishment that only the Mother Church could provide. The solution flows from their wide-open mouths, spilling into the street below—nourishment and fluency falling away as an emetic stream, a parody of religious literacy, a travesty of the lactating Church.[3]

Modern technological innovations like baby bottles and formulas make it possible for babies to reject their mothers' *alma ubera*. What might be called a thickening of the child's development through contact and deep nourishment ceases at that moment of the separation of the baby from its mother. A certain grotesqueness sets in, fluency takes on the shady character of gray water. This may seem far-fetched, to argue by a seven-hundred-year old analogy, but certainly a good many young people these days have taken on a gargoyle ferocity. They stand outside the classic institutions, continually spouting, as if a general outpouring were the equivalent of fluency, creating a nuisance for everyone who comes in contact with them. But in the course of their lives they have taken in little that is nourishing. Indeed, in many cases they refuse to be nourished, for they see nothing off in the distance but a grim and bleak future.

I "read" that aberrant behavior as a sign that young people want something better in their lives, that they need something more nourishing. I view their stance as a plea for help—a positive sign. That dismal future they stare into, every one of us shares with them.

To effect changes in literacy levels in this country, nothing short of the ideal can be tolerated, because the ideal describes what used to be called normal. Everyone who reads this has a choice: The eradication of drugs and violence and illiteracy is possible, but not through some governmental program, or some bureaucratic agency. Bureaucracies and agencies have caused the problem. The solution can come only if teachers and parents and administrators first hold a vision of what life should look like, and then be willing to work to realize it.

Every mother—from poor mothers who need to work to

---

[3]For an analysis of gargoyles, see Michael Camille, *Image on the Edge: The Margins of Medieval Art.*

survive, to rich mothers who work as a luxury—needs to return to the home, at least until their babies move out of infancy. Even after that they need to make their presence felt in the home. If healthy, these mothers need to breast-feed their infants. That means, of course, economic stability in the house and adequate nutritional levels for the mother. It also means that the mother cannot live on the streets but must take up full residence in the home.

How can we possibly make a structural change of such staggering proportions? I certainly do not intend for authorities to enforce the return of mothers back into the house. Rather, the question is How can we create the conditions—in a sense, how can we, with the most benign effort, remove all the hindrances to the mother's presence—to make it possible for mothers, and fathers, to carry on normal social roles inside their houses with their children?

I do not argue for the family because of some intrinsic importance I think it holds, or because I subscribe to something called "family values"—a code hiding a conservative political and social agenda. I am interested in the family insofar as it has created a particular form of literacy, which in turn has shaped the human being we know and, even more crucially, have come to expect.

Like all relationships, the one between family and literacy is reciprocal. Literacy has kept the family alive—through discussions, critical analysis, stories, arguments, and conversation. Insofar as the computer has helped to erase the inner core of the human being—conspiring, that is, in the obliteration (*ob-littera* = "the erasure of letters") of stories and storytelling—it has hastened the destruction of the family. The family wraps itself around the dynamic core of orality. Each member of the family, like a member of a tribe, carries those shared stories with them. The family narrates a life together.[4]

---

[4]For a discussion of the narrated self, see Jerome Bruner, "Autobiography and the Self," in his *Acts of Meaning*. Bruner discusses the ways in which young children become socialized into certain narrative patterns. These patterns, he contends, shape the child's soul, in a certain way "create" the child's life.

That's the first step—a mother and a father. Once the child moves off to school, however, the family's influence needs to follow the child and surround him or her. Play is a slow-moving stream that carries the child from home through the earliest years of schooling. Any attempt to truly educate, to teach young children to read and write dams up that stream. Preschool and kindergarten and Head Start programs—however well intentioned they might be—interrupt a child's flow of education.

As teachers become increasingly desperate about literacy levels in this country, they cannot wait to get their hands on young children in nervous anticipation of teaching them to read and write. Teachers react by seizing control of the child at the age of three, or even two. That is simply too early a time to bring them to literacy. It is a time before they have experienced a full immersion in orality born out of that intimate connection with their mothers, without the intervention of words, letters, writing, and texts.

As nerve-wracking as it might be, parents have to take a big risk and be willing to hold off the time when they expect their children to take up reading and writing. They will struggle, in their hearts, with a most serious question: Have I launched my daughter on her way to literacy? I have two responses. First, placing pressure on a child's eye to read a text rather than training the ear to listen carefully and to repeat orally only inhibits full literate development. It disregards an absolutely crucial and necessary stage in the developmental process in which oral practice becomes the close companion of the word visually read.

My second response: Confronted with an almost endless variety of electronic gadgets—from TVs to CDs, from videos to video games—children must be allowed sufficient time to express themselves. A fertile imagination may be the best protection—

indeed, it may be the *only* protection—against an onslaught of technologically delivered images. It may be the only way of carrying our youngest generations of citizens back from the very edge of despair.

For virtually every mother and father, every politician running for election or reelection, every principal and teacher, "full literacy" is a desired and stated goal. But they all seem to look past the paradoxical nature of literacy. The way to literacy does not lie through literacy. An early immersion in literacy in fact only blocks the way. As teachers and parents become more and more nervous about their children's ability to read and write, they need to back off from the natural desire to increase the pressure for more literacy instruction.

Let history teach us its powerful lesson. Let us take youngsters out of the linguistic limbo they find themselves in and move them back into the key experience they have missed—orality. The clues to a developed adulthood may lie in this key shift, moving out of the home and infancy into a primary school environment. This is the lesson that my dyslexic student, Maxwell, offers all of us the chance to learn. The teaching of literacy has to be founded on a curriculum of song, dance, play, and joking, coupled with improvisation and recitation. Students need to hear stories, either made up by the teacher or read out loud. They need to make them up themselves or try to retell them in their own words. Teachers need to provide continual instruction in the oral arts—from primary school, through the upper grades, and on into college. Past generations were more literate because they learned to speak well, and acquired an increased vocabulary through rhetorical practice. Good readers grow out of good reciters and good speakers.

One of the miracles of literacy, as I said earlier, is the future tense. Whether we feel responsible for the current social mess or not, let me report that for young people today, the future is a tense one: they don't feel they have much of one. Of course the solutions are difficult and maybe even impossible. But if young people are careening toward disaster, they are taking us with them.

That should give everyone pause. To reach a solution, we must first of all want to reach one. Otherwise, nothing can help. And to determine that course, only the simplest technique will help to get us there, one born out of the very bedrock of literacy.

We need to gather into small groups—textual communities— and discuss this most devastating issue, the time bomb that has already gone off, and figure out how to minimize the damage, and more important, how to make certain that future generations do not self-destruct. And here we can benefit from literacy's other miracle, the counter-factual. In those small groups it is extremely important to imagine, to describe in the most vivid and concrete detail, what the world might look like. Indeed, what we want it to look like. The future tense and the counter-factual —if those two wither and die, if we can no longer, as adults, dream purposively about the future, then all is lost. Then literacy has surely drained out of this culture. And this book is nothing more than an irrelevant dream.

WORKS CITED

ABRAHAMS, ROGER D. "A Performance-Centered Approach to Gossip." *Man: The Journal of the Royal Anthropological Institute* 5 (1970): 280–95.

ACKERMAN, DIANE. *A Natural History of the Senses.* New York: Random House, 1990.

ANDERSON, DAVID C. "Street Guns." *New York Times Magazine,* February 14, 1993.

APPLE, RIMA D. *Mothers and Medicine: A Social History of Infant Feeding, 1890–1950.* Madison: The University of Wisconsin Press, 1987.

APTED, MEHADEV L. *Humor and Laughter: An Anthropological Approach.* Ithaca: Cornell University Press, 1985.

ARMEN, JEAN-CLAUDE. *Gazelle-Boy.* New York: Universe Books, 1974.

AUGUSTINE. *Opera Omni.* 7 vols. Paris: J.-P. Migne, 1887.

AUSTIN, JOHN L. *How to Do Things with Words.* Cambridge: Harvard University Press, 1962.

BAIN, BRUCE, ed. *The Sociogenesis of Language and Human Conduct.* New York and London: Plenum Press, 1983.

BAKHTIN, MIKHAIL. *The Dialogic Imagination: Four Essays.* Ed. Michael Holquist. Austin: University of Texas Press, 1981.

BEATTIE, JAMES. *Essays: On Poetry and Music, as They Effect the Mind; On Laughter and Ludicrous Composition; On the Utility of Classical Learning.* Edinburgh: W. Creech, 1778.

BENEDICT. *Acta Sanctorum Ordinis S. Benedictii.* 9 vols. Paris: 1668–1701.

BENJAMIN, WALTER. *Illuminations: Essays and Reflections.* Ed. Hannah Arendt. Trans. Harry Zohn. New York: Schocken Books, 1969.

BETTELHEIM, BRUNO. *The Uses of Enchantment: The Meaning and Importance of Fairy Tales.* New York: Vintage Books, 1977.

BING, LÉON. "Confessions from the Crossfire." *L.A. Weekly,* May 6–12, 1988.

———. *Do or Die.* New York: HarperCollins, 1991.

BLEDSTEIN, BURTON J. *The Culture of Professionalism: The Middle Class and the Development of Higher Education in America.* New York: W. W. Norton, 1978.

BLY, ROBERT. "What the Mayans Could Teach to the Joint Chiefs." *New York Times,* July 23, 1993.

BONAVENTURE, BROTHER. "The Teaching of Latin in Later Medieval England." *Medieval Studies* 23 (1961): 1–20.

BROWNLEE, W. ELLIOT, and MARY M. BROWNLEE. *Women in the American Economy: A Documentary History, 1675 to 1929.* New Haven: Yale University Press, 1976.

BRUNER, JEROME. *Acts of Meaning.* Cambridge: Harvard University Press, 1990.

———. *Child's Talk: Learning to Use Language.* New York: W. W. Norton, 1983.

———. "The Ontogenesis of Speech Acts." *Journal of Child Language* 2 (1975): 1–18.

BRUNER, JEROME, and V. SHERWOOD. "Early Rule Structure: The Case of Peekaboo." In Mary Gauvain and Michael Cole, eds., *Readings on the Development of Children.* New York: W. H. Freeman and Company, 1993.

BRUNER, JEROME, and SUSAN WEISSER. "The Invention of Self: Autobiography and Its Forms." In David R. Olson and Nancy Torrance, eds., *Literacy and Orality.* Cambridge, Eng.: Cambridge University Press, 1991.

BURGESS, ANTHONY. *On Going to Bed.* New York: Abbeville Press, 1982.

BUZZELL, KEITH A. *The Neurophysiology of Television Viewing: A Preliminary Report.* Privately distributed.

CAILLOIS, ROGER. *Man, Play, and Games.* New York: Free Press, 1961.

CAMILLE, MICHAEL. *Image on the Edge: The Margins of Medieval Art.* Cambridge: Harvard University Press, 1992.

————. "Seeing and Reading: Some Visual Implications of Medieval Literacy and Illiteracy." *Art History* 8, no. 1 (March 1985): 26–49.

CANDLAND, DOUGLAS KEITH. *Feral Children and Clever Animals: Reflections on Human Nature.* New York: Oxford University Press, 1993.

CASE, ROBBIE. *Intellectual Development: Birth to Adulthood.* Orlando, Fla.: Academic Press, 1985.

CETRON, MARVIN, and MARGARET GAYLE. *Educational Renaissance: Our Schools at the Turn of the Twenty-first Century.* New York: St. Martin's Press, 1991.

CHIARO, DELIA. *The Language of Jokes: Analysing Verbal Play.* London: Routledge, 1992.

CHOMSKY, NOAM. *Rules and Representations.* New York: Columbia University Press, 1980.

CIXOUS, HÉLÈNE. "The Laugh of the Medusa." Trans. Keith Cohen and Paula Cohen. *Signs* (Summer 1976): 150–67.

CLARK, EVE W., and HERBERT H. CLARK. *Psychology and Language: An Introduction to Psycholinguistics.* New York: Harcourt Brace Jovanovich, 1977.

CLARKE-STEWART, ALISON. "Infant Day-Care: Maligned or Malignant?" *American Psychologist* 44, no. 2 (February 1989): 266–73.

CLONINGER, ROBERT. "Three Brain Chemical Systems." *Science* 236: 410–16.

CONDON, WILLIAM, and LOUIS SANDER. "Neonate Movement Is Synchronized with Adult Speech: Interactional Participation and Language Acquisition." *Science* (1974): 99–101.

CROSSLEY-HOLLAND, KEVIN, ed. *The Exeter Book Riddles.* New York: Penguin Books, 1979.

CURTISS, SUSAN. *Genie: A Psychoanalytic Study of a Modern-Day "Wild Child."* New York: Academic Press, 1977.

DAVIDSON, CATHY, ed. *Reading in America: Literature and Social History.* Baltimore: The Johns Hopkins University Press, 1989.

DAVIDSON, DONALD. *Truth and Interpretation.* New York: Oxford University Press, 1984.

DIL, ANWAR S., ed. *Language, Structure and Language Use: Essays by Charles H. Ferguson.* Palo Alto: Stanford University Press, 1971.

ECKHOLM, ERIK. "Teen-Age Gangs Are Inflicting Lethal Violence on Small Cities." *New York Times,* January 31, 1993.

EHRMANN, JACQUES, ed. *Game, Play, Literature. Yale French Studies* 41 (1968): 5–167.

ELLIS, GODFREY J. "Youth in the Electronic Environment: An Introduction." *Youth and Society* 15, no. 1 (September 1983): 3–12.

ELMER-DEWITT, PHILIP. "Cyberpunk!" *Time,* February 8, 1992.

FARAL, EDMOND. *Les Jongleurs en France du Moyen Âge.* Paris: H. Champion, 1964.

FERNALD, ANNE, et al. "A Cross-Language Study of Prosodic Modifications in Mothers' and Fathers' Speech to Preverbal Infants." *Journal of Child Language* 16, no. 3 (October 1989): 472–501.

FEUERBACH, ANSELM VON. *Kaspar Hauser: An Account of an Individual Life in a Dungeon, Separated from All Communication with the World, from Early Childhood to about the Age of Seventeen.* London: Simpkin & Marshall, 1833.

FINE, MICHELLE. "Dropping Out of High School, An Inside Look." *Social Policy* (Fall 1985): 43–50.

FISKE, EDWARD B. *Smart Schools, Smart Kids: Why Do Some Schools Work?* New York: Simon & Schuster, 1991.

FOUCAULT, MICHEL. *The Order of Things: An Archaeology of the Human Sciences.* New York: Random House, 1970.

FREUD, SIGMUND. *Jokes and Their Relation to the Unconscious.* New York: W. W. Norton and Company, 1960.

FUCHS, VICTOR. *Women's Quest for Economic Equality.* Cambridge: Harvard University Press, 1988.

GARDNER, JOHN. *October Light.* New York: Alfred A. Knopf, 1976.

GASS, WILLIAM H. "Human, All Too Human." *New York Review of Books* 35 (February 4, 1988): 35.

GEBER, MARCELLE. "The Psycho-Motor Development of African Children in the First Year and the Influence of Maternal Behavior." *Journal of Social Psychology* 47 (1958): 185–95.

GEERTZ, CLIFFORD. *The Interpretation of Culture.* New York: Basic Books, 1973.

GORDIMER, NADINE. *The Essential Gesture.* New York: Alfred A. Knopf, 1988.

GRAUBAUD, STEPHEN R., ed. "America's Childhood." *Daedalus* (Winter 1993).

GREENFIELD, P. M., and J. SMITH. *The Structure of Communication in Early Language Development.* New York: Academic Press, 1976.

HALLIDAY, M.A.K. *Learning How to Mean.* London: Arnold, 1975.

HAVELOCK, ERIC. *The Literate Revolution in Greece and Its Cultural Consequences.* Princeton: Princeton University Press, 1982.

―――. *The Muse Learns to Write: Reflections on Orality and Literacy from Antiquity to the Present.* New Haven: Yale University Press, 1986.

HEILMAN, SAMUEL C. *Synagogue Life: A Study in Symbolic Interaction.* Chicago: University of Chicago Press, 1976.

HEISIG, KARL. "Muttersprache: Ein romanistischer Beitrag zur Genesis eines deutschen Wortes und zur Enstehung der deutsch-franzoesischen Sprachgrenze." *Muttersprache* 22, no. 3 (1954): 144–74.

HIGGINS, TORY E. "Self-Discrepancy: A Theory Relating Self and Affect." *Pyschological Review* 94 (1987): 319–40.

HOEFER, C., and M. C. HARDY. "Later Development of Breast Fed and Artificially Fed Infants." *Journal of the American Medical Association* 96 (1929): 615–19.

HUIZINGA, JOHANN. *Homo Ludens: A Study of the Play Elements in Culture.* New York: Beacon Press, 1955.

HUNGERFORD, T.A.G., ed. *Australian Signpost.* New York: F. W. Cheshire, 1956.

ILLICH, IVAN. *Deschooling Society.* New York and London: Harper & Row, 1972.

―――. *H$_2$O and the Waters of Forgetfulness.* Berkeley: Heyday Books, 1988.

―――. *In the Mirror of the Past: Lectures and Addresses, 1978–1990.* New York and London: Marion Boyars, 1992.

————. *Medical Nemesis*. New York and London: Marion Boyars, 1975.

————. *Shadow Work*. New York and London: Marion Boyars, 1981.

————. *Tools for Conviviality*. New York: Harper & Row, 1973.

————. *Toward a History of Needs*. New York: Pantheon Books, 1978.

ILLICH, IVAN, and BARRY SANDERS. *ABC: The Alphabetization of the Popular Mind*. San Francisco: North Point Press, 1988.

JACK, IAN, ed. *Browning: Poetical Works, 1833–64*. New York: Oxford University Press, 1970.

JANKOWSKI, MARTÍN SÁNCHEZ. *Islands in the Street: Gangs and American Urban Society*. Berkeley and Los Angeles: The University of California Press, 1991.

JENKINS, JOHN WILLIAMS. "Infant Schools and the Development of Public Primary Schools in Selected American Cities Before the Civil War." Unpublished Ph.D. dissertation. University of Wisconsin, 1978.

KAESTLE, CARL F., and MARIS A. VINOVSKIS. *Education and Social Change in Nineteenth-Century Massachusetts*. Cambridge, Eng.: Cambridge University Press, 1980.

KENNEDY, C. W., trans. *The Poems of Cynewulf*. Cambridge: Harvard University Press, 1949.

KLEIN, MALCOLM. *Street Gangs and Street Workers*. New York: Prentice Hall, 1971.

KOZOL, JONATHAN. *Savage Inequalities*. New York: Crown Publishers, 1991.

KROEBER, THEODORE. *Ishi*. Berkeley and Los Angeles: The University of California Press, 1976.

LA BONTY, JAN. "College Students as Readers." Presentation at the Fortieth Annual Meeting of the National Readers' Conference, Miami, Florida, November 1990.

LANE, HARLAN. *The Wild Boy of Aveyron*. New York: Random House, 1978.

LANGER, SUSANNE K. *Philosophy in a New Key*. New York: Charles Scribner's Sons, 1942.

LANHAM, RICHARD. *The Motives of Eloquence: Literary Rhetoric in the Renaissance.* New Haven: Yale University Press, 1976.

LARSON, ERIK. "The Story of a Gun." *Atlantic Monthly,* January 1993, pp. 48–78.

LASCH, CHRISTOPHER. Untitled review. *New York Review of Books,* November 24, 1977, pp. 15–18.

LEFEBVRE, HENRI. *The Production of Space.* Trans. Donald Nicholson-Smith. Oxford and Cambridge, Eng.: Basil Blackwell, 1991.

LEISS, WILLIAM. *The Limits to Satisfaction.* Toronto: University of Toronto Press, 1976.

LICHTENBERG, JAMES. "Reading: Does the Future Even Require It?" *Liberal Education* 79, no. 1 (Winter 1991): 4.

LURIA, A. R. *Cognitive Development: Its Cultural and Social Foundations.* Ed. Michael Cole. Trans. Martin Lopez-Morillas and Lynn Solotaroff. Cambridge: Harvard University Press, 1976.

MACLEAN, PAUL D. "The Triune Brain in Conflict." In P.O. Sifneos, ed., *Psychotherapy and Psychosomatics.* Basel, Switzerland: S. Karger, 1977.

MALSON, LUCIEN. *Wolf Children and the Problem of Human Nature.* New York and London: Monthly Review Press, 1972.

MANNING, STEPHEN. "Rhetoric, Game, Morality, and Geoffrey Chaucer." *Studies in the Age of Chaucer* I (1979): 105–18.

MARKUS, HAZEL, and PAULA NURIUS. "Possible Selves." *American Psychologist* 41 (1986): 954–69.

MARROU, HENRI IRENÉE. *A History of Education in Antiquity.* New York: Sheed and Ward, 1956.

MATURANA, HUMBERTO R., and FRANCISCO J. VARELA. *The Tree of Knowledge: The Biological Roots of Human Understanding.* Cambridge: New Science Library, 1987.

MICHELSEN, G. F. *To Sleep with Ghosts: A Novel of Africa.* New York: Bantam Books, 1992.

MILLER, GEORGE A. "Dictionaries in the Mind." *Language and Cognitive Processes* (Spring 1986): 171–85.

MILLS, D. L., S. A. COFFEY, and H. J. NEVILLE. "Language abilities and cerebral specializations in 10–20 month-olds." In C. Nelson, ed., *Neuro Correlates of Early Cognition and Linguistic Development Symposium*. Society for Research and Child Development, 1992.

MITCHELL, STEPHEN. *Relational Concepts in Psychoanalysis*. Cambridge: Harvard University Press, 1988.

MONTAGU, ASHLEY. *Touching: The Human Significance of Skin*. New York: Columbia University Press, 1972.

MOORE, JOAN W. *Going Down to the Barrio: Homeboys and Homegirls in Change*. Philadelphia: Temple University Press, 1991.

MOSKOWITZ, BREYNE ARLENE. "The Acquisition of Language." In William S-Y. Wang, ed., *The Emergence of Language: Development and Evolution*. New York: W. H. Freeman and Company, 1991.

MULKAY, MICHAEL. *On Humor: Its Nature and Its Place in Modern Society*. Cambridge, Eng.: Basil Blackwell, 1988.

MUMFORD, LEWIS. *The Culture of Cities*. New York: Harcourt Brace and World, 1970.

NEBRIJA, ELIO ANTONIO DE. *Gramatica Castellana*. Texto establecido sobre la edition "princeps" de 1492, por Pascual Galendo Romeo y Luis Ortiz. Madrid, 1946.

NELSON, C. "Neuro Correlates of Early Cognition and Linguistic Development Symposium." In C. Nelson, ed., *Neuro correlates of early cognition and linguistic development symposium*. Presented at Society for Research in Child Development, Seattle, Washington, 1991.

NEWMEYER, FREDERICK J. *Grammatical Theory: Its Limits and Its Possibilities*. Chicago: University of Chicago Press, 1983.

NICOLL, ALLARDYCE. *Masks, Mimes and Miracles: Studies in the Popular Theatre*. London: George G. Harrap and Company, Ltd., 1931.

OGILVY, J.D.A. *"Mimi, scurrae, historiones:* Entertainers in the Early Middle Ages." *Speculum* 38, no. 4 (1963): 603–19.

OLINICK, STANLEY L. "The Gossiping Psychoanalyst." *International Review of Psycho-Analysis* 7 (1980): 441–43.

OLSON, DAVID R., and NANCY TORRANCE, eds. *Literacy and Orality.* Cambridge: Cambridge University Press, 1991.

OLSON, GLENDING. *Literature as Recreation in the Later Middle Ages.* Ithaca: Cornell University Press, 1982.

O'NEILL, MOLLY. "Arming the Armani Set." *New York Times,* January 3, 1993.

ONG, WALTER J. *Orality and Literacy: The Technologizing of the Word.* London and New York: Methuen, 1982.

ORING, ELLIOT. *Jokes and Their Relations.* Lexington: The University Press of Kentucky, 1992.

PALMER, GABRIELLE. *The Politics of Breastfeeding.* London: Pandora Press, 1988.

PANOFSKY, ERWIN. *Idea.* Berlin: Teubner, 1924.

PATTON, R. G., and L. I. GARDNER. *Growth Failure in Maternal Deprivation.* Springfield, Ill.: Charles C. Thomas, 1963.

PEARCE, JOSEPH CHILTON. *Evolution's End: Claiming the Potential of Our Intelligence.* San Francisco: Harper San Francisco, 1992.

PEARS, D. F. *The Development of Wittgenstein's Philosophy.* Oxford: Oxford University Press, 1987.

———. *Wittgenstein.* Cambridge: Harvard University Press, 1986.

PENCE, ALAN R. "Infant Schools in North America, 1825–1840." In *Advances in Early Education and Day Care.* Greenwich, Conn.: JAI Press, 1986.

PHILLIPS, ADAM. *On Kissing, Tickling, and Being Bored: Psychoanalytic Essays on the Unexamined Life.* Cambridge: Harvard University Press, 1993.

POSTMAN, NEIL. *Amusing Ourselves to Death: Public Discourse in the Age of Show Business.* New York: Viking Penguin, 1985.

PRATKANIS, ANTHONY R., STEVEN J. BRECKLER, and ANTHONY G. GREENWALD, eds. *Attitude Structure and Function.* Hillsdale, N.J.: Lawrence Erlbaum Associates, 1989.

PROVENZO, EUGENE F., JR., *Video Kids: Making Sense of Nintendo.* Cambridge: Harvard University Press, 1991.

PULGRAM, E. "Spoken and Written Latin." *Language* 26 (1950): 458–66.

PUTNAM, HILARY. *Mind, Language and Reality.* Philosophical Papers, vol. 2. Cambridge: Cambridge University Press, 1975.

RADIN, PAUL. *The Trickster.* New York: Greenwood Publishers, 1956.

REICH, HERMANN. *Der Mimus.* Berlin: n.p., 1903.

RHEINGOLD, H. L., and H. W. STEVENSON, eds. *Early Behavior: Comparative and Developmental Approaches.* New York: John Wiley & Sons, 1967.

RIFKIN, JEREMY. *Biosphere Politics: A New Consciousness for a New Century.* New York: Crown Publishers, 1991.

RODRIGUEZ, LUIS J. *Always Running: La Vida Loca, Gang Days in L.A.* Willimantic, Conn.: Curbstone Press, 1993.

RYMER, RUSS. *Genie: An Abused Child's Flight from Silence.* New York: HarperCollins, 1993.

SCOTT, MONSTER KODY. *Monster: The Autobiography of an L.A. Gang Member.* New York: Atlantic Monthly Press, 1993.

SELNOW, G. W. "Playing Videogames: The Electronic Friend." *Journal of Communications* 34 (1984): 148–56.

SHAKUR, SHANYIKA. *Monster.* New York: Atlantic Monthly Press, 1993.

SHATTUCK, ROGER. *The Forbidden Experiment: The Story of the Wild Boy of Aveyron.* New York: Farrar, Straus & Giroux, 1980.

SINGAL, DANIEL J. "The Other Crisis in Education." *The Atlantic Monthly,* November 1991.

SINGH, J.A.L., and ROBERT M. ZINGG. *Wolf Children and Feral Men.* New York: Harper and Brothers, 1942.

SIPCHEN, BOB. *Baby Insane and the Buddha.* New York: Doubleday, 1993.

SIRAISI, NANCY G. "The Music of Pulse in the Writings of Italian Academic Physicians (Fourteenth And Fifteenth Centuries)." *Speculum* 50 (1975): 689–710.

SMITH, J. *The Structure of Communication in Early Language Development.* New York: Academic Press, 1976.

SNOW, CATHERINE, and CHARLES A. FERGUSON, eds. *Talking to Children: Language Input and Acquisition.* Cambridge: Cambridge University Press, 1977.

SONTAG, SUSAN. *On Photography.* New York: Farrar, Straus & Giroux, 1977.

SPACKS, PATRICIA MEYER. *Gossip.* New York: Alfred A. Knopf, 1985.

STEINER, GEORGE. *Real Presences.* Chicago: The University of Chicago Press, 1989.

STERN, DANIEL N. *The First Relationship: Infant and Mother.* Cambridge: Harvard University Press, 1977.

STEVENSON, H. W., ed. *Concept of Development. Monograph of the Society for Research and Child Development* 31, no. 5 (1966).

STOCK, BRIAN. *The Implications of Literacy: Written Language and Models of Interpretation in the Eleventh and Twelfth Centuries.* Princeton: Princeton University Press, 1983.

TOLES, TERRI. "Video Games and American Military Ideology." *The Critical Communications Review* 30. In Vincent Mosco and Janet Wasko, eds., *Popular Culture and Media Events.* Norwood, N.J.: Ablex, 1985.

TWAIN, MARK. *The Adventures of Huckleberry Finn.* Ed. and with an introduction by John Seelye. New York: Penguin Books, 1985.

VINOVSKIS, MARIS A. "Early Childhood Education: Then and Now," in *America's Childhood. Daedalus* (Winter 1993).

VON FRANZ, MARIE-LOUISE. *An Introduction to the Interpretation of Fairy Tales.* New York: Spring Publications, 1970.

VYGOTSKY, LEV. *Thought and Language.* Cambridge: MIT Press, 1962.

WANG, WILLIAM S-Y., ed. *The Emergence of Language: Development and Evolution.* New York: W. H. Freeman, 1991.

WASSERMANN, JAKOB. *Caspar Hauser.* Trans. Michael Hulse. New York: Bantam Books, 1992.

WATT, WILLIAM, trans. *Augustine's Confessions.* Loeb Classical Library, London: W. Heinemann, 1919–22.

WEISSBERGER, L. "Ist Muttersprache eine germanische oder eine romantische Wortpraegung." *Proceedings of the British Academy* 62 (1938): 428–37.

WEKKER, HERMAN. *The Expression of Future Time in Contemporary British English: An Investigation into the Syntax and Semantics of Five Verbal Expressions Expressing Futurity.* Holland: North-Holland Publishing Co., 1976.

WHITMAN, WALT. *Leaves of Grass.* New York: Dolphin Books, 1955.

WINNICOTT, D. W. *The Child, the Family, and the Outside World.* New York: Addison-Wesley Publishing Company, Inc., 1964.

————. *Home Is Where We Start From: Essays by a Psychoanalyst.* New York: W. W. Norton, 1986.

WITTGENSTEIN, LUDWIG. *Tractatus Logico-Philosophicus.* Trans. D. F. Pears and B. F. McGuinness. New York: Humanities Press, 1987.

WRIGHT, ROGER. "Speaking, Reading, and Writing Late Latin and Early Romance." *Neophilologus* 60, no. 17 (1976): 178–89.

ZBORAY, RONALD J. "Antebellum Reading and the Ironies of Technological Innovation." In Cathy Davidson, ed., *Reading in America: Literature and Social History.* Baltimore, Md.: The Johns Hopkins University Press, 1989.

ZIGLER, EDWARD, and JEANETTE VALENTINE, eds. *Project Head Start: A Legacy of the War on Poverty.* New York: The Free Press, 1979.

INDEX